Sweetheart Killers

Sweetheart Killers

Chloë Castleden

Magpie Books, London

Constable & Robinson Ltd
3 The Lanchesters
162 Fulham Palace Road
London W6 9ER
www.constablerobinson.com

This edition published by Magpie Books,
an imprint of Constable & Robinson Ltd, 2008.

A copy of the British Library Cataloguing in
Publication Data is available from the British Library

ISBN 978-1-84529-791-6

Printed and bound in the EU

3 5 7 9 10 8 6 4 2

PEFC/16-33-111
CATG-PEFC-052
www.pefc.org

Contents

Introduction: Lovers who Kill

The Dangers of Imagination

Perhaps humanity's greatest blessing is also its greatest curse. We are fortunate to be a highly creative species. We have the imagination to think of stories, to picture possible futures, to solve problems and think of new ways of doing things.

It is our creative imaginations that have given us myths, art, folk tales, and philosophy. Even science is driven by the imagination. Someone had to imagine flying to the moon before they started to wonder exactly how that could be achieved.

However imagination has a much darker side. We can tell us ourselves nasty, evil stories as well as pleasant ones. We can think of every kind of human and sexual transgression, and create an image of it. And once it has been imagined it is often only a matter of time before someone puts the idea into practice.

Terrorism, murder, abuse and torture are all expressions of someone's imagination. In each case, the evil takes the form of an idea before it is enacted. Perhaps this is why the idea of couples who love one another but who also kill is so very

1

disturbing. One of our most exalted narrative forms is the love story in which a pair of humans find each other and fall in love. The whole idea of love is to some degree a romanticization, a fairy tale, but one that we recognize because it appeals to what is best in us. As humans we can feel love, empathy and compassion.

However when this is perverted into murder by those rare couples who choose to act out the nightmarish side of their imaginations, it becomes a mockery of love. Love is a celebration of life, so how can it be in any way associated with the urge to kill?

There are a variety of ways in which two people who have a relationship can be drawn into murder. These can range from mundane motives such as greed for money or the desire for revenge, to such strange phenomena as vampirism and trophy killing.

Within this book we see couples such as Holly Harvey and Sandy Ketchum who killed in the hope of being together. We also see partners who are trying to protect their lovers, as in the case of Sheilagh Farrow and Trevor Hardy. Probably the most common theme in the book is those cases where couples kill to sate the sexual perversions of one or both parties. The Gallegos, the Wests, and the case of Paul Bernardo and Karla Homolka all exemplify this theme.

What is frequently true of couples who kill is that there is some kind of feedback mechanism at work. Maybe both of the partners are morally prone to murder, or maybe only one starts out that way. In some cases here, the first murder is an accident. But once the couple are drawn into a situation where they are mutually guilty, either because they are both complicit in murder, or because one is covering up for the other's crimes, then there is a lethal combination of self-protection and self-justification.

In the end, writing about couples who kill often draws us into a philosophical examination of love and passion, and the way that humans can influence one another to perform evil acts. In wartime a whole society can descend into murderous rage, in which entire nations or peoples can be seen as the enemy. When couples kill, they have often created their own warlike mentality of 'us against the world'. In this state of mind, the couple suspends the usual laws of morality and acts in a bubble of their own making. The unfortunate victims are the ones who suffer as a result.

What about the Victims?

Writing about murderers creates some difficult moral ambiguities. In many ways, one feels that the story should really be about the victims. After all, the real tragedy in a murder is that someone has been robbed of his or her life. It would be nice to be able to focus on the life of the person who was innocent and who died for whatever senseless reason, rather than on the killers.

However, the stories of the victims can be hard to tell. Their lives are hopefully remembered by their friends and families, and they were often people who might have gone to live full, wonderful lives. But their story is a simple one, at least with regards to the story of murder. They lived their life until one day someone took that life from them. No matter how fascinating that life was, the story of a murderer will inevitably centre on the killer rather than on the people they killed.

This brings in the next problem. When we write about killers, we are struggling to understand what happened and why it happened. The bare facts are often appalling beyond belief. So we try to come to some level of comprehension. We look to the background, the childhood or earlier life of the killer to try and see what changed them from an ordinary, possibly damaged person, into a murderer or murderess.

And in the process of trying to understand, the killer becomes the central character in the story. We inevitably tell the story from their point of view to some degree, because when we are talking about the period in which they were killing without being caught, that is the only way to tell the story. They are the antiheroes, and if we are not very careful we can even end up treating them as heroes, albeit flawed heroes.

In film, television and fiction, this tendency has gone so far that in films such as *Silence of the Lambs,* or the television series *Dexter,* we are expected to empathize with the killer, more than with the victim. But this tendency is an ever-present risk in any writing about killers. It is a hard task to draw a clear line between understanding how crimes happened and seeking to excuse killers for their crimes.

In writing or reading about killers, we start to see the world from their point of view, to wonder what they would do next, maybe even to forgive them. And this is a very dangerous path. No matter that they are the centre of the story, no matter how much we might be able to comprehend the causes that drove them to murder, we have to remember that the most important story here is the story of the victims.

With every murder, a life is cut short. We may not always know or be able to tell the story of that life, even briefly. But we always have to remember that as these killers drifted through life, taking lives and eventually succumbing to justice (or not), the victims weren't bit-part players. They were the heroes of their own life stories, and in their cases they often deserved to be treated as heroes, even if they end up being relegated to minor roles in the stories we are telling here.

I'd like to dedicate this book to every victim of the crimes that are described herein. Many of the victims are mentioned only briefly. The policemen murdered by Clyde Parker were all real people who had families and friends who were no doubt devastated by their deaths. The victims of horrific sex criminals like the Wests and the Gallegos did nothing to deserve their treatment. The victims of Walter Kelbach and Myron Lance just happened to be in the wrong place at the wrong time.

They all died in the service of monstrous desires and appetites, or selfish, childish and desperate motivations. And many of those mentioned in this book are still remembered by people who loved them.

There are times when attempting to understand the story of murderers leads one to adopt a flippant tone or one that is overly sympathetic towards the criminal. In some cases one can perceive a spectrum of good and evil in which one perceives (for instance) Martha Beck as less culpable than Myra Hindley, or Sheilagh Hardy as less guilty than Charlene Gallego.

But in the end, these people all shared responsibility for the most heinous crime a human can commit, which is murder.

The people who should ultimately be remembered are the victims. We should recall the killers only as failed human beings, who made the world a worse place through their selfish, evil actions. The victims are the ones we should care about.

Serial Killer Couples

Introduction

The term 'serial killers' first entered the popular argot as a result of murderers like Ted Bundy and David Berkowitz. Going further back into history, Jack the Ripper was another classic example of a case of serial killing, albeit one in which the killer remained unidentified.

There isn't an absolutely clear distinction between a serial killer and a multiple murderer. Trevor Hardy, who is included in the next section of this book, showed signs of a serial killer mentality and might have become one if he had not been apprehended after three killings. But the main thing that defines what we think of as a serial killer is the use of a repetitive modus operandi. A serial killer tends to have a single fixed idea that they act out repeatedly, using trademark habits that may include specific types of mutilation, methods of abduction and habits of treatment of their victims.

Not all serial killers exhibit a sexual element to their deviant behaviour, but all of the killers in this section were partially sexually motivated. There is a strong tendency for one or both partners to be obsessed with transgressive sexual practices, and to have achieved their desires by subjugating and then murdering their victims.

Theories about serial killers often focus on ideas of compulsion and control. The killer wants to control a situation in a way that they are only able to do through violence, and this develops into a murderous habit.

There is also an element of emotional underdevelopment that is common in serial killers. Either because of events in childhood, as with Gerald Gallego and Ian Brady, or because of other factors, a killer fails to develop emotionally, and exhibits basically childish behavior, but with the addition of an all too adult ability to inflict pain and death.

For Fred West, a head injury seems to have compounded with a strange childhood to create a disturbed man, with evil motivations. While in the case of a killer like Paul Bernardo, there seems to be no obvious reason why he should have turned into a serial rapist and killer.

The interesting and troubling aspect of these killers from the point of view of this book is how the monstrous ideas and motivations of one or both partners in a couple came to be realized in a mutual killing pact.

It is often the male partner whose sexual desires are the motivating force in the killings, as they certainly were with David Birnie and Doug Clark. But the partners of these two killers, Catherine Birnie and Carol Bundy, became guilty of horrific crimes. Were these women merely tools of their lovers, who only wanted to keep their man happy no matter how awful his desires? Or is there more to the question? Was the submissive nature of these women part of the catalyst that led to the killing?

This is the first question we need to confront as we explore the stories of these couples. But along the way there are other moral questions that are hard to avoid. In the cases of Charlene Gallego and Karla Homolka, the issue of plea bargaining becomes the crucial moral issue. In both cases the female partner received a lesser punishment, and was eventually paroled, because she assisted the authorities in obtaining a conviction of her ex-partner.

However both of these women were guilty of crimes that,

in isolation, would be judged as being deserving of more severe sentences. Was it right to allow them to plead for lighter sentences in order to minimize the risk of their partners evading justice?

The final question that comes up in any consideration of couples who kill together is the very basic issue of moral responsibility. Many of the killers in this book attempted to blame their partners after they were apprehended. Some of the women tried to claim that they were battered wives who acted out of fear, indeed some of them may have been telling the truth.

In other cases, such as the case of Myra Hindley, one wonders whether their passive acquiescence might actually have been the catalyst that turned a transgressive fantasy into reality. Would Ian Brady have become a murderer without the admiration and devotion of a woman who was prepared to tolerate his most lunatic ideas?

We can't possibly know the answer to that question. Few of these cases are clear-cut when it comes to how the moral responsibility should be shared. In the end one can only return to the sixth commandment, 'Thou Shalt Not Kill' and conclude that anyone who is involved in a murder in any way, whether they were the passive assistant, cheerleader, or active partner, is still guilty of a terrible crime.

Fred and Rosemary West

The House of Horrors

Some crimes are so revolting they almost defy belief. The case of Fred and Rosemary West is a prime example. Over a twenty-year period from the late 1960s this married couple murdered and dismembered at least twelve girls, mostly in their small three-storey house in 25 Cromwell Street in Gloucester, in the west of England. In several of the cases the women had been raped and tortured before being killed. Several of the victims were lodgers or nannies, living transient lives that meant that their disappearance was not immediately connected to the Wests.

The 'House of Horrors' is no longer standing. After the terrible things that happened there, the only reasonable course of action was to raze it to the ground. Nothing other than a bleak, landscaped area with a footpath now marks the location of some of the worst crimes of the period. Beneath the surface there are five concrete masses, used to fill in holes from which the police had removed human remains. The bones had been buried in an upright position in these holes. The heads and limbs had been removed from the corpses and stuffed down into the holes beside the torsos,

12

which by the time of the police excavations were in an advanced state of decay. In each case a kneecap or finger bone had been kept by Fred West as a keepsake.

For all the gruesomeness of such details, the truly horrifying details of the case centre on the couple's treatment of their own children. One daughter, Heather, was amongst the murdered children as was a step-daughter in their care, Charmaine. Over a period of many years the couple indulged in terrible abuse of their children, which only fully came to light after they were finally brought to justice. After Fred West had raped another one of his daughters and videoed the abuse in 1992, the girl's schoolfriends picked up on some of the gruesome details of the household from conversations with her. This was the start of the trail that led police to start putting together the pieces of the tragic jigsaw of the case.

It took another twenty-one months of determined police investigation, including a few false starts, before the Wests' downfall started to develop on 24 February 1994, when police obtained a warrant to dig up the garden at Cromwell Road. It was the discovery of bones there that led on to the final grisly discoveries in the cellar. As Fred and Rosemary's explanations started to crumble, the police excavated greater areas and discovered more and more human remains. At one stage Fred confessed to the murder of his daughter Heather, only to retract the confession. However it soon became clear to the investigating police that this went far beyond a case of child abuse or a single murder

What leads a married couple into such an evil existence? Both Fred and Rosemary had strange childhoods, and it is rumoured that both came from families with a history of incest. To even begin to understand how they turned into serial killers it is necessary to consider the lives they had led before meeting each other.

*   *   *

13

Fred West was born in 1941, to a family of farm labourers in the village of Much Marcle in Herefordshire, between Ross-on-Wye and Ledbury. His parents were Walter and Daisy West. The family were poor, and Fred had six brothers and sisters. By all acounts he was close to his parents, especially his mother. As he grew older he started to take on the rather strange simian look that is so familiar from the photographs of him in later life, with a large jaw and irregular teeth.

He left school when he was fifteen with very little education, unable to read well, and worked as a farm hand. He had been unpopular at school, teased for having a strange, overweight mother who would visit the school when Fred got into his regular bouts of trouble. As a young man he was already known as someone who aggressively chased women.

It is hard to know if there is any truth in the allegations of incest in either family. Fred used to boast that his father had slept with his sisters and that he had himself impregnated at least one of his sisters. In a similar vein it would later be alleged that even while Rosemary West was with Fred, her father would visit to sleep with her, with Fred's knowledge. No one can know if such suggestions are true. They may merely reflect West's rather strange mentality even at a younger age, before he had moved on to murder.

Several accidents in Fred's younger days seem to have had a lasting effect on him. At seventeen he was in a coma for a week after a bad motorcycle accident, which also left him with a metal plate in his skull. This also left him with an uneven gait, as the broken leg didn't fully recover. Some of those who knew him at the time reported that his temper was affected – he became prone to sudden rages and lost what little self-control he had had.

The following year Fred suffered another head injury at a local youth club. He had tried to force his attentions on a girl and she pushed him off the fire escape. Once again he lost consciousness. We can't be certain about this, but it widely believed that the combination of the two accidents left him with some damage to the brain, which may have been a factor in his inability to control his horrific urges as he aged.

It was around this time that Fred started to get into trouble with the police. He was caught with a friend, stealing from a jewellery shop. He was also accused of having sexual relations with a local thirteen-year-old girl who became pregnant as a result. The shame of this, combined with Fred's unrepentant response led to Fred being estranged from his family for a while.

He continued to have problems with the law, going on to further cases of stealing and under-age sex. The case of the thirteen-year-old girl led to a trial, where he managed to avoid prison after it was claimed that he was epileptic.

Thus Fred's last few teenage years had left him with a record both for theft and child-molestation. It was in this period that Fred first met an attractive Scottish girl called Rena Costello. She would return to Scotland, but later on she came back into his life with tragic consequences. Rena also had a record for stealing and had worked as a prostitute.

While she was back in Scotland Fred was allowed back in to the family home, in spite of his disgrace. In the summer of 1962, Rena returned from Scotland, pregnant with a mixed-race child. Fred didn't care about this and the couple got back together. They married secretly late in the year and moved away to Scotland.

Charmaine was born in March 1963. Fred's parents wouldn't have approved of his taking on another man's child, let alone a mixed-race one. In an attempt to deal with this Rena wrote to them explaining that the baby they had believed was Fred's had died, and that they had adopted a mixed-race child.

Like Fred's later lies to the police, there is a childlike element in this transparent fabrication. Fred's lies were so pathetically easy to see through in later years that it sometimes seems extraordinary that his and Rosemary's crimes remained undetected for so long, especially given that she was not especially intelligent herself.

*   *   *

She was born Rosemary Letts in 1953 in Devon, England. Her father Bill was apparently a schizophrenic, while her mother Daisy was a depressive who was treated with electro-shock therapy even while she was pregnant with Rosemary.

Bill was an authoritarian bully prone to administering violent bouts of 'punishment' to his wife and children. The family were poor and seem to have lived a fairly miserable existence. One of Rosemary's brothers later remembered it thus: 'If he felt we were in bed too late, he would throw a bucket of cold water over us . . . We were not allowed to speak and play like normal children. If we were noisy, he would go for us with a belt or chunk of wood. He would beat you black and blue until mum got in between us. Then she would get a good hiding.'

It was this brutal existence which led to Daisy's depression and hospitalization. There is not a great deal of research as to the effects which electroshock therapy, applied to the mother, might have on an unborn child. Daisy had the treatment, now discredited as a cruel, arcane practice, on repeated occasions while she was carrying Rosemary. It is impossible to know if this may have had an effect on the unborn child, though from a modern point of view it seems astonishingly cruel to subject a pregnant woman to this practice.

While she was a child, the family decided that Rose was 'a bit on the slow side'. She developed habits that are psychologically interesting. While in the cot, she would rock repetitively, thumping the cot to and fro. Later on she would bang her head against a wall while indulging in a similar repetitive routine. These behaviours resemble the stereo-typed behavior of unhappily caged animals, something which is supposed to relieve their stress and boredom while caged. Similar behaviors are often observed in autistic children, possibly as a soothing mechanism in a strange and confusing world.

Rose grew up to become her father's favourite, and escaped many of the beatings administered to her siblings. But her school life was not happy. She was not unattractive, although she had a slight tendency to obesity. This was the reason why she was bullied at school and had few friends, getting into periodic fights with those who tormented her. At home she was obedient and her father spared her some of his most aggressive behavior, but it can't have been a pleasant home life.

There was nothing obviously violent or criminal in Rose's upbringing. It may be that, as someone who had enjoyed her father's attention and favouritism, she was naturally keen to please, so went along with her eventual husband's fantasies, or it may have been that she had become psychologically damaged even before she met her match in Fred.

It is hard to judge such things, and an unhappy childhood is no excuse for the kinds of crimes we are examining here. But the roots of evil often stretch back to childhood experiences, and in Rose's case one can see elements that may have laid the seeds of the murderess she would become.

*   *   *

Meanwhile, whilst Rose was still growing up, Fred was living in Scotland with Rena. She had worked as a prostitute, but West's fascination with deviant sex still seems to have been something that revolted her at times.

The respected writer Colin Wilson wrote in *The Corpse Garden* about West's demands: 'He wanted oral sex, bondage and . . . sodomy . . . at all hours of the day and night.' In pursuit of his sick fantasies West pursued women whenever he could. He was charming enough to frequently seduce girls he met. He was at this time working in an ice cream van, which gave him freedom to roam.

He was often unfaithful to Rena, but like many unfaithful men, he was nonetheless aggressively possessive about both Rena and her young daughter Charmaine. Rena had another child, Fred's this time, in 1964. Both children would go on to suffer torments at the hands of Fred and West. Of the mother and two daughters, only Anne Marie, the younger child, would survive the years of murder and torture that lay ahead.

Fred and Rena's relationship suffered from a series of further strains over the ensuing period. A young boy died in an accidental collision with the ice cream truck that Fred drove, and he decided that he would move back to Gloucester. He doesn't seem to have been to blame for the accident although he felt he might lose his job as a result.

He had met a young woman called Anna McFall. She moved with the family back to Gloucester, having recently been bereaved when her boyfriend died. Fred was not yet a murderer, but nonetheless his life seemed surrounded by death and tragedy.

This tendency took a macabre new turn when Fred took a new job in Gloucester in a slaughterhouse. Some have pointed to this period as being the turning point, when Fred's already disturbed personality took a turn for the worse. Daily exposure to corpses, and the experience of seeing the blood and dismemberment that is a slaughter-house's daily business may well have given him new grist for his fantasies.

It is likely that this spell of work also influenced his later treatment of corpses, which he would defile in necrophiliac practices, and also mutilate. As we'll see, it would become a standard part of his murderous routine to remove fingers and toes from the corpses he disposed of.

Rena was unhappy in Gloucester. Fred refused to let her take the two daughters with her back to Scotland, even though Charmaine was not even his own blood child. She gave in to his demands and returned home on her own. However she missed the children and returned to Gloucester. Meanwhile Fred and Anna McFall had taken up together and were living in a local trailer.

There is no firm evidence linking Fred to the assaults, but at least eight unsolved sexual assaults in the local area. In each case, the suspects were of an appearance that bore some resemblance to West.

When Rena returned to Gloucester, she went to the local police and talked to Constable Hazel Savage. Savage would eventually become a crucial member of the team that brought Fred to justice, although it would be a quarter of a century before she was finally given the satisfaction of bringing to justice the man of whom she first became aware through Rena's report.

Rena told Savage that Fred was a pervert, that he shouldn't be allowed to look after children and that he was potentially violent. But before things could be taken much further, Rena ended up going back to Fred, and Savage was unable to pursue these reports as a result.

Rena's reunion with Fred came after the disappearance of Anna McFall. Fred's relationship with her had succumbed to instability. Anna was pregnant and wanted Fred to marry her. This would have involved a divorce from Rena. No one knows the full story but so far as anyone knows this was the catalyst for Fred's first descent into murder.

His murder of Anna was a horrific slaughter. He buried her near the trailer park, but not before violating her body by subjecting it to a prolonged dismemberment. He cut off her fingers and toes, a pattern that would become typical of his disposal of his victims. The unborn foetus was buried with her, the first of his children to die as a result of his crimes.

Rena, who was unaware of what had happened, temporarily moved back in with Fred once it became clear that Anna was gone, although she would not stay with him for much longer, as she left town once more, leaving her children with Fred. It was around this time that another possible victim of West disappeared.

On 5 January 1968 Mary Bastholm vanished from a snowy bus stop in Gloucester. She had been going to meet her boyfriend to play the board game Monopoly with him. There were signs of a struggle, with some of the pieces of the game left scattered near the bus stop. Fred's son Stephen would later say that Fred had confessed to this murder in jail before his death.

After his eventual arrest West would also claim to have killed another 20 victims who wouldn't be found. He made this confession to the volunteer worker Janet Leach, whose appearance at the trial of Rosemary West had a major impact on the course of that trial.

West was known for bragging and for lying, so it is hard to trust every detail of his confessions or his denials. But in this case it seems very likely that he was the killer. He knew Mary from the café where she worked. He would later abduct women from bus stops in similar circumstances, and he tended to follow similar patterns in his abductions. Mary Bastholm was only fifteen years old when she was taken so suddenly from her family and friends.

It seems that by this time, Fred West was developing the habits of abduction and murder, having moved on from sick fantasy to reality. This progression would go a step further once he met his future wife Rose Letts in 1968.

* * *

As a teenager, Rose had developed some odd sexual behaviour. She displayed herself naked to her brothers and on at least one occasion climbed into bed with them. Her father wouldn't allow her to date boys of her own age. She went along with this on the surface but transferred her sexual interest to older men, something which may also fit in with her curious relationship with her own father.

When Mary Bastholm disappeared, girls of Rose's age were unnerved by the fear of an abductor on the loose. There had been a rash of sexual assaults in the area, and it seemed prudent to avoid strange men. However Rose continued to pursue older men, including strangers. Her mother finally became brave enough to walk out on her violent, controlling husband, and moved in with Rose's sister Glenys and her husband Jim Tyler. Rose moved with her. Jim later reported that Rose had tried to seduce him and had been involved with several other men at this time. One man reportedly raped her after she had trusted him in this period.

During this period, Fred West was working as a delivery driver, and this was his occupation when he met Rose. Her father Bill Letts was against the relationship from the start. Rose had moved back in with him, another sign of her ambiguous relationship with older authority figures. On the one hand she was rebellious, yet she seemed eager to please the older men she pursued.

Letts even went to Fred's trailer to threaten him and try to separate the couple. The problem was temporarily solved as Fred served a term in prison for minor offences. However it became apparent that Rose was pregnant with West's child. She now left her father's home and moved into the West house where she looked after Rena's two children Charmaine and Anne Marie.

Her own daughter Heather was born in 1970. She now had three children to look after, and Fred West was often absent as he had constant problems with the law. The next step on the murderous journey of the couple came during one of the periods when he was in prison.

Fred had already killed his own unborn child when he murdered Anna McFall. Now Rose killed one of his step-children, Charmaine. Anne Marie later reported that Rose had no self-control and was subject to violent rages. It seems that she killed Charmaine in one of these rages, when the kind of beating that she was familiar with from her own childhood home went too far and the child ended up dead. She was still a child of primary school age, but the woman who was supposed to be in care of her had taken her life.

In many ways this seems to have been a pivotal event in the relationship between the Wests. Fred was probably only involved in burying the body beneath the floor of the kitchen of the Midland Road house where they lived at that stage. Again he removed keepsakes: fingers, toes and kneecaps.

Now Rose knew that he was capable of such evil. But she also knew that he could say the same of her. This was a secret that bound her to him, because they could now destroy each other. At one stage, when her parents tried to persuade her to leave him, she said 'You don't know him! There's nothing he wouldn't do – even murder!' But she was the partner who had taken the first step within that relationship that led to their murderous co-dependence.

Rose also told Charmaine's sister Anne Marie that their mother Rena had taken Charmaine away, to explain away the disappearance. This lie would lead on to another problem, to which the solution was once again murder.

When Rena next visited, it was clear that the story Rose had told was untrue. Rena attempted to discover the truth, even tracking down Fred's father to look for answers (his mother had died a few years before). Fred feared discovery and cold-bloodedly chose to murder Rena, probably after getting her drunk to make the task easier for him. The actual deed resembled his earlier murder of Anna McFall. Rena was buried in a similar area, and once again the body was mutilated.

*   *   *

We live in a strange world today. The internet has made the strangest and most dangerous of sexual obsessions and imagery an everyday occurrence for those who choose to seek out the material. In some respects this makes it hard to explain how deviant the West's sexual behavior was back in the 1970s when the public attitudes to pornography were far less tolerant.

Some of their activities were simply voyeuristic or salacious, while others spilled over into violence and violation. This fact makes one wonder how much damage is being done to young minds today by the pornographic clichés and bullying misogyny to which they can easily be exposed, and how brutalized some vulnerable imaginations will become.

This kind of brutality, and normalization of transgressive, horrific behaviour was a central part of the way in which the Wests' relationship developed. Rose would tolerate, participate in and encourage Fred's sickest fantasies, and this was a defining feature of their life together. The sexual deviancy of the Wests also became increasingly extreme as they embarked on a lifetime of murder.

Fred would run advertisements in magazines for 'swingers' with erotic photos of Rose attached. Rose regularly participated in sexual acts for money, or simply to satisfy Fred's voyeuristic desires. They often brought men from Gloucester's West Indian community back to the house, and Fred drilled peepholes so that he could observe the bondage, multiple partners, sadism or whatever.

Where this deviant behaviour spilled over into torture and

abduction was in their treatment of young girls. One babysitter, Elizabeth Agius, recounted that when she had asked the Wests where they had been one night, they replied that they had been cruising for young girls to pick up, in particular virgins. Agius took this for a joke, but was herself later propositioned by Fred and she was also allegedly drugged and raped on another occasion.

After the birth of their daughter Mae in 1972, the Wests moved from Midland Road to Cromwell Street, to the house that would become the 'House of Horrors'. It was a larger house with a garage and cellar, suitable in these respects for Rose's prostitution and Fred's fetishes. It was also large enough for them to take in lodgers.

It was here that the Wests would increasingly turn to torture and outright abuse. Fred converted the cellar into his 'torture chamber'. Amongst other vile acts, he raped his own eight-year-old daughter Anne Marie, while Rose held her down after helping to tie and gag her.

It is hard to speak of such repulsive evil, but Anne Marie would go on to be treated in similar fashion on many occasions. Her book *Out of the Shadows* is a brave but harrowing account of the treatment she received. At the time, she was cowed into silence by threats of severe beatings if she told anyone what had happened and this wall of fear and silence in the family would unfortunately protect the parents for many years.

The Wests came close to being caught in 1972. They hired Caroline Owens, a seventeen-year-old girl, as their nanny, in which role she was to live in their house. When they made advances to her she rejected them. Eventually, when she decided she was leaving as a result of their behaviour, they forced her to strip and Fred raped her. Fred threatened her that if she didn't comply, he would keep her in the cellar and allow his sex circle to use her, then kill and bury her.

When she returned home, Caroline's mother, alarmed by

her bruises, managed to persuade her to confess what had happened, in spite of her fear. The police were called and the case went to court. Tragically, the case failed.

Caroline was too scared to testify, submitting a statement instead, and when the magistrate believed Fred's cover story that Caroline had participated willingly, the couple escaped with a fine. No wonder women then and now often feel that the law is inadequate when it comes to achieving convictions for the crime of rape, when such a repugnant man could walk free simply because the magistrate took his word over that of a terrified girl.

There were a number of occasions in the 1970s when a more adequate police response might have put an end to the Wests' crimes. On several occasions the police received information that Anne Marie might be a victim of abuse, and a simple medical inspection would surely have confirmed this.

However no action was taken. This may have been from mere incompetence on the part of the officers involved. Some have suggested that Fred's role as an occasional informer may have protected him, or even that police officers who had attended sex sessions in the house might have turned a blind eye. The full story can't be known, but while the eventual police investigation into the Wests was a model of dogged professionalism, the legal system and the police let down the Wests' children and victims too many times in the 1970s and 1980s.

At this stage, when Rose was nineteen, she was pregnant with her third child, Stephen. At such a young age she had already participated in many vile acts, and now the couple must have felt impregnable, since even a clear report of their behaviour failed to lead to any punishment.

From here on, the case of the Wests becomes a procession of young girls who became victims. Perhaps, after the trial and close escape they had been through, they decided that the only safe route was to kill anyone whom they had abused. Whatever the reason, there were few survivors of their abuse after this time.

In telling the story of such prolific murderers, it is easy to forget that each one of their victims was a real person, someone who had friends and family and who would otherwise have gone on to live a normal life. The victims become a blur of names, who we will list here, but we should always remember that each one of these names conceals yet another individual and collective tragedy.

*   *   *

Linda Gough

Linda Gough had been friends with some of the Wests' lodgers. Aged nineteen, in 1973 she had an argument with her parents and moved into the house. Rose was five months pregnant with her son Stephen at this stage, having also given birth to another daughter, Mae, in 1972.

Linda's death came after she was taken into the cellar, tied up with tape and rope and assaulted. She was killed and dismembered in Fred West's usual manner. She was buried in the shed, over which Fred would eventually build a bathroom extension.

When Linda's concerned parents came to look for her, Rose first denied all knowledge of the girl, although she was wearing a pair of slippers that had belonged to Linda. Later she told them that she had remembered, and that Linda had moved away to Weston-super-Mare (the same excuse she would use later to explain Heather's disappearance).

She told the children a different story, that Linda had been hitting Anne Marie so Rose had thrown her out. Rose's complicity in lying to cover up Linda's disappearance was a clear sign that she was either involved in the murder or in concealing the crime.

Carol Anne Cooper

Carol Anne Cooper was only fifteen when the Wests abducted her from a bus stop, just as Fred had allegedly done with Mary Bastholm. As with many of the Wests' crimes, the only clues as to what ordeals she underwent came from her corpse, when it was found in the cellar in 1994. Her head had suffered a deep wound, although this may have been after she died as Fred dismembered the body.

She had been gagged with surgical tape, and the rest of her body had been bound with tape and clothes line. She had probably died either from strangulation or suffocation.

Lucy Partington

Lucy Partington is one of the better known victims of the Wests, simply because by a coincidence she was a relative of the novelist Martin Amis, who wrote about her in his book *Experience*.

On 27 December 1973 Lucy, who was twenty-one, set off to catch a bus, and was never seen again. Again the exact details of her death are conjectural, but as with other victims, she was buried with remnants of the gags and ropes that had been used to restrain her.

Fred West visited hospital a week later for treatment for a

deep cut, which may have happened as he dismembered the body, suggesting that as with other victims, the Wests kept Lucy a prisoner and abused her for several days before finally killing her.

As well as Fred's usual act of removing the fingers and toes of the corpse, other bones were missing, including a kneecap, ribs and a shoulder blade.

Theresa Siegenthaler

In April 1974 the Wests abducted and killed another twenty-one-year-old, Theresa Siegenthaler. She was on her way to visit a friend of hers, a local priest. Theresa was a strong girl, trained in self-defence, but she was nonetheless overpowered and imprisoned.

She died with her feet bound and a silk mask covering her face. When Fred dismembered the body he chopped up the longer bones to fit them into another hole in the cellar, close to the room that was supposed to be the children's playroom.

Shirley Hubbard

Shirley Hubbard was fifteen, a pretty young girl who had been in and out of foster homes, but who had found a work-experience position as a beautician at the time of her abduction.

She seems to have suffered especially heartless abuse, possibly because Rose was jealous of her good looks. The mask on her face completely obscured her features, leaving only room for two straws that were inserted into her nose, presumably so that she could breathe under such constricted circumstances.

She was also buried in the cellar, along with her decapitated head, limbs, and with toes and fingers missing.

Juanita Mott

Juanita Mott was an eighteen-year-old who had previously been a lodger of the Wests. When she was out hitch-hiking in the spring of 1975 she was picked up or abducted by the Wests and suffered the same fate as the increasingly tragic list of previous victims.

She was once again buried in the cellar of the house. Her skull had been caved in by a hammer, probably the fatal blow. Seventeen feet of rope was found with her, suggesting an unusually complex form of bondage. The rope was criss-crossed around her entire body, and she had probably been suspended from the ceiling of the cellar during her ordeal.

Miss A.

Miss A. is an exception in this list of victims, in that she survived her abuse by the Wests. She was given the name Miss A. at the trial of Rose West, where she gave evidence of her treatment. She was from a local girls' home, and was enticed to Cromwell Street by the Wests. She was taken to a room where two naked girls were being held prisoner. She was raped by Fred, assaulted sexually by Rose, and witnessed other acts of torture and abuse against the two other girls. It is likely that one of the girls was Anne Marie

West who was regularly abused both by Fred and also by friends he brought home to the house.

For whatever reason Miss A. was not killed and her evidence made up a crucial part of the case against Rose West, the best part of two decades later.

Shirley Robinson

Shirley Robinson was an ex-prostitute who moved into the West house as a lodger, and who also looked after the children. She had relationships with both Fred and Rose. During this period Rose became pregnant, not by Fred, but by one of her clients. The child, when it was born, would be the first of four mixed-race children she had over the following years. Fred didn't mind this and had a perverse fascination with what he saw as the greater virility of black men.

However Rose was far less happy when Shirley became pregnant with Fred's child. Shirley was aware of Rose's hostility and started sleeping in another lodger's room in the hope of protecting herself from assault. But she had nowhere else to go and hoped to stay with Fred.

In May 1978 she disappeared. Unlike previous murders, she hadn't been tied up and assaulted, but had been taken to the cellar and strangled. Again her body was dismembered. The foetus was near to term and was cut from her body and buried with her disfigured corpse in the garden, in an echo of the earlier burial of Anna McFall, who had also been carrying Fred's child. The cellar was by now too full for further burials.

Alison Chambers

Alison Chambers, who was seventeen when she died, had escaped from life in an orphanage in Wales and had been relocated in a local facility for young women. The Wests invited her to stay with them as nanny, and she wrote to her family to say she was living with a loving family in the country.

Sadly the truth was that she was at Cromwell Street and, in September 1979 she became the latest victim of sexual abuse and murder, finally being buried in the garden. She was the last victim to be buried at the site for eight years, although it is very likely that the Wests continued to murder and to bury their victims elsewhere.

*   *   *

This litany of victims is both pathetic and horrifying. The West's remorseless behaviour also extended to their own family, and to other young children. Anne Marie became pregnant by Fred, although it was an ectopic pregnancy that had to be aborted.

Through this period, as well as the regular murders, the couple also abused a number of children whom they would bring back to the house from a local children's home. Rose in particular seemed driven to touch and abuse younger girls and there were numerous instances of such behaviour.

The relationship between the Wests in this period started to change in terms of the balance of power. Bound together by mutual guilt as they were, Rose nonetheless started to become more assertive and more unstable. She became angered easily and with so many children now in the house, she often lashed out and beat them.

Fred continued to work obsessively, both at his manual labour and at home on further extensions to the house. He

31

had few interests outside of sex, abuse and his building work, not being especially sociable and not liking to drink lest he should lose control. Of course he had no control over his base instincts, but he needed to avoid giving too much away about his crimes. He would boast and drop sinister hints, but still feel that he was the one who was in control.

The next time a victim was buried at the house was a pivotal moment in the story of the Wests. Their daughter Heather was now a teenage girl, who still suffered heavily at their hands. Her brother Stephen later reported that she was regularly raped by Fred for years before her death.

In May 1987 she left school and applied for a job abroad. She was devastated when she didn't get the job, presumably because she had seen it as a way to escape her horrific childhood. The Wests must have feared that, away from the family home, the web of terror that had prevented the children from telling others about events in the house would no longer keep her quiet.

She had also confided in a friend the previous year about some of the things that had happened to her. The friend's parents were friends of the Wests, so they knew that her silence was a fragile one.

The exact facts are unclear. At one point Fred claimed to have killed Heather alone, although his testimony was notoriously unreliable and he was probably protecting Rose. There are also the reports from both Stephen and Anne Marie that Rose had on occasions nearly strangled them in anger, and this may have been the cause of Heather's death.

In addition there is the upsetting report from Barry, one of Rose's children, who saw Heather fall to the floor, after which he said that Rose stamped repeatedly on her head.

One part of Fred's account which may be partially reliable is his story of the dismemberment of Heather. He claimed that an argument had got out of hand, and he had grabbed her by the throat to stop her laughing at him, until she turned blue and stopped breathing (this part of the account is probably false as he gave it when he was attempting to deflect blame from Rose, and was trying to make the death seem accidental).

Then he described putting her in the bath, and strangling her again to make sure she was dead. He didn't want her to suddenly turn out to be alive while he was cutting her up.

He cut the head off, not want her to be 'looking at him' while he worked. Then he twisted the foot to break the leg before removing both legs. Dismembered in this way, he could fit her corpse into a rubbish bin, which he rolled into the garden, burying her behind the children's Wendy house, whilst being careful to avoid the roots of a young tree that was growing there.

The verbatim account of this dismemberment gives an insight into Fred West's mind – part callous murderer, part childish boaster, revealing his own inability to perceive moral perspective in the details he chooses to reveal. He even asked one of his sons, Stephen, to help dig the hole in which his sister was to be buried. The children were told that Heather had left home. They would later sometimes joke that Heather was 'buried under the patio', without knowing how close this was to the truth.

*   *   *

It was in 1992 that the Wests' luck finally ran out. After a young girl told the police that her friend had been assaulted by Fred, the case was assigned to Detective Constable Hazel Savage. Savage remembered the stories she had heard from Rena about Fred's perverted behaviour. Finally the Wests were to be investigated by an officer who had the persistence and drive to uncover the truth.

On 6 August 1992, police took a search warrant to 25 Cromwell Street looking for evidence of child abuse. They

33

found large quantities of pornography and Rose was arrested for assisting in the rape of a minor. Fred was also arrested, for rape and sodomy of a minor.

Savage went to work interviewing the family and friends of the Wests. Anne Marie told her the appalling story of her abuse. She also mentioned her concern about Charmaine, whom Hazel had also known from her earlier meetings with Rena.

Hazel was now in a position to bring child abuse charges. However she broadened the enquiry to include disappearances of Charmaine, Rena and Heather. Heather had apparently disappeared without leaving any trace. There were no national insurance, tax or medical records for her, which would be almost impossible if she were still alive and hadn't left the country.

Savage persisted with a long, detailed investigation. By February 1994 she was in a position to take the next step, and a police team was sent to the house at Cromwell Street. When Rose saw their warrant, she immediately called her husband and told him to come home. The police were there to dig up the garden and search for Heather.

Fred wasn't visibly alarmed at first. He visited the police station, asking them not to make too much of a mess of his garden. He told them that Heather had been a lesbian, with drugs problems, and that she had disappeared in 1987.

However the implacable digging of the garden continued. The Wests clearly had a long conversation that night, as by the morning Fred's position had shifted. First thing the next day he confessed to the murder of Heather to Hazel Savage. This was when he gave the police his horrific cold-eyed account of her dismemberment and burial.

He was insistent that Rose had known nothing about the murder. It seems that this was a last-ditch attempt by the Wests to salvage their position. If he had been able to persuade the police that he had killed Heather accidentally on his own, Rose might have escaped prison, and he would have been able to prevent the police from discovering their many other murders.

However he was inconsistent even in this confession, denying everything he had said within an hour, possibly in a panic again. And now the police had discovered three human bones in the garden, and they weren't Heather's.

The younger children were put into care at this stage. Fred was kept in custody. Rose attempted to overdose on sleeping pills, but was saved by her son Stephen.

At this stage there was a brief hiatus in the case. Two potential witnesses in the abuse case declined to give evidence, and there was no immediate murder case to be made, although Savage remained deeply suspicious.

Fred was temporarily allowed out of jail, but Savage proceeded to seek clearance for the media-sensitive task of full-scale digging in the garden (the earlier excavations had been more limited). The case was being overseen by Detective Superintendent John Bennett, whose book *The Cromwell Street Murders* provides a fascinating, detailed account of the exhaustive police work that goes into a major murder enquiry.

There was still no certainty about Heather's fate. The West children were questioned with sensitivity. They had been threatened by Fred that if they talked, they would end their days 'under the patio like Heather', so it was understandably hard for the police to decode their information.

At one point, when the police finally started digging on a bigger scale, Fred told his son Stephen that he would be going away, and that he had done something bad. Stephen later recalled, 'He looked at me so evil and so cold. That look went right through me.'

Gradually the police uncovered the remains of Shirley Robinson, Heather and a third woman. They also started to investigate the disappearances of Rena and Charmaine. Fred at this point owned up to the murders, though he still tried to protect Rose. He also pointed the police towards the additional bodies in the cellar. For some reason, Fred would accept the charge of murder but insisted that he was innocent of rape, claiming that the sex with the girls had been consensual. Given all the other details that were emerging this was a curiously pointless, self-serving lie, but one that again shows the subnormal self-absorption of this callous man.

Nine sets of bones had now been found, including those recovered from the cellar. The police had the unpleasant task of attempting to identify the bodies. In most of the cases Fred was unable to provide them with names, so they had to attempt to match the remains against the files of missing persons. Around the country, families who had lost touch with young female family members were left in fear that they would hear the worst from the police.

Rose was actively trying to present herself as a victim in these crimes, an innocent bystander who had been fooled by a vicious husband. The police weren't convinced and kept working to tie her in to the case, in spite of Fred's defence of her. He continued to co-operate with the police, even boasting at times about his prolific murders.

He let them know where to find Rena, Anna McFall and Charmaine. However when it came to Mary Bastholm, he stopped co-operating and failed to provide a location for the possible burial.

To Fred's dismay, Rose now abandoned him personally. Perhaps she was merely trying to act the part, but she refused to touch him at a joint hearing, and refused to return his letters. On 13 December 1994, Fred was charged with twelve murders. He wrote to Rose, 'We will always be in love . . .You will always be Mrs West, all over the world.'

On New Year's Day 1995, Fred took his own life at Winson Green Prison in Birmingham, during the guards' lunchtime. He used a torn-up bedsheet to hang himself. A

callous killer in his life, he chose the coward's w̶
avoiding justice. Few mourned his passing, but one
regret that he didn't stand up in court to be faced with
vileness of his crimes. He also hoped that, by dying a̶ ̶
taking the blame, he might yet be able to save his wife from
the justice she so richly deserved.

The police now had a difficult problem. There was not
much evidence to link Rose directly to the murders, and in
Fred's absence she could lie all she wanted without fear of
contradiction. The case came to court on 3 October 1995.
Several witnesses, including Caroline Owens, Miss A., and
Anne Marie gave evidence, demonstrating that Rose had
been fully involved in many sadistic and perverted assaults
on young women.

The defence aimed to show that while Rose may have
been involved in sexual crimes, she was innocent of the
murders and didn't know about Fred's disposal of the bodies.

Rose made an unimpressive witness in her own defence,
leading the jury to see her as a selfish woman who had
treated her children badly at best. Taped confessions from
Fred were also played, and obvious inconsistencies were
revealed in his statements that attempted to exonerate Rose.

The key witness was Janet Leach, who was called because
she had attended Fred West's police interviews as an 'appropriate adult'. Fred had privately confessed to her that he was
taking the blame to protect his wife. He had told her that
Rose was the murderer in the cases of Charmaine and Shirley
Robinson.

This private confession was a terrible burden for Janet
Leach. She had been made ill by the stress and the moral
dilemmas it raised. After Fred's death she felt able to tell the
police and the court all that he had said. It was clearly a very
difficult act for her, and she collapsed, and had to be taken to
hospital, after the stress of her testimony.

Her evidence turned the tide. If the jury had ever been

willing to believe Rose, they could now clearly see the horrible truth.

Rose was found guilty and given a sentence of life in prison on ten counts of murder. She is still alive at time of writing. However, in conclusion, let's not remember her, or her evil husband.

Instead, let's end by remembering the known and unknown victims of their callous deeds. The names given in this chapter include those who are known to have been killed by them, but it is almost certain that more innocents died at the hands of this couple. In addition they brought misery to the lives of many, in their own family and elsewhere, whose lives were affected by their vile deeds.

Gerald and Charlene Gallego

The Sex Slave Killers

One of the most horrifying cases of an American couple who were serial killers was that of Gerald and Charlene Gallego, from Sacramento in California. This pair killed ten victims, mostly teenaged girls. The victims were kept as slaves before being brutally murdered. Charlene's involvement was mostly as a passive accomplice, but it is hard to forgive or even comprehend her involvement in these brutal crimes on that basis.

A later pair of killers, James Daveggio and Michelle Michaud would turn out to be virtual copycat criminals, who mimicked some of the Gallego's most vile crimes, although Daveggio and Michaud's spree of crime in the 1990s resulted in fewer deaths. In their case they assaulted seventeen or more girls in horrific ways, but did not kill their victims with the same regularity. But for the Gallegos murder seemed to come all too easily.

*   *   *

Gerald Armond Gallego was born in 1946 and grew up in Sacramento. If it is ever fair to say of a man that he was 'bad

39

to the core', it seems reasonable to say that of him. He was always likely to become a criminal as so many others in his family had already done. His mother, Lorraine Pullen Bennett Gallego, was a Sacramento prostitute. Her family included members who had been charged with murders and child molestation. Meanwhile Gerald's father (also called Gerald) was in San Quentin, and would never meet his child. When he was released he ended up killing two police officers in Mississippi and was executed in the gas chamber there.

The young Gerald had already been charged with burglary and sex offenses when he was as young as six. He acted as a runner for pimps who his mother knew, and when he was twelve he was charged with coming lewd acts with a six-year-old-girl and placed in a detention centre for children.

Once he was released, he was re-arrested within a year for armed robbery, a crime he committed with his half brother. After escaping and being recaptured, he served over a year in captivity before he was paroled in 1963.

All of this had taken place while Gerald was under the age of eighteen. He clearly wasn't someone who was going to grow up to be a model citizen.

Between 1963 and 1966 Gerald went through four short-lived marriages. From the first one, he had a child called Krista, who stayed with his mother after the marriage failed. From the age of six, she would be abused by her father. She would eventually file charges against him in 1978, for incest, sodomy, oral copulation, and unlawful intercourse.

He married a second time in 1966, but the bride left within a month. Gerald had beaten her and threatened her with a knife, and she wisely chose to leave him at the first opportunity.

The third and fourth marriages also failed, and in both cases it was Gerald's bizarre and violent behaviour towards women that was the catalyst.

In 1969, Gerald was once again apprehended for armed

robbery. Just as before, he was working with his half-brother David. They robbed a motel in Vacaville, California, and Gerald was sentenced to a five-year stretch. He escaped once, early in his time in jail, but ended up serving the full term before being released in 1974. He promptly got married again, and once again the marriage failed due to his behaviour.

Clearly Gerald was attractive to women. He never had difficulty in meeting new women, and he married them often enough. It was just that he was so unstable and violent, and so obsessed with strange sexual fantasies, that very few women would put up with him for long.

Finally, in 1977, Gerald met the woman who would become his partner in horrific crimes, Charlene Adell Williams. They met at a poker club in the September of that year and immediately embarked on a relationship.

*　　*　　*

There was nothing to suggest that Charlene would grow up to be a murderer. Born in 1956, she came from Arden Park, one of the nicer areas in Sacramento, from a middle-class family. Her father Charles was a successful executive in the grocery business, her mother was called Mercedes.

As a child Charlene seemed to be a model pupil. She had a high IQ and was a gifted violinist. She did go off the rails somewhat as a teenager. She became involved with drugs, alcohol, and what her parents regarded as unsuitable boys. She graduated from high school (with poor grades) and then flunked out of college.

She also went through some short-lived failed marriages, two in succession after leaving college. She had a sweet appearance and was short with blonde hair. This was the twenty-one-year-old girl to whom Gerald Gallego was immediately attracted on their first meeting.

41

From the start, the difficulties of being married to Gerald became apparent. He insisted that Charlene would work at the supermarket, and that he would take the money she earned. He was controlling in many details of her life, including how she dressed and what make-up she could wear.

Their sexual relationship was also complex. Gerald was often unable to achieve an erection and he would blame and abuse her for this problem. He openly slept with other women, and Charlene was expected to put up with this. But when he caught her once in bed with a young girl, he was furious, and took out his violent resentment on her.

However in spite of all of these details, Charlene didn't leave him as his previous five wives had done. Perhaps she thought she loved him, or perhaps the streak of teenage rebellion that she had retained meant that she found the transgressive nature of their life together more interesting than 'normality'. Either way, she stayed and soon the relationship would move on to the crimes for which the couple are now remembered.

In July 1978, Charlene became pregnant. Gerald would force her to abort the child during September, but by then their story had moved on to murder.

*   *   *

Gerald had always harboured violent sexual fantasies, and had discussed these with Charlene. On 11 September 1978, the couple turned these sick fantasies into reality for the first time.

They drove their Dodge van to the shopping centre at Sacramento's Country Club Plaza. Charlene, who was still pregnant at this stage, lured two teenage girls into the van, promising them marijuana. Seventeen-year-old Rhonda Scheffler and sixteen-year-old Kippi Vaught were the two unfortunate girls who climbed into the back of the van, only to find Gerald waiting for them with a gun.

Charlene appears to have been reluctant at first in this venture, and only went ahead with finding the girls for Gerald after he threatened her. If she didn't already know how violent he could be she was soon to find out.

He tied the girls' hands and feet with tape, and Charlene watched over them while he drove the van to a quiet area in the countryside, in the foothills of the Sierra Nevada mountains.

Gerald took the girls away from the van, instructing Charlene to wait for him. The full details of what he did to the girls in the next few hours are unknown, but given his later behaviour, one must assume he assaulted them sexually. Later he returned to give Charlene further instructions. She took the van back into town and visited some friends, in order to establish an alibi, then returned driving the couple's Oldsmobile instead of the van.

Gerald was waiting with the girls who were still bound. They were forced into the car. Charlene then followed Gerald's directions to a woodland area near Baxter in California. Gerald was talking as though the girls would be released, but when he asked Charlene to stop the car, he ordered them out, clubbed them with a tyre iron and then shot each of them dead while they lay unconscious on the ground.

Their bodies would be discovered two days later by farm workers in the area. It was on or close to this day that Charlene had an abortion under instructions from Gerald.

*   *   *

At the end of the month, Gerald's teenage daughter Krista filed charges of abuse against him. As a result, Gerald and Charlene decided to leave town.

Surprisingly, they were helped in this by Charlene's parents, Charles and Mercedes Williams who were of course unaware that Gerald had committed the recent murders. They helped Charlene to dishonestly use her cousin's birth certificate so that Gerald could take on the identity of Stephen Feil, and obtain a driving licence in that name. Charles Williams also used his contacts to find a job for Gerald driving a truck for a supermarket in Houston. Presumably Charles and Mercedes preferred to get Gerald out of town rather than see their daughter's name dragged through the mud in Sacramento where Gerald faced charges of child abuse. They were always protective towards their daughter, whatever they might think of her taste in husbands.

On the way to Texas, they got married in Reno. For a while both held down jobs and there were no further murders, but having started killing, Gerald was always likely to kill again, and by 24 April 1979 he had given in to the urge once again.

The modus operandi was the same as for the first killings, although these victims were even younger. At Washoe County Fair, Charlene enticed fourteen-year-old Brenda Lynne Judd, and thirteen-year-old Sandra Kay Colley to the couple's van. This time her cover story was to tell them she'd pay them to distribute leaflets and that she needed to return to the van to fetch them.

Once again Gerald was waiting for them with a gun, and tied them up. He bought a hammer and a shovel on the way. Charlene continued to drive, while Gerald stayed in the back of the van and assaulted the girls. Then he took over driving and they went further into the hills. Finally they stopped in a lonely spot, and Gerald forced the girls one by one to walk away from the van. He killed and buried them with the tools he had bought.

When Charlene cleaned out the van, on their return, Gerald kept the tools, in spite of the danger of them being incriminating evidence. However, the investigation into the disappearance of the two murdered girls didn't make any progress and for the time being the couple were safe. They even felt confident enough to return to Sacramento, under the assumed name of Feil.

Back in their home town Gerald was distracted for a few months by an affair he had with a local woman. By this stage of their marriage, Charlene was relieved when Gerald found a new sexual partner, as it relieved the pressure on her, both in his desire for sex slaves and also because their own sex life suffered from problems with Gerald's tendency to impotence.

However Gerald's desires resurfaced and on 24 April 1980 he ordered Charlene to help him once again. Stacey Ann Redican and Karen Twiggs were both seventeen, and were unlucky enough to run into Charlene while she was prowling round the Sunrise Mall in Citrus Heights, which is close to Sacramento. The two unfortunate girls were coming out of a bookstore when she approached them and offered them some drugs in her van.

Gerald was becoming more confident in his violent practices. Rather than tying them up, he ordered the girls to undress and started raping them in the back of the van, while Charlene drove on into the east along the interstate highway. They ended up at Limerick Canyon, twenty miles from Lovelock in Nevada. Gerald once again walked the girls away from the van one at a time, and killed them with the hammer. This time Charlene insisted on getting rid of the murder weapon, and it was thrown out of the window on the return journey.

For the first time, Gerald also insisted on Charlene viewing the graves. She was distressed and thought she saw movement although he assured her the girls were dead. He was perhaps trying to involve her more deeply in his murderous guilt at this stage, rather than leaving her to be a remote accomplice who waited in the van.

45

The remains of Karen and Stacy remained undiscovered until picnickers stumbled on them. The corpses had been mutilated by coyotes, but it was still clear at the autopsy that they had been raped and then murdered with a blunt instrument.

*　　*　　*

From this stage onwards, Gallego's behaviour became more careless; he was more likely to act on the spur of the moment, and the murders became more frequent. Like so many killers who are not caught early on, he had a ludicrously elevated view of his own ability to evade justice, and believed he could not be caught if he kept doing the same thing.

The couple remarried under his assumed name, further cutting their ties to the past. Charlene became pregnant again, and this time Gerald didn't force her to have an abortion.

Only six weeks after he had murdered Karen and Stacy, the 'Feils' were driving to Oregon for a holiday when he stopped the van to pick up a hitch-hiker that they passed. Her name was Linda Aguilar, and she was four months pregnant. Charlene had asked him not to pick her up she could see that the twenty-one-year-old was pregnant. Gerald merely joked that he liked his women pregnant. Linda was only making a trip to the store but accepted the ride home. Gerald forced her into the back of the van and assaulted her while Charlene drove.

The couple found a nearby patch of woodland. Charlene waited near the van while Gerald marched Linda into the woods. Without his hammer, he used a rock to bludgeon her before strangling her.

Her body would be found within a few weeks. Her boyfriend had previously beaten her and he came under serious suspicion for the murder, all of which helped to prevent the police from connecting the case to Gallego's other victims.

There was another six-week break in the killings before Gerald made his next attack. On 16 July 1980, the couple spent the day drinking. They ended up in West Sacramento at the Sail Inn, where they knew people and were on familiar terms with the bar staff.

The bartender, Virginia Mochel, was a thirty-four-year-old mother of two children, who were nine and four at the time of her death. She was friendly with the couple, and had no reason to fear them. At two in the morning, the Gallegos waited outside for her to come out after closing up. Gallego was drunk, but not to such an extent that he couldn't handle his gun. He abducted Virginia as she was about to start up her car to return home. It was his thirty-fourth birthday and the only thing he could think of doing to celebrate, other than drinking, was to rape and murder yet another innocent girl.

They drove to the Gallego's house. He tied her hands with fishing twine, then raped and assaulted her in the back of the van, while Charlene inanely and callously went inside to watch television. Virginia was left crying for mercy and asking why he didn't just kill her. Inevitably this was exactly what he did. The Gallegos dumped her body near to Clarksville.

There were several respects in which this was a turning point in Gerald's killing spree. Charlene's role in the whole series of events had been one of casual, if occasionally guilty compliance. To see Gerald kill someone who was not just a random young girl, but someone they knew, whom she knew had children, took her distress to a new level.

Secondly, this victim alerted the police to the possibility that the murders were more than a series of random disappearances or murders. Virginia Mochel did not seem like the sort of person who would simply wander off, so it was immediately assumed she had been abducted. And when her body was found, in October, the twine on her wrists suggested the nature of her abduction and started to ring alarm bells that she was one of a number of victims of a serial killer.

The police tracked down 'Stephen Feil' and his girlfriend in the course of their investigations, simply because they had been seen drinking in the bar, and the police wanted to trace all possible witnesses. Gerald denied all knowledge. However Charlene's alibi, that she and 'Stephen' had been fishing that day, created further suspicions because of the fishing twine that had been found on the victim's corpse.

However there was no further evidence and the suspicions had to be shelved until further events moved the investigation on.

*   *   *

Gerald's casual murder of Virginia Mochel seems to have awoken Charlene's slumbering conscience to some degree. The couple started to have regular arguments, in which Gerald would often lose control and hit her. In September, after a bad summer, Charlene left Gerald and temporarily moved back in with her parents. Gerald went off on his own and visited a former girlfriend out of town.

However he came back to town and demanded to see his wife. She assented and they arranged to meet on 1 November. They borrowed her parents' Oldsmobile, saying that they were going out to dinner. Instead they went to a bar and got drunk.

Gerald decided he wanted to look for another victim. Charlene was reluctant, but it seems clear that Gerald was both intimidating and testing her loyalty with this plan. They went to Arden Fair shopping center. There was a Founder's Day dance at the Carousel Restaurant, which was attended by many students from the California State University, which is in Sacramento.

Two seniors from the university, Craig Miller, twenty-two, and Mary Elizabeth Sowers (also known as Mary Beth), twenty-one, left the restaurant shortly after midnight, just as Gerald and Charlene were passing. They were a model couple who were engaged to be married.

Charlene was not willing to get out of the car and had been urging Gerald to give up for the night. But he wouldn't accept this idea, as he was determined to abduct someone. In the absence of her assistance, he resorted to brazen, brute force. He got out of the car and approached the couple, then pulled a gun on them and ordered them to get into the car.

They complied, fearing the wild-eyed drunk who was accosting them, and hoping to calm him down. One of the other college students, who knew Craig and recognized that he wasn't in his own car, stopped by the open window of the car and asked where they were going. They were scared of provoking Gerald and didn't answer immediately.

Charlene started shouting at Gerald and drove the car away at speed. However Craig's friend had time to make a note of the licence number of the car. Charlene drove the car out of town until Gerald told her to stop. He ordered Craig out of the car, then shot him in the head in front of his terrified fiancée.

Drunk and out of control, Gerald had lost all sense of caution. Having killed so often it had become a mere habit to him. Charlene drove him back to his apartment, and watched television while he raped Mary Beth in the bedroom.

Then they once again drove out into the country and Gerald shot Mary Beth. Then they went back to the apartment where Charlene helped him to clean up and try to conceal any forensic evidence.

When it was discovered that the couple hadn't returned home, Craig's friend gave the licence plate number of the Oldsmobile to the police. They came round to the house the next day to investigate, before Charlene had made it home. Charlene was unprepared and lied fairly transparently about where they had been the night before. She claimed they had driven the red Triumph car, even though detectives had already visited the house and seen it sitting unused in the driveway. Then she changed her story and claimed that she had been so drunk she couldn't remember which car she'd used.

She called Gerald to let him know that the police were closing in on them. He decided first to go back to Craig's body, to conceal the corpse, which, unusually, he had not done at the time, in his impatience to get back to assaulting the victim's poor fiancée.

However when they returned to the scene of the crime, the body had already been discovered and removed. In a panic, they decided to flee. They drove to Reno, and abandoned their car there before boarding a bus to Salt Lake City.

From this point the case against them moved far more quickly. Craig's friend identified Gerald as the man who had been in a car with the murdered couple. Confronted with the possibility that Gallego was a murderer, Charles Williams decided he had to tell the police that Stephen Feil was an alias for Gerald Gallego. The bullets from Craig Miller's body were also identified as having been fired from a gun that belonged to Gerald. The police had all they needed to make an arrest, other than a knowledge of the whereabouts of the suspects.

This didn't hold them up for long, though. Charlene called her parents from Salt Lake City and asked them to wire her some money. They had always felt that they had to protect her in the past, but it was apparent to them that it was no longer acceptable to do that. They promised to wire the money, then alerted the police to the transaction.

The couple were apprehended at the Western Union office in Omaha, where they had moved on to via Denver. FBI agents made the arrest. The couple surrendered without attempting to escape or fight.

*　　*　　*

It took some time for the trial to come to court. To start with there were some obstacles in the way of prosecuting Gerald for murder. Charlene was by now heavily pregnant, and gave birth to a son, also called Gerald, in January 1981. Charles and Mercedes Williams were granted custody of the child.

The case could have been held in several states, as the murders had ranged across their territories. There were funding problems in the legal system in California, and at one point a public appeal was launched which raised over $25,000 towards the costs of prosecuting Gallego.

The final problem was that most of the evidence in the case was dependent on Charlene's willingness to bear witness against her husband. She accepted early on that this was the best path for her, but the process of cutting the deal was torturous. Many politicians called for her to prosecuted for the murders without the complication of a plea bargain, but the prosecution took the view that it was more important to build as strong a case as possible against Gerald, the prime mover in this murderous relationship.

The final arrangement was that she would plead guilty to the murders of Craig Miller and Mary Beth Sowers. For this she was given a sentence of sixteen years, eight months, the minimum sentence applicable to a first-degree murder charge in California at the time. (The charge would eventually be dropped, although she still received the full sentence in return for co-operation and a guarantee she wouldn't face further charges in any other state).

She reached a similar deal with Nevada authorities, pleading guilty to the second-degree murder of Karen Twiggs and Stacey Redican and receiving the same sentence.

The Oregon authorities decided that it would be a super-fluous expense to run a third case, so didn't press charges. So in the end Gerald Gallego would be tried for these four murders, and the other murder charges would never come to court.

Gerald's behaviour at his two trials in California and Nevada was erratic. He decided he would be better at defending himself than any lawyer, a disastrous decision that reflected his egotism and over-confidence in his own abilities.

From the start he made a hash of his attempt to be a legal eagle. He declined to make an opening statement, thus giving the prosecution the advantage of telling the jury the full story first. When Mercedes Williams came to the stand and gave damning evidence against him, he failed to cross-examine the witness.

However he did spend six days cross-examining Charlene in an attempt to undermine her evidence. She had already given an account of why she had failed to restrain his vicious behaviour. Her account was that he had had a strong psychological hold over her and that she had feared him. She gave a harrowing account of occasions on which he had beaten her or threatened to do so. She explained how he had kept all her money and how, when she had questioned any of his decisions, he had accused her of not being the girl he had married, of letting him down.

All in all, her statements may have failed to justify her own shameful acquiescence in the murder spree. But she had given an eloquent and convincing account of a marriage in which she was psychologically and physically abused.

So Gerald's cross-examination of her came across as being the act of exactly the kind of bullying, manipulative husband she had described. He tried to persuade the court that she was a drug addict, and forced her to confess to a lesbian affair she had had while still in prison. He read out a love letter that she had sent him after they had been captured.

In general he was attempting to portray her as a low-life who was only giving evidence against him to save her own skin. However his manner of attempting this only convinced most observers that he was the kind of man she had claimed that he was. The jury need not have believed that Charlene was a paragon to accept that the evidence she gave about the murders was essentially correct.

Gerald also took the stand himself, and was caught out in a series of obvious lies and conflicting statements. Any sane lawyer would probably have kept him from testifying, as he was bound to be a bizarre and unpredictable witness. But as his own counsel, he believed he could persuade the jury to believe him.

In his closing statement he acknowledged that he had been given a 'legal licking' but made a feeble appeal to the jury to trust him, and take his word that he was innocent. To no one's surprise, the jury chose not to do this, and found him guilty of the first-degree murders of Craig Miller and Mary Beth Sowers. He was sentenced to death.

He was then extradited to Nevada, to be tried for the murders of Stacy Redican and Karen Twiggs. This trial was slightly less bizarre as Gerald accepted a defence lawyer rather than representing himself. Once again his counsel tried to discredit Charlene, but once again her evidence was too compelling to be diregarded. She had directed the police to a ball of string in Gerald's van, which was a perfect match for the string with which the girls' wrists had been bound. This evidence, taken in tandem with her account of the murders led to a second death penalty in June 1984.

*   *   *

In spite of being the first prisoner ever to be awaiting the death penalty on death row in two separate states, Gerald Gallego was never executed. He remained in prison until his death from rectal cancer on 18 July 2002. A series of appeals were issued by or for him, and the process of competency hearings and evaluation tribunals ticked away over the years. At one point he succeeded in having the Nevada verdict overturned on the basis of a technicality. But the state promptly held a second trial at which he was once again convicted and sentenced to death. In the end his death curtailed the process.

The one interesting theory that came out of the evaluations was the evidence given by a psychiatrist, Dr David Foster. He stated that Gallego's behaviour resulted from two main causes. Firstly he had the delusion that there was 'a herd of people from the dark side who are his enemy.'

He also asserted that Gallego had post-traumatic stress disorder as a result of an abusive childhood. He also suggested that a childhood head injury might have inhibited his 'ability to plan, problem-solve, comprehend and make judgments.'

It is hard to know what to make of these kinds of theories. We know from the evidence of a number of serial killers, including Fred West and Raymond Fernandez, that head injuries can be a contributory factor to vicious behavior, uninhibited by social norms or morality. However it seems almost too convenient an explanation.

And however awful Gerald Gallego's childhood might have been, his experiences pale into insignificance when compared to the horrors he inflicted on his victims as an adult.

When such a monster is on the loose, the best one can hope for is that those around him will restrain him or inform the authorities of his actions. In this case the horrendous truth is that Charlene's silence and acquiescence contributed to the deaths of all ten of Gallego's victims. She may never have murdered herself, but she will have those ten deaths on her conscience until she dies. She may deserve some under-standing, but there is a difference between understanding and forgiveness.

Charlene Gallego (who had reverted to her maiden name of Charlene Adell Williams) was released from prison in August 1997, after serving her sentence. She was forty years old at the time of release.

Her mother and lawyer released statements saying that she would not be returning to Sacramento and that she intended to 'pursue positive goals' in an undisclosed location. She didn't indicate where she was going, but she must be registered as a felon wherever she lives, so her whereabouts are known to the authorities.

Perhaps she deserves some credit for at least trying to pursue positive goals, but a lifetime of good works still won't bring back Gallego's victims or heal the grief of their relatives and friends.

Myra Hindley and Ian Brady

Murder on the Moors

One of the most intriguing and disturbing aspects of murders committed by couples is the way in which two lovers can create a mutually reinforcing fantasy world. We may be familiar with this phenomenon from personal experience or observation – two people who become romantically involved often take on elements of each other's belief systems and behaviours, and it can become hard to disentangle who influenced who in many ways.

This is a natural psychological effect – a relationship depends on some give and take and also requires us to develop a mutual understanding and view of the world. But when a couple indulges in murderous behavior, it is harder to understand how this turns into a vicious circle of reinforced behaviour.

One example of this is the case of the Moors murderers, Ian Brady and Myra Hindley. When they met, Brady was a fairly intense, private young man who liked to play with ideas of amorality and Nietzschean immunity to petty herd behavior, but he had done little to act out his ideas. Hindley had been an apparently religious girl, who had been trusted by local parents as a babysitter.

Yet, after these two met each other, they tortured and killed five children. Four of their victims were buried on Saddleworth Moor, a bleak area of moorland that rises above the northern English industrial city of Manchester.

In the 1960s Manchester was a fairly bleak place, still recovering from the decline of industry, the closures of mills, and the bombing of the Second World War. Against this backdrop and the harsh moors that surround the city, the murders had a baleful, powerful effect on the British public, who were deeply shocked by the involvement of a young girl like Hindley in such abhorrent crimes.

As a result, the murders have been examined repeatedly in film, songs and books. For many years newspapers would rake over the details of the crimes, often in connection with Hindley's long campaign to be released from prison. While many multiple murderers do eventually get released from prison, the British public and political establishment was uncomfortable with the possibility that Hindley might ever be freed and she eventually died whilst still imprisoned. But even fifty years later it is hard to truly understand the motivations and actions of this couple.

By the time their murderous activities were discovered, they had sunk so deeply into a mutual shared *folie à deux*, that they insouciantly killed their last victim in front of a seventeen-year-old witness, David Smith.

*   *   *

Smith was married to Hindley's sister Maureen. On 6 October 1965, the couple were visited by Myra Hindley. She said she didn't want to walk home alone, so Smith accompanied her to 16 Wardle Brook Avenue, Manchester, where she lived with Ian Brady. She invited him in to share some wine, then left him in the kitchen.

A loud scream came from the living room, and Myra shouted to him. Smith went into the room and found Brady holding a large figure. It was initially unclear what the figure was, but Brady dropped it against the sofa, and Smith saw that it was a young man. The young man was alive and groaning. Ian Brady was holding an axe and proceeded to hit the young man twice in the head with it, apparently killing him.

Brady then covered the youth's head, put wire round his neck and tightened it, whilst cursing him. Finally he stopped and said 'That's it, it's the messiest yet.' Hindley and Brady proceeded to swap jokes about the whole event, while Hindley made a cup of tea. Smith was horrified, but also terrified, and concluded that he was personally in serious danger.

As a result of this, he went along with the conversation, and even helped them to clear up the mess and move the body. Brady had previously boasted to him about killing people, but he presumed it was a black joke. And now Hindley told him a story about how they had been burying someone they had killed on Saddleworth Moor and had nearly been apprehended by a passing policeman.

For some time, Brady had been gradually drawing Smith into the sick fantasies and moral theories that were the foundation for the couple's murders, and it seems that they wanted to involve him in their murderous behaviour. Smith was known as a local ruffian, and the Hindley family didn't approve of him. To some extent he had been under Brady's spell, but he retained enough connection to reality to see that what was happening went far beyond what he should tolerate.

Finally David Smith managed to leave the house and return home. He was terrified and physically sick, and told Maureen everything. Armed with a knife and a screwdriver in case Brady turned up, they went out together to a public phone and called the police.

The case was dealt with by Superintendent Bob Talbot, who had to be called back from an imminent vacation by Detective Inspector Wills. David and Maureen told him their story at the police station in Hyde. Talbot went to the house in Wardle Brook Avenue, assisted by a number of officers. Hindley let him in and allowed them to unlock the upstairs bedroom, where the body and murder weapon were discovered.

The young man was later identified as Edward Evans, a seventeen-year-old who had been lured to the house by Brady. The final cause of death had been the strangulation rather than the axe blows.

Brady was immediately arrested. His initial story was that he had carried out the murder with Smith after an altercation with Evans. He protected Hindley by denying she had been involved, and Hindley initially backed up this story. It was not until a few days later, when a document was found in her car describing their murderous plans, that she was also arrested. This was the moment when the case broke through into the wider public consciousness as a murder committed by a young couple.

But how had Brady and Hindley reached the stage where they could behave in this horrific manner?

*　　*　　*

Myra Hindley was born in 1942 in Manchester. As a child she was religious, attending church regularly and apparently got along well with other children and liked animals. When she was young, she and her mother had lived with her grandmother, while her father served in the war. When her sister was born in 1946, her father Bob had bought them a home, but was struggling to adapt to peacetime. Myra was sent back to stay with her grandmother, who doted on her.

Myra's relationship with her father seems to have suffered as a result of their various absences in her childhood – they

59

remained distant as she grew older. It could be argued that in later life this was one influence that led her into seeking a relationship with the dominating figure of Brady.

At school, Myra performed reasonably well, preferring sport, arts and creative activities. She didn't get into the grammar school, and had to go to the inferior secondary modern, perhaps because of her frequent absences from junior school, absences that were tolerated by her grandmother who enjoyed her company. But she was usually in the 'A' streams of the secondary school and was rarely in trouble. Her good relationships with younger children led to her being frequently used as a babysitter by local parents.

When she was fifteen Myra was friendly with a younger thirteen-year-old boy called Michael Higgins. He was a quiet, timid youth and Myra took to treating him protectively as though she were an older sister. She was deeply affected by his death in a local swimming hole. He had asked her to go swimming with him that day and she had declined the offer, something that made her feel guilty for his death as she was a stronger swimmer than him.

Her reaction to his death was extravagant and somewhat hysterical. She dressed in black, attended church regularly and cried frequently. She even converted to Catholicism in this period.

It didn't look as though Myra would do well in her exams and she left school at sixteen. She worked for a local engineering firm for a while. This was the period in which she acquired bleached hair and started to wear the heavy make-up that would later become familiar from police photographs.

She was briefly engaged to be married to a local boy when she was seventeen, but she appeared restless and bored by her life and by the prospect of following her mother into an ordinary domestic lifestyle. She considered joining the armed forces although never went far in pursuing the idea, and also moved to London briefly before moving back to Manchester. There, she took a new job as secretary at Millward Merchandisers. This was where she met Ian Brady.

* * *

Brady had been born in 1938 in the Gorbals region of Glasgow, a rough slum in the industrial Scottish city. His mother Peggy was unmarried, which was still considered a stigma. She worked as a waitress for low pay, and found herself unable to cope with a child, often having to leave the young Ian at home on his own.

She advertised for someone to look after the baby for her, and he was unofficially adopted by Mary and John Sloane. They already had four children. Peggy arranged for them to receive Ian's support money. For a long time she would visit on Sundays, but they didn't tell Ian that she was his mother. Eventually she visited less often and then moved to Manchester with a new husband, Patrick Brady.

This strange situation led to the young Brady being emotionally remote. He didn't seem to fit in with the Sloane family, no matter how hard they tried to make him feel part of the family. He was withdrawn and emotionally turbulent, often having violent temper tantrums.

At school he was described as intelligent, but an under-achiever. As a teenager he started to get into trouble, smoking, missing school, and failing to do his work. He became obsessed with the Nazi regime in Germany, the one subject he really studied in this period.

By the age of sixteen he had been charged with breaking into houses three times. Eventually he was given the choice of a custodial sentence or moving to live with his mother Peggy and her husband, whom he had never met, in Manchester. He took his stepfather's surname, although they were not close.

He found it difficult to adjust to life in Manchester, and was treated as an outsider because of his dense Glaswegian accent. He started to read more widely, exploring writers such as Dostoevsky, Nietzsche and de Sade. In these writers he found themes of alienation and of the re-evaluation of the norms and morals of bourgeois society. In de Sade, he also found early hints of the sadistic sexual appetite that would become a powerful part of his later relationship with Hindley.

Brady's new start in Moss Side didn't transform him and soon he drifted back into crime. When he was working in a brewery he was arrested for theft and aiding and abetting and sentenced to two years in borstal, the British penal institution for underage criminals.

He spent the first three months in the adult jail Strangeways in Manchester, as no borstal places were available. Strangeways was a notoriously dangerous, rough prison, and this must have been a harrowing time for a teenager.

After being moved on to Hatfield borstal he got into a fight with a warder and was sent to yet another tough institution in Hull. Brady spent much of his time in prison trying to come up with criminal schemes that would make him rich, but he also studied book-keeping while he was there.

When he left prison, Brady took a while to find work, but eventually, after a spell as a labourer, he got a job using his book-keeping skills. This was as a stock clerk at Millward's Merchandisers. He had been working there a year when Hindley arrived as the new secretary.

Hindley was immediately attracted to Brady and pursued him without success for months. She saw his withdrawn, silent nature as 'enigmatic, worldly and a sign of intelligence.' She had been looking for something different in her life and saw Brady as something more exciting and fascinating that the boys she had known before. He was uninterested for some time, but eventually asked her out after a Christmas party.

From the start the relationship revolved around Brady's personal fascinations. Hindley would later write that 'the strength of my love for Ian Brady was part of the reason I allowed myself to be pushed into murder. He had such a powerful personality, such overwhelming charisma. If he'd told me the moon was made of green cheese or that the sun rose in the west I would have believed him.'

In this statement, Hindley was as usual trying to blame Brady for her own crimes. But there seems to be some truth in what she wrote. Brady introduced her to his Nazi fixation, showing her film of the Nuremberg trials, and giving her *Mein Kampf* to read.

He also introduced her to the ideas of his favourite writers, or at least to his interpretation of those ideas. In writers such as Dostoevsky and Nitzsche he saw a rejection of moral norms, and an invitation to the individual to triumph over others by all means necessary. In de Sade he found a writer who resonated with his own sado-masochistic fantasies.

Those who knew Hindley recalled that she changed from the time she started to go out with Brady. She started to reject the ordinary life of her friends, to say she hated normal families and babies. She started dressing in a miniskirt and long boots.

In private they were indulging Brady's sexual fantasies. They took pornographic photographs of each other. But the danger of their mutual psychological reinforcement grew when Brady talked to Hindley of his other beliefs. She stopped attending church when he told her that there was no God. Brady described murder as the 'supreme pleasure', and said that rape wasn't wrong, and again Hindley fitted in with his attitudes. She was in thrall to him to the degree that she adopted all of his beliefs as though they were her own, regardless of how dangerous or immoral. Brady rejected morality in the same way as Nietzsche – as an imposition the weak place upon the strong. But where Nietzsche was looking to create new values, Brady misinterpreted his writing as a sweeping justification of immorality.

It is unclear how strong a part Hindley played in building this mutual world in which rape and murder became acceptable. When there was a possibility of Hindley being released from prison in later life, Brady wrote the following about their relationship.

> Myra Hindley and I once loved each other. We were a unified force, not two conflicting entities. The relationship was not based on the delusional concept of *folie à deux*, but on a conscious/subconscious emotional and psychological affinity. She regarded periodic homicides as rituals of reciprocal innervation, marriage ceremonies theoretically binding us ever closer. As the records show, before we met my criminal activities had been primarily mercenary.
>
> Afterwards, a duality of motivation developed. Existential philosophy melded with the spirituality of death and became predominant. We experimented with the concept of total possibility. Instead of the requisite Lady Macbeth, I got Messalina. Apart, our futures would have taken radically divergent courses . . .
>
> When I learned . . . this week that she was now claiming I had threatened to kill her if she did not participate in the Moors murders, I considered that the lowest lie of all. The fact that she continued to write several lengthy letters a week to me for seven years after we were imprisoned contradicts this cynical allegation. Perhaps her expedient demonomania now implies that I exercised an evil

influence over her for seven years from my prison cell three hundred miles distant?

In character she is essentially a chameleon, adopting whatever camouflage will suit and voicing whatever she believes the individual wishes to hear. This subliminal soft-sell lured the innocent and naïve.

When their accounts differ, it can be hard to know who to trust. Brady himself pointed out in his letter that he had never sought parole, so could speak the truth, whereas Hindley was motivated by the desire to achieve her ambition of a parole. This may mean that we can trust his words. Either way it does seem that their relationship was the trigger that pushed Brady from being a solitary brooding petty criminal into the terrible crimes that would follow.

Perhaps it was Hindley's unquestioning adoration and belief in him that gave him the confidence to carry out his fantasies, or perhaps their fantasies merged and became strengthened by the fact they were together.

*   *   *

In 1963 Brady first explored Hindley's capacity for crime, when they started planning a bank robbery together. On Brady's suggestion, Hindley learned to drive, joined a gun club and bought two guns. The plan was for Hindley to be the getaway driver.

They never carried out this plan, but it is clear that the planning helped to develop the trust between them – it became apparent to both that they were willing to co-operate on activities that were outside the law.

Inspired by his understanding of his literary heroes, the existentialists and writers such as Dostoevsky, Brady now saw himself as the outsider in society who could do as he chose. He later said that he felt he had 'reached the stage where, whatever came to mind, get out and do it . . . I led the life that other people could only think about.'

The time had now come when the two would turn their secret life into reality. Over the following year, they started their murderous partnership.

Brady and Hindley's first victim was Pauline Reade, who was sixteen years old at the time. On 12 July 1963 she was on her way to a dance at a local social club. Three friends of hers had been planning to go to the dance, but after their parents found out that alcohol would be served the situation had changed. Nonetheless two friends followed Pauline to the dance, and after taking a short cut on the way, they realised that Pauline hadn't arrived as planned.

Pauline's parents went out to search for her when she failed to arrive home. They called the police in the morning, but their search also failed to find any trace of the missing girl.

It was Myra Hindley who had abducted Pauline. Just as when she was younger, she knew how to talk to young people and win their trust. She had promised Pauline some records and then tricked her into going to Saddleworth Moor with her in the minivan on the pretext that she was looking for a missing glove.

Brady followed behind on a motorbike, knowing that the child would more easily trust a woman on her own. He joined up with the couple on the Moor, pretending it was a chance meeting.

The details of Pauline's final moments are unknown. The certain facts are that she was sexually abused by Brady either before or after she died. She died after her throat was cut from behind. Hindley and Brady together hid the evidence and Brady buried the body in a shallow grave on the Moor.

It is uncertain whether the murder of this poor girl was intended as a one-off or the first of many. But as so often with serial killers, the first victim was followed by others. Once the line of taboo had been crossed by Brady and Hindley together, it was all but inevitable that they would continue with their horrific activities.

On 11 November of the same year a second child disappeared. Twelve-year-old John Kilbride had been watching a film at the cinema with his friend John Ryan. After the film they visited the local market, where stallholders would sometimes give them money to help out. That was the last place where John Ryan saw his friend. Like Pauline Reade before him, he simply disappeared.

His parents Sheila and Patrick called the police and once again a major search was instigated. Once again the search found nothing.

Again, it was Hindley who had won the trust of the young boy. Seeing him helping with the market stalls she had offered him some money to help her move some boxes.

As before, Brady joined up with them on the Moor. He tried cutting John's throat with a serrated knife. But when this didn't work, he used his shoelace to strangle the boy. He also assaulted John sexually. While this was going on, Hindley kept watch from the car on the road, using the headlights to signal to Brady if the road was clear. John Kilbride was also buried on the Moor.

The couple took photographs at the scene of the crime. One became symbolic of the Moors Murders. At first sight it is merely a picture of Hindley cradling her dog. But the picture was taken over the child's freshly buried body as a keepsake. This vision of gloating arrogance helped to establish the image of Hindley as evil and callous in the minds of the British public when it was later printed in the newspapers.

Again the couple waited for a few months before they killed another victim. But their confidence was growing as they came to believe that they were invulnerable. Neither of the previous victims had been found and they believed that as long as they weren't they would not be caught. They were also aware that, since capital punishment had been abolished the year before, the worst sentence they could face would be life imprisonment.

The third murder victim was Keith Bennett, who was twelve at the time of the murder. He was on his way from his mother's house to his grandmother's. His mother was going out to the bingo and Keith was old enough to walk the mile by himself. Tragically he never made it as he was intercepted by Hindley.

The alarm was only raised the next morning – his grandmother had assumed that his mother had changed her mind about going out. The police search was once again fruitless.

Hindley had used the same ploy as she had used with Pauline Reade, asking Keith to help her search for her glove on Saddleworth Moor. Brady then lured the boy into a ravine. He sexually assaulted the child, killed him by strangling him with a piece of string. While this was happening, Hindley callously watched from the top of the ravine. The couple once again took photographs at the scene, which Hindley managed to destroy in the gap between Brady's arrest and hers.

*　　*　　*

Vile as the pair's activities had been up to this point, they descended even further into evil with their next victim. The murder of Lesley Ann Downey haunts the city of Manchester like an evil black stain to this day. No one who has heard the details can be left in any doubt as to the vicious, evil nature of both Hindley and Brady.

The modus operandi started out following the pattern of previous crimes. Lesley Ann, a pretty ten-year-old girl with curly black hair, had gone to a local fairground on Boxing

Day. She only had a sixpence with her and wasn't expected to stay long at the fair. Her mother would later describe her as a 'good child who always did her homework, a perfect child any mother would be proud of'.

Myra followed her around the fair, waiting for an opportune moment. She pretended to drop a bag of groceries and Lesley Ann helped her pick them up. At this stage Brady arrived and, trusting Hindley, the girl helped them take the shopping to the car.

Here the murderers' pattern of behaviour changed. Instead of going straight to the Moors, they took Lesley Ann to their home. She was forced upstairs, where she tied, gagged and attacked. Brady initially claimed that Hindley had not been involved in the attack, but a slip of the tongue at the trial revealed that Hindley had been fully involved in both the torture and sexual abuse.

For whatever perverted reason, Hindley chose to record the attack on a spool tape recorder. This was the tape recording that would so tragically be played to Lesley Ann's mother when the police needed her to identify her daughter's voice. What worse torture could there be for a mother than to be made to listen to her own child being assaulted in this way?

After the attack Lesley Ann died at Brady's hands, choked with a ligature. They washed the body, wrapped it in a sheet and took it to the Moors where Lesley Ann was buried in a shallow grave.

Meanwhile Lesley Ann's mother Ann and her boyfriend Alan had raised the alarm as soon as Lesley Ann failed to return from the fair. But their search would be as fruitless as those of the Brady and Hindley's earlier victims.

*   *   *

The next time the couple killed would be the murder that led to their arrest. Following Brady's arrest for the murder of

69

Edward Evans, the police searched the house where Brady and Hindley had lived. They found a ticket concealed in a prayer book, and this led on to the discovery of two suitcases in a locker at the station in Manchester.

In the suitcases were several pieces of incriminating evidence. There were pornographic photographs of Hindley, a notebook which contained the name of John Kilbride, the photograph of Hindley with her dog posing on one of the graves on Saddleworth Moor (although it only became certain that this was the location after later investigations).

The suitcases also contained the tape-recording of Lesley Ann Downey pleading for her life. Shocked detectives were reduced to tears by this tape and by the cold, callous nature of the male and adult female voices also captured. Brady and Hindley were identified by their voices, and after Lesley Ann's mother had been put through the awful ordeal of identifying her own daughter on the tape, the police were sure that that several murders were now involved.

The photographs of the Moors led to extensive police searches, and within a few weeks the body of John Kilbride was discovered – Lesley Ann Downey's had already been found in the previous searches that followed Brady's arrest and the discovery that the two had frequented Saddleworth Moor. This was the period in which the newspaper and television coverage of the grim search and investigations created public outrage.

The trial was held in April 1966 at the crown court in Chester. At the trial, both Brady and Hindley attempted to implicate David Smith in some of the murders, whilst Brady did what he could to deflect blame from Hindley. But the evidence was too compelling.

Brady was found guilty of the murders of Edward Evans, John Kilbride and Lesley Ann Downey. Hindley was found guilty of murdering Downey and Evans and of harbouring

Brady, knowing that he was the murderer of John Kilbride. Both were sentenced to life imprisonment.

The bodies of Pauline Reade and Keith Bennett had not been found. The police suspected that the pair were the killers of these two children but were unable to put forward sufficient evidence for the court. Pauline Reade's body was not found until 1987, after Brady finally confessed to the murders in 1986, while that of Keith Bennett has never been located.

The judge, Mr Justice Fenton Atkinson, had clearly been affected to some degree by Brady's attempts to take the blame. He called the pair of defendants 'sadistic killers of the utmost depravity'. However, while he expressed the opinion that Brady was 'wicked beyond belief' and incapable of reform, he suggested that this wasn't true of Hindley, once she had been removed from Brady's influence.

The British public felt somewhat differently. Brady was clearly evil. However there had not been a case within living memory where a woman had been so deeply involved in the murder of children. In addition, the fact that Hindley had been involved both in winning the children's trust and in their horrific mistreatment made her a target of especially intense hatred in the media and public.

Brady accepted his fate more stoically than Hindley. Over the years he has made it clear that he does not wish to be released, and has, through various hunger strikes and suicide bids, shown a preference for death.

But Hindley campaigned endlessly for her own release. In the early years of her imprisonment she wrote long letters to Brady. But later on she chose to present herself as a reformed Christian, capable of returning to normal life.

The prison campaigner Lord Longford took up her case; indeed many feel that he was somewhat of a dupe for doing so, and his public reputation suffered as a result. Hindley continued to deny personal responsibility for the crimes she had committed, preferring to blame Brady, and to say that he had influenced her or even forced to take part in the murders. Like her earlier lies about David Smith, it seems clear that she was being self-serving.

Brady, who had no obvious reason to lie, seems to have been the more truthful of the pair during his incarceration. For all his depravity and in spite of the bouts of mental breakdown he was subject to in prison, his accounts of Hindley's complicity probably have more claim to be believed than her attempts at self-justification.

During one of Hindley's bids to win release he wrote a letter to the then Home Secretary, which we have already quoted from. He made it clear that Hindley was a 'chameleon' personality, capable of taking on whatever characteristics she needed to win the trust of others. He also made it clear how deeply complicit she had been in their mutual crimes.

After the confession regarding Pauline Reade and Keith Bennett, both Hindley and Brady were taken back to the moors to try to help identify the locations of the graves, to no avail in the case of Keith Bennett.

In 1990 the Home Secretary made a ruling that Hindley should never be released. It took her until 1994 to discover this via a Law Lords judgment on her case. She continued to campaign for release, but there was little political will to support the release of such a notorious killer.

Hindley died in 2002, having been taken from prison to hospital, suffering from pneumonia. The 'most hated woman in Britain' was finally released from imprisonment by death, not freedom. Brady is still alive at the time of writing, although it is reported that his only desire is death. At one point he threatened to sue the prison service after they used force feeding to thwart a hunger strike.

Many of the families of the victims were also denied their desires and rights. They lost the right to see their loved ones grow up. In the case of Keith Bennett's mother, she was even denied the chance to see her child given a final resting place as the body remains undiscovered. The families went through awful grief and many of them never recovered from the shock. It is impossible to feel any pity for Brady, knowing the suffering he and Hindley caused together.

There is a terrible irony, but possibly some kind of justice in the fact that his final choice of death has been for so long denied him, just as he denied the gift of life to the children that he tormented and killed.

Carol M. Bundy and Doug Clark

The Sunset Slayer

During the late spring and early summer of 1980, Los Angeles police were on the lookout for a serial murderer. The bodies of two young girls were found near Sunset Boulevard. Teenage stepsisters Gina Marano (fifteen) and Cynthia Chandler (sixteen) were found dead on 12 June. They had vanished on 11 June from Huntington Beach, on their way to meet up with some friends. Their bodies were found the next morning beside the Ventura Freeway near Griffith Park, in Los Angeles.

Each sister had been shot in the head with a small-caliber pistol. On 24 June the bodies of two more young women were found. Exxie Wilson and Karen Jones were discovered separately, Wilson had been decapitated, her head was missing and her body had been put in a wooden box and placed in the driveway of a nearby house. Because of the location of the murders newspapers began calling the killer 'The Sunset Slayer'.

The police felt that they were making some progress when Carol Bundy, a divorced thirty-seven-year-old with two children living in the San Fernando Valley, told police that her lover, Doug Clark, had told her he had killed several young women.

All had been shot with a gun Bundy had purchased. Bundy claimed initially that she knew nothing of the murders, 'only what he [Clark] told me'.

At first sight this appeared to be one of those cases where a woman had tolerated and perhaps protected her partner in spite of his murderous and perverted activities. However, police would soon discover the extent of Carol's involvement in what was a brutal sexually motivated string of killings. She may have started out being drawn into Clark's sick fantasies, but she was far from innocent in the matter herself.

*   *   *

Douglas Clark had been in the US military and had lived in many different countries by the time he settled in Southern California. He liked to call himself 'the king of the one-night stands', and his typical conquest was a frumpy middle-aged housewife.

Carol Bundy fitted the bill perfectly. She was an overweight clinical nurse who had taken her two children and left her abusive husband three years earlier. Soon after leaving her marriage, she fell for her apartment building supervisor, forty-five-year-old John Murray. Murray worked nights as a country-and-western singer and was the type of man who would always help someone in need.

Alone as a single parent Bundy badly needed money. Murray helped her claim $620 a month for her visual disabilities (she suffered from severe cataracts and carried a white cane) and helped her to be fitted for glasses, greatly improving her sight.

Alone and clingy, Carol started asking the supervisor round to her apartment to fix minor problems. She even began clogging the toilets and drains just to get a visit from Murray. They became lovers, but Murray was married and refused to leave his wife. Desperate, Carol approached his wife and offered her $1,500 to disappear. Murray was so furious that he broke off the affair and threw her out of her apartment.

Still obsessed with him, she began to visit the bar where Murray worked and it was there that she met Douglas Clark. On the rebound, Bundy began a relationship with Clark that same night, and the two began living together. By day Clark worked in the boiler room of a Burbank soap factory but at night dwelled in his sordid fantasies. Privately he dreamed of rape and murder, mutilation and necrophilia.

As his fantasies escalated he began looking for women with whom he could act them out. Carol turned a blind eye when he brought younger women home for sex and obediently took photographs when he asked her to.

Eventually kinky sex began to give way to paedophilia; he even brought home an eleven-year-old girl wearing roller-skates, but Carol was so enslaved by him that she never complained. Needing something more to get his kicks, Clark began discussing death and mutilation.

*   *   *

After the murders of Marano and Chandler, Clark confessed to Bundy, excitedly sharing the gruesome details of how he had forced the girls to perform oral sex on him, then shot each girl in the head as she brought him to orgasm.

Ten days later he killed again. Karen Jones was a twenty-four-year old prostitute. She was found behind a Burbank steakhouse, murdered by a single gunshot to the head. Later that morning, the headless corpse of twenty-year-old Exxie Wilson was found. Whilst Bundy's sons were out of the house Clark brought Wilson's head out of the refrigerator and forced Carol to put make-up on it.

Later in her confession she told police, 'We had a lot of fun with her. I was making her up like a Barbie with make-up.' Clark then proceeded to perform oral sex with the dead woman's head. It became a pattern, Douglas Clark would strike a deal for oral sex with a girl and during the act, shoot her in the head. He would then engage in sexual acts with their dead bodies.

The 'Sunset Slayer' was already making headlines when Exxie Wilson's head was found in a Hollywood alley, stuffed into an ornate wooden box. The box had been thoroughly scrubbed clean to avoid leaving any clues to identify the murderer.

On 27 June the mummified corpse of a seventeen-year-old prostitute was found near Hollywood. Marnette Comer was a runaway from Sacramento and had last been seen alive around three weeks earlier. Comer had been known to work the Sunset Strip just like Clark's other victims. The murders continued when an unidentified young woman was found with two bullet wounds in her head on Sunset Boulevard on 25 July. Later the same month, another unidentified body was found near Malibu, again with a bullet wound in the head.

Unknown to Doug Clark, Carol Bundy had continued visiting John Murray at the country-and-western bar where he performed by night. Whilst extremely drunk one night she confessed all to him. Murray was shocked and wanted to tell the police. Bundy panicked. On 5 August she met Murray at midnight as usual in his van she stabbed him to death and cut off his head. His torso was found in his van but his head has never been discovered.

*   *   *

A few days after she had killed Murray, reality seemed to set in for Bundy. The magnitude of what she had done overwhelmed her and she broke down at work, sobbing to a fellow nurse, 'I can't take it any more. I'm supposed to save lives, not take them.'

When her colleague told the police, Carol Bundy told them about Doug Clark and the murders, initially pretending that she had nothing to do with them. When police called on Bundy at home, they found three pairs of panties removed from victims as trophies, along with snapshots of Clark engaged in sexual acts with an eleven-year-old girl.

Clark was arrested immediately. Four days later, police retrieved a pistol from the boiler room at the soap factory. Ballistics tests would prove that the gun was the same weapon that had been used to kill the 'Sunset' victims.

Under questioning, Clark claimed that Bundy and Murray committed the murders and he was merely Bundy's fall guy. Police began to question Carol Bundy. Bundy eventually confessed to the murder of John Murray but claimed it was self-defence.

Under further intense questioning Bundy also admitted that she had been present during one of the murders for which Clark was charged. That murder took place in East Hollywood in a car parked behind a gas station. Bundy claimed Clark shot a prostitute in the head while the prostitute was performing oral sex on him.

Bundy had hired the girl as a present for Clark's birthday. Clark denied he had shot her, telling police that Bundy had been the shooter. Both agreed however, that they had disposed of the body together. Bundy plea-bargained by agreeing to testify at Clark's trial in return for a lesser jail sentence.

*   *   *

Clark's trial became a media sensation. The press constantly reported the seedy world in which Bundy and Clark carried on their sexual adventures. Clark admitted that he had been having an affair with the thirteen-year-old girl who babysat Carol Bundy's children. Bundy told a shocked courtroom how Clark had put the head of one of his victims in the refrigerator then played with it, performing sexual acts with it in the shower.

Doug Clark initially waived the right to an attorney and represented himself in court. Blaming Bundy and Murray for the murders he told the jury, 'We have to vote for the death penalty in this case. The evidence cries out for it.'

The jury didn't believe his first claim, but were happy to comply with the latter. On 28 January 1983, Clark was found guilty on six counts of first-degree murder as well as one count each of attempted murder, mayhem, and mutilating human remains. He was sentenced to death and is still on California's death row. No date has yet been set for his execution.

Carol Bundy pled insanity but later admitted to her role in the killing of John Murray and one of the unidentified female victims. According to her statement, she removed John Murray's head to remove ballistic evidence, a trick she'd learned from Doug Clark. She also admitted to handling Clark's gun when her fingerprints were identified on it. Convicted on the basis of her own confession, Bundy was sentenced to twenty-seven years for one count of murder and twenty-five years on the other. The sentences were to run concurrently. Carol Bundy died of heart failure on 9 December 2003, in the Central California Women's Facility in Chowchilla. She was sixty-one years old.

Catherine and David Birnie

The Willagee Killers

On 10 November 1986, shoppers in a small retail complex in the quiet district of Willagee on the outskirts of Perth, Western Australia, were shocked to see a half-naked teenager stumbling out of the woods. Clearly terrified, the girl asked a shopkeeper to call the police saying she had been raped and held hostage at knifepoint by a couple living nearby.

At the time, the police were searching for twenty-one-year-old Denise Brown who had gone missing five days earlier. They thought they had finally found their missing girl. What was about to transpire, however, was far more disturbing. It revealed a spate of sexually related murders covering the previous four or five weeks eventually resulting in the discovery of four dead women. The young girl in the grocery store had clearly initially been destined to be the fifth.

The girl led police to 3 Moorhouse Street, the home of David and Catherine Birnie. It was a dilapidated bungalow, made of white brick, with a garden that was overrun with weeds. This was the address where the couple tortured, raped and subsequently murdered four young women. According to police it was the worst looking house on the street, an address which would gain notoriety as the love-nest, torture chamber and execution room of a husband-and-wife serial killer team.

The Birnies' victims were chosen on the spur of the moment. The couple didn't really care who they murdered. Their victims simply had to be young and female. Whenever the Birnies felt like killing someone they would drive along the highways of Perth and pick up hitchhikers or, pretending to be friendly, offer young women a lift. Their victims never suspected the 'kind' couple until it was too late.

At knifepoint they were taken back to Moorhouse Street, tied to a bed and sexually abused as the Birnies carried out their sordid fantasies. Then they were murdered. The lucky ones were put to sleep with an overdose of sleeping pills and then strangled. The less fortunate victims were either stabbed or bludgeoned to death with a knife or an axe.

The murders were not the first time that the couple had been in trouble with the law. Both had a long history of criminal activity and both had suffered very mixed up, deprived childhoods.

It would seem that they always felt that they had in common a transient and unaffectionate background. Psychiatrists would later report that the two had an unusually high level of emotional dependence on each other.

*　　*　　*

David John Birnie was born in 1951, the eldest of several children. Both his parents, Margaret and John Birnie, suffered from chronic alcoholism and for all of their young lives, the authorities periodically took the children away from their parents and placed them in government institutions.

David's parents divorced when he was ten years old.

Apparently, neither parent wanted or claimed custody of him and he subsequently became a ward of the state.

He was a short, slightly built boy who looked nothing like a stereotypical serial killer. The only time that it looked like he might make a success of himself was in the early 1960s when he trained as an apprentice jockey with trainer Eric Parnham.

Parnham recalled Birnie as a pale, sickly looking boy who he took on through kindness just to give him a job. When Birnie was recommended to him as an apprentice prospect, Parnham went to pick the boy up at his home. According to Parnham, the house was a derelict slum surrounded by a pack of dogs.

Birnie worked in the stables for almost a year and showed enough ability to become a good jockey. Parnham eventually sacked him when he was alleged to have robbed and tried to sexually abuse the elderly owner of a boarding house wearing nothing but a pair of tights over his head.

By the time he was an adolescent, David had already been found guilty of several crimes and had spent time in jail for various misdemeanors and felonies. As an adult, he was known to the authorities as a sexual addict, pornography addict, and a paraphiliac (having a disorder characterised by sexual fantasies, feelings or activities involving a non-human object, a non-consenting partner such as a child, or pain and humiliation of oneself or one's partner). He had one childless marriage prior to his common-law marriage with Catherine.

*   *   *

David and Catherine first met when they lived next door to each other as young children. Catherine, too, was born, in 1951, into a life of doom and despair. She was ten months old when her mother died, and her father took her to live in South Africa with him.

At the age of two, she was sent back to Australia to live with her grandparents who legally fostered her. Neighbours from the time recall that the child rarely laughed and had few pleasures. She never had a playmate and other children were not allowed to play with her because they were not allowed in her grandparents' house.

Catherine would later watch her grandmother die in the throes of an epileptic seizure when she was fifteen years old. Subsequently she was sent to live with an aunt and uncle where again her loneliness and sadness is what most people remember about her. Even before she reached high school it would seem that her mind was scarred by loneliness.

David Birnie was reunited with Catherine when they were both in their teens, during the time she was living with her aunt and uncle.

Catherine thought she had found a friend in Birnie, a relationship that she would later identify as love. So was so used to being alone that she would do anything David wanted her to do. David had watched his family falling apart since he was ten years old. He showed an early taste for crime, and Catherine fell in line with anything he wanted. Together they went on a minor crime rampage that would later land them both in jail.

Even by the time he developed his teenage friendship with Catherine, David already had an extensive record for juvenile offences. By the age of sixteen, Catherine was helping David burgle a string of shops and small factories in Perth.

Both were eventually arrested and on 11 June 1969, David and Catherine pleaded guilty in the Perth Police Court, to eleven charges of breaking, entering and stealing goods worth nearly $3,000. They admitted to stealing oxyacetylene equipment and using it to try to crack a safe at the Waverley drive-in movie theatre.

At their trial the court heard that Catherine was already

pregnant by Birnie. Accordingly, Catherine was placed on probation and Birnie was given a three-year sentence in Karnet Prison. He wasn't incarcerated for long. On 21 June 1970, David Birnie managed to break out of jail and teamed up with Catherine once again. When they were re-apprehended on 10 July they were charged on fifty-three counts of stealing, receiving stolen goods, breaking and entering, being unlawfully on premises, unlawfully driving motor vehicles and unlawfully using vehicles.

In their possession police found clothing, wigs, bedding, radios, food, books, 100 sticks of gelignite, 120 detonators and three fuses. This time at their trial Catherine said that she knew that what they had done was wrong but that her love for David was so strong that she would do anything for him. This time Birnie was sentenced to a further two-and-a-half years in prison and Catherine received six months. Her newborn baby was taken from her by welfare workers.

*   *   *

On her release from prison a few months later, Catherine went to work as a live-in domestic servant for a family in Fremantle. Although she and David remained casual lovers into their late teens, Catherine eventually married Donald McLaughlin, the son of her employers, on 31 May 1972, her twenty-first birthday.

On first impression it would seem she had been lucky and freed herself from the influence of David Birnie and a life of crime, but the happiness didn't last. Not long after the marriage Catherine gave birth to the first of their six children. The couple called their first-born son 'Little Donny' after his father.

At the age of only seven months Donny was crushed to death by a car in front of his mother. Catherine was distraught and it seemed that the marriage thereafter went downhill. Certainly no one would have described it as happy.

Catherine obviously still pined for David Birnie. By this time David was out of prison and was back on the streets. He had one failed marriage behind him and his brief career as a jockey was over after the claims of sexual intimidation and theft. In 1984 he reunited himself with Catherine and the two began an affair. A year later it came as no surprise when Catherine abandoned her husband and children and moved in with David Birnie.

The McLaughlin family had been living in a State Housing Commission home in the working-class suburb of Victoria Park. Catherine had to look after her unemployed husband, their six children and her father and uncle. Friends and relatives said that the place was like a rubbish dump. Catherine was not house-proud nor did she ever care much about how her kids looked. There was little money for food.

Eventually, Catherine simply phoned her husband one day and said she wasn't coming back. After thirteen years apart, she returned to her first love and later had her name changed by deed poll to Birnie, becoming his common-law wife.

*   *   *

It is almost unanimously agreed that Catherine became completely emotionally dependent on David, who by this time had become embroiled in a world of bizarre sexual fantasy. He had a sexual appetite that was seemingly insatiable. He began demanding intercourse six times a day. He wanted Catherine to be his compliant sex slave.

It would seem to have been a condition that ran in the family. David's younger brother James had also served prison sentences for sex offences. James stayed with the couple for a short time when he was released from prison after serving five months for indecently interfering with his six-year-old niece.

He told a reporter after the couple's arrest: '[The six-year-

85

old] led me on. You don't know what they can be like. When I left prison, I had nowhere to go. I couldn't go back to my mother's place because I had assaulted her and there was a restraining order out against me. I had a couple of fights with mum and the police chased me off. Mum has alcohol problems. So David and Catherine let me move in. They weren't real happy about it and David kept saying that he was going to kill me to keep me in line.'

James also added that David Birnie seemed to have had few friends, was heavily into kinky sex and had a big pornographic video collection. 'He has to have sex five or six times a day,' James said of his brother. 'I saw him use a hypodermic of that stuff you have when they're going to put stitches in your leg. It makes you numb. He put the needle in his penis. Then he had sex. David has had many women. He always has someone.'

It is also rumoured that when David moved in with James, during a brief separation from Catherine, he sodomised his brother as a substitute for an available female. In addition to this it is claimed that David loaned Catherine to James to be treated however he liked for James's twenty-first birthday. Clearly, the Birnie household was far from normal. In 1986 however, kinky turned to killing, possibly after David and Catherine had exhausted everything together sexually and were in need of fresh kicks.

Catherine later confessed that at this point they began discussing abduction and rape. Birnie persuaded her that she would enjoy watching him penetrate another woman who was bound and gagged. Catherine was prepared to go along with him.

*   *   *

They snared their first victim on 6 October. Mary Neilson was a twenty-two-year-old psychology student at the

86

University of Western Australia. She worked part-time at a local delicatessen and was hoping eventually to get a job as a counsellor with the Community Welfare department. Her parents were both TAFE (college for Technical and Further Education) lecturers and were in the United Kingdom on holiday when their daughter disappeared.

Neilson had first approached David Birnie at the garage where he worked to buy some spare tyres. Birnie suggested that he could offer her a better bargain if she stopped by his house. It would turn out to be a very bad bargain indeed. The last sighting of Mary Neilson was when she left the delicatessen on that Monday to attend a lecture at her university. She never made it.

Her car, a Galant sedan was discovered six days later left in a riverside car park ironically directly opposite police headquarters. David Birnie would tell police after his arrest that he had driven it there himself. Mary Neilson was seized at knife-point as soon as she entered the Birnie house.

She was forced into the bedroom, where she was stripped, bound and gagged before being chained to the bed. Then Catherine Birnie watched as her lover repeatedly raped the girl. Whilst the rape was taking place Catherine asked him questions about what turned him on the most. She later told police that by doing so she would know what to do to excite him.

Catherine admitted that she knew that Mary Neilson would probably eventually have to die but said it was something that she and Birnie hadn't yet discussed, that it wasn't pre-meditated. Later that same night they took the girl to the Gleneagles National Park where Birnie raped her again then, as Catherine watched, wrapped a nylon cord around her neck and slowly tightened it with a tree branch. Mary Neilson was strangled. Birnie then stabbed her through the body (he believed it would stop the body swelling, allowing gases to escape the body as it decomposed) and buried her in a shallow grave.

*   *   *

It was two weeks before the couple killed again. Around 20 October, they picked up a pretty fifteen-year-old called Susannah Candy as she hitchhiked along the Stirling Highway in Claremont. Susannah was said to be a brilliant student at Hollywood High School. She lived in the fashionable district of Nedlands with her parents and two brothers and a sister. The daughter of one of the leading ophthalmic surgeons in Western Australia her disappearance was a very public affair.

The Birnies forced her to send letters to her family to assure them that she was all right. Her family though, always feared the worst. The Birnies later confessed that they had been driving around for hours looking for a new victim and after seeing Susannah, stopped and offered her a lift. They bound and gagged her within seconds of her getting into the car then drove her back to their house in Willagee.

Like Mary Neilson, Susannah was stripped, tied to the bed and repeatedly raped by David Birnie. This time however, after David had finished with the girl, Catherine Birnie got into bed with them. David had told her that this turned him on. David Birnie later tried to strangle Susannah with nylon cord, but she fought back with all her strength and the Birnies had to subdue her. They eventually forced sleeping pills down her throat and once Susannah was unconscious, David put the cord around her neck and asked Catherine to prove her love for him by murdering the girl by tightening the cord around her neck.

Catherine obliged and tightened the cord until Susannah stopped breathing. This time David Birnie watched. When asked later why she had done it, Catherine Birnie said:

88

'Because I wanted to see how strong I was within my inner self. I didn't feel a thing. It was like I expected. I was prepared to follow him to the end of the earth and do anything to see that his desires were satisfied. She was a female. Females hurt and destroy males.'

It is interesting, if distressing, to see that she had internalised David's beliefs to such a strong degree that she identified with his point of view more than she identified with a member of her own sex. After killing Susannah Candy, the couple drove her body to the State Forest and buried her near the grave of Mary Neilson.

The Birnies found their third victim on 1 November. She was a woman they were already acquainted with, thirty-one-year-old Noelene Patterson. On that day she was standing beside her car on the Canning Highway, East Fremantle because she had run out of petrol.

Noelene lived with her mother in the leafy suburb of Bicton on the shores of the Swan River, and worked as bar manager at the Nedlands Golf Club. Members of the Golf Club remembered her as a very polite and charming young woman. She had previously worked for nine years as an air hostess. She had even worked for corporate tycoon Alan Bond as a hostess on his private jet for two years.

Since she already knew the couple, Noelene had no qualms about getting into the Birnies' car. However, once inside it was the same story as before. Noelene had a knife held to her throat and was tied up and gagged. The Birnies drove her to Moorhouse Street where she was dragged into the bedroom, chained to the bed and repeatedly raped by David Birnie.

This time however, the scenario was a little different. Noelene was a beautiful, elegant lady who had clearly enchanted David Birnie from the outset. Catherine took an immediate dislike to her. Noelene was everything Catherine wanted to be: good-looking, graceful and popular. This time

89

David kept putting off the murder and Catherine became infuriated. Insecure and emotionally dependent on him, she felt as if she was losing him.

She told police that she even held the knife to her own heart and threatened to kill herself unless he killed Noelene. Noelene was kept prisoner in the Moorhouse Street house for three days before she was killed. Again, sleeping tablets were forced down her throat and David strangled her under the watchful and determined eye of Catherine. When they took her body to the forest to bury her Catherine said she took great pleasure in throwing dirt in the dead woman's face.

*   *   *

The Birnies struck again almost immediately, on 5 November, when they abducted their fourth victim. Denise Brown was waiting for a bus on Stirling Highway. The twenty-one-year-old was known as a happy and fun-loving girl who loved dancing and going to nightclubs.

She worked part-time as a computer operator in Perth and shared a flat in Nedlands with her boyfriend and another couple. On the night she was picked up by the Birnies, she had been at the Coolbellup Hotel for a drink with a girlfriend. A friend later told journalists, 'She was someone who would do anything to help anyone. She trusted too many people. Perhaps that is why she didn't think twice about taking a lift.'

Denise was abducted at knifepoint and, like the other victims, taken to the Birnies' house in Willagee where she was chained to the bed and raped. The next day the Birnies took her to the Wanneroo pine plantation.

Hidden in the forest, David Birnie raped Denise in the car as the couple waited for nightfall. After dark they pulled her out of the car and sexually assaulted her again. As Catherine guided him with her torch, David Birnie stabbed Denise

Brown in the neck whilst raping her. It was to be their blood-iest murder.

Denise didn't die straight away after being stabbed. Catherine gave David a bigger knife and he plunged it into her again until she lay silent on the forest floor. Thinking that she was dead the Birnies dug a shallow grave and put her body in it. However, as they were covering her body with soil, Denise sat up.

David Birnie then took an axe and smashed her skull with it. Denise sat up one more time and eventually Birnie split her skull open with the axe and she finally died.

*   *   *

Police were later to find out that the Birnies nearly abducted another girl on their way to Wanneroo Forest. The Birnies had offered a lift to a nineteen-year-old student as she was walking along Pijar Road, Wanneroo. The girl later recognized the couple from newspaper photographs.

She told police that as she was walking a car pulled up beside her. There was a couple in the front and someone slumped on the seat in the back. The person in the back was almost certainly Denise Brown.

The girl told police, 'I felt uneasy. I didn't recognize the car. There was a man driving and a woman in the front seat of the car. The man kept looking down, not looking at me and the woman was drinking a can of UDL rum and coke. I thought the fact that she was drinking at that time of day was strange. He didn't look at me the whole time. It was the woman who did all the talking. She asked me if I wanted a lift anywhere. I said, 'No, I only live up the road.'

'They continued to sit there and I looked into the back seat where I saw a small person with short brown hair lying across the seat. I thought it must have been their son or daughter asleep in the back. The person was in a sleeping position and from the haircut, looked like a boy, but for some reason I got the feeling it was a girl. I told them again I didn't want a lift because walking was good exercise. The man looked up for the first time and gazed at me before looking away again. By this time more cars had appeared and I started to walk away but they continued to sit in the car. Finally the car started and they did another U-turn and drove up Pinjar Road towards the pine plantation. It wasn't until I saw a really good photo of Catherine Birnie that I realised who they were. Somebody must have been looking after me that day. I don't know what would have happened to me if I had got into that car.'

*   *   *

The messy murder of Denise Brown seemed to have badly affected Catherine Birnie. She told police that she enjoyed the sex they had with their victims and didn't mind them being strangled or stabbed to death. However, after the brutal murder of Denise she decided that she didn't want to go through that again. This could be why she left their next victim unchained and alone in their bedroom.

Victim number five survived their attack and by informing the police of the Moorhouse Street address led to the Birnies' arrest and finally their conviction. She was a sixteen-year-old girl and her name has never been released because she was a juvenile at the time.

She ran into the grocery store in a small Willagee shopping complex on 10 November 1986, half-naked, crying and demanding to be taken to the police station. The girl was taken to Palmyra police station where Detective Ferguson and Detective Sergeant Vince Katich were following up leads on Denise Brown's disappearance.

They hoped that it was the breakthrough they had been so desperately waiting for and expected the girl to be Denise

Brown. Instead they found a teenager with an incredible story. The frightened girl told the police how she had been abducted at knife-point by a couple who had taken her back to their house and stripped and chained her to a bed by her wrists and feet where the man repeatedly raped her as the woman watched.

She also said that she remembered the man talking about injecting something into his penis. She was kept chained to the bed all night but in the morning the woman untied her and forced her to telephone her parents and tell them that she had spent the night with a friend. While she was using the phone she had the good sense to note the number.

She was subsequently able to give police a full description of her attackers, along with their telephone number and address. The girl said that the woman went to answer the door leaving her unchained and that she escaped through the bedroom window.

The information that the girl gave the police led a team of armed detectives to the scruffy and dilapidated house in Moorhouse Street. When she told police about being forced to telephone her parents, Detective Ferguson and his partner Detective Sergeant Katich began to suspect that the couple were the kidnappers of the other young women because they had been forced to do the same thing.

They also felt sure that since the girl had seen their faces and knew their address, the couple had intended to murder her and it was likely that they had done this before.

The police immediately went to the Birnies' house but when they arrived there was no one home. Two detectives hid inside a van and eventually arrested Catherine Birnie as she arrived home. Initially, Catherine refused to answer any questions until her husband was with her.

She told the police of the car yard where David worked as a labourer and he was arrested soon afterwards. When the police brought him home, the couple claimed that the girl had not been abducted, but had willingly come to the house to smoke cannabis with the Birnies, and that all sexual activity had been consensual.

They vehemently denied the girl's allegations and although she had apparently hidden a packet of cigarettes in the bedroom to prove that she'd been there the police had little other evidence to back the girl's claims.

The police detained the Birnies for questioning all day. Eventually they decided to interrogate David and Catherine separately, hoping that intense questioning would weaken their will and give the detectives a confession.

Bizarrely enough, it was an attempt at a humorous comment that finally led to David Birnie's confession. Towards evening, Detective Sergeant Katich joked to him, 'It's getting dark. Best we take the shovel and dig them up.' According to police, David Birnie amazed them by replying immediately, 'Okay. There are four of them.'

When she was told of her lover's confession, Catherine Birnie also broke her silence. She explained to the detectives: 'I think I must have come to a decision that, sooner or later, there had to be an end to the rampage. I had reached the stage when I didn't know what to do. I suppose I came to a decision that I was prepared to give her a chance.

'I knew it was a foregone conclusion that David would kill her, and probably do it that night. I was just fed up with the killings. I thought if something did not happen soon it would simply go on and on and never end.

'Deep and dark in the back of my mind was yet another fear. I had a great fear that I would have to look at another killing like that of Denise Brown, the girl he murdered with an axe. I wanted to avoid that at all costs. In the back of my mind I had come to the position where I really did not care if the girl escaped or not. When I found out that the girl had escaped, I felt a twinge of terror run down my spine. I thought to myself: 'David will be furious. What shall I tell him?'

David and Catherine Birnie agreed to take police to where the bodies were buried not far from the city. Police reports describe the couple as appearing excited and even proud to show police the graves of their four victims. As the convoy of police vehicles drove along Wannneroo Road towards the dense pine forest David was relaxed and chatty about his crimes.

He led police about 200 yards into the forest where he pointed at a mound of earth and told them to 'dig there'. Minutes later, police discovered the corpse of Denise Brown who had been reported missing only five days earlier.

A guard was placed next to Denise's shallow grave and Birnie led the police south to the Glen Eagle Picnic Area on the Albany Highway near Armadale. David Birnie then guided police into the forest and along a narrow track.

About forty yards from the track, police uncovered the decomposing body of twenty-two-year-old Mary Neilson, who had gone missing on 6 October. Further down the same track, David Birnie pointed out the burial site of fifteen-year-old Susannah Candy who hadn't been seen since 19 October.

Detective Sergeant Katich later said that he was astonished that neither David nor Catherine Birnie showed any emotion or guilt while the bodies were being uncovered. If anything, he said, they appeared to enjoy being the centre of attention as they pointed the graves out to police.

Catherine Birnie wanted her turn next. She pointed out where they had buried thirty-one-year-old Noelene Patterson, whom they had kidnapped and murdered on 30 October. Catherine Birnie was determined to explain to police that she disliked Noelene from the moment that she and David had abducted her. She even said that she was glad that Noelene was dead.

According to police reports, as she pointed out the grave, she spat on it. Detectives said that she showed a great deal of pride in being able to find the grave by herself. It was as if she didn't want David Birnie to get all of the credit. As they left the graves, David Birnie is said to have commented to Katich: 'What a pointless loss of young life.' Whether he was referring only to Noelene Patterson's death or all four murders has never been made clear.

*   *   *

As the couple were being charged with multiple murder, there was absolutely no doubt in the detectives' mind that if the young girl hadn't escaped earlier in the day, the killings would have gone on. On 12 November 1986, David John Birnie and Catherine Margaret Birnie appeared at Fremantle Magistrates' Court and were charged with four counts of murder.

The public was so outraged at their crimes that a crowd gathered outside the court. The holding cell leading to the courtroom had to be heavily guarded by police. As the trial began, psychiatrists attached to the case agreed that Catherine Birnie could not have killed on her own. She just wasn't the type. But the quiet mother of six children was totally obsessed with David Birnie and would do anything for him, including murder.

David Birnie was a completely different story. He had been in and out of institutions and prison all of his life and was always going to end up in jail for a long time. It was impossible however, to have foreseen the magnitude of his crimes.

David Birnie was led into court handcuffed to a policeman. He was wearing a faded pair of blue overalls with trainers and socks. Catherine, barefoot and handcuffed to a policeman, wore faded blue jeans and a faded shirt. Neither of them made any comment as the charges were read out and neither of them wanted any legal representation.

They entered no plea to the court and bail was officially

refused. The Birnies were remanded in custody until their trial. Catherine Birnie was asked if she wanted to wait eight or thirty days before her next court appearance. She apparently turned to David and said, 'I'll go when he goes.'

The trial date was set for 10 February 1987 at Perth Supreme Court. A crowd outside called angrily for the death penalty. As the prison truck carrying the Birnies arrived there were shouts of 'Hang the bastards' and 'String them up.' The couple were led into the court holding cells under a heavy police guard.

Bill Power covered the Birnies' crimes and trial for the Perth *Daily News*. Power later recalled the Birnies' appearance in the Perth Supreme Court as one of the most chilling experiences of his career. 'There was nothing distinctive about David and Catherine Birnie when they first appeared in court to face multiple murder charges of the serial killings which brought to an end the mystery of young women going missing off Perth streets.

'They were a rather nondescript, ordinary-looking couple you might find running a petrol station in a country town. David was a weedy little man and Catherine his drab, slightly buxom wife with a very sour face. Both were accompanied by male police officers.'

He recalled that David Birnie had been the first to appear on the stairs that led to the holding cell underneath the court, looking out of place in the rather grand surroundings of the Perth Supreme Court.

Birnie stood in the dock watching the police, media and crowd as Catherine made her entrance. The court appearance was a brief one. Power wrote that 'the erstwhile angelic Catherine, who moments before had acted out such a show of dedication, was dragged kicking and screaming and spitting down the wooden staircase to a prison van waiting beside the court. Perhaps she never wanted another man besides David to touch her.'

97

At his trial David Birnie pleaded guilty immediately to four counts of murder and one count of abduction and rape. He was asked why he was pleading guilty and in response gestured towards the victims' families and said, 'It's the least I could do.'

Mr Justice Wallace sentenced David Birnie to the maximum sentence of life imprisonment with strict security. He told the court: 'The law is not strong enough to express the community's horror at this sadistic killer who tortured, raped and murdered four women. In my opinion, David John Birnie is such a danger to society that he should never be released from prison.'

David Birnie stood silently in the dock as the sentence was passed. His arrogance returned as he was led to the prison van under tight security. With the angry mob calling for his blood, David Birnie is said to have put his hand to his lips and blown them a kiss.

Catherine Birnie had not been required to plead as her barrister was awaiting a psychiatric report to determine her sanity. She was remanded to appear later that month. Found sane enough to plead, Catherine Birnie admitted her part in the murders and was sentenced on 3 March 1987 in the Perth Supreme Court.

A psychiatrist to the court said that Catherine was totally dependent on Birnie and almost entirely vulnerable to his evil influence. He told the court, 'It is the worst case of personality dependence I have seen in my career.' Mr Justice Wallace had no hesitation in handing down the same sentence as that imposed on David Birnie.

He said: 'In my opinion you should never be released to be with David Birnie. You should never be allowed to see him again.'

*   *   *

In their first four years in prison the couple exchanged 2,600 letters, but they were denied the right to marry, have personal phone calls to each other or to have contact visits. In Fremantle prison David Birnie was repeatedly beaten up and attempted suicide later in 1987. He was eventually moved to Casuarina maximum security prison for his own protection.

In 1993 David Birnie's personal computer was confiscated from his cell in the protection unit when it was found to contain pornographic material.

He was found dead in his cell in October 2005. He had hanged himself.

At the time of the trial, Bill Power of the *Daily News* had written: 'As the heinous charges of abduction, rape, torture and murder were being read out against him, Catherine Birnie bent forward, stretched out her right hand and gently stroked the ball of David Birnie's thumb behind his back. There has probably never before been such a declaration of undying love in the Western Australian Supreme Court dock.'

Once again, this is a case that challenges our notions of love and evil, as the two were so inextricably entwined in the relationship between the two killers. It is disturbing to see that a couple who were clearly in love with each other, after some fashion, could act in such horrific ways towards the women they abducted and murdered.

And as with other killers in this book, it seems that the only appropriate way to end the story of the Birnies is to remember the victims rather than the killers.

Each of the women listed below had her life stolen to satisfy a man's sick fantasy. Each victim died knowing that a woman had acquiesced or participated in her vile abuse for the gratification of her man. And each of them would probably still be alive today if they had never met the Birnies.

The Victims

Mary Frances Neilson (age twenty-two)
Susannah Candy (age fifteen)
Noelene Patterson (age thirty-five)
Denise Karen Brown (age twenty-one)

Paul Bernardo and Karla Homolka

Ken and Barbie Killers

Paul Bernardo, a killer and convicted rapist, together with his wife and accomplice, Karla Homolka, claimed at least three young women's lives, and raped and assaulted countless others. The two were to become Canada's most reviled criminals. Outwardly, one would never think them capable of such crimes. To the general public they looked like a perfect Barbie and Ken couple.

Bernardo and Homolka met in Scarborough in Toronto, Ontario, in 1987. Bernardo was by then already the unknown perpetrator of a series of rapes being investigated by the FBI. The couple began a relationship characterised by sexual perversion and fantasies that would run out of control. They even involved Homolka's fifteen-year-old sister Tammy as a victim in their bizarre sexual practices, something that sadly ended in tragedy.

Paul Bernardo doesn't seem to fit the usual profile of the perpetrator of violent sexual assault or murder, which is possibly why he went undetected for so long, even after police had been alerted to his possible involvement. He was born into a financially well-off family on 27 August 1964.

However, there are reports that his father Kenneth Bernardo was himself abusive to his wife, Paul's mother Marilyn. The couple ran a highly successful marble and tile company and were affluent and privileged to all appearances. But there was a rumour that Paul's mother had an affair with her first love after she was married to Kenneth and that it is her lover not Kenneth who is Paul's father. According to this theory, the elder Bernardo was tolerant of the affair and even put his name on the birth certificate.

Paul's father had personal sexual issues of his own. He fondled a girl and was charged with child molestation in 1975. He was suspected of being the neighbourhood peeping tom and it is reported that he also abused his own daughter. Bernardo's mother later sank into clinical depression because of her husband's abuse and gained weight.

She seemed to withdraw from family life, eventually taking refuge in the basement of their Scarborough home. Young Paul Bernardo didn't initially appear to affected by the turmoil in his family.

When Bernardo was sixteen, his mother is said to have told him of his actual parentage and described the way that they had covered it up by putting his father's name on his birth certificate. This is a difficult age for such revelations, and Bernardo seems to have responded with contempt rather than with understanding.

From this time onwards Paul began openly to call his mother 'slob' and 'whore' and had little to do with her, possibly why he eschewed the family business and decided to follow his own path. He decided instead to become an accountant.

He graduated from Sir Wilfrid Laurier Collegiate Institute and went to work for Amway. He began to fantasise about becoming rich and powerful. According to one book which deals with the case, *Deadly Innocence*, by Scott Burnside and Scott and Alan Cairns, he started to buy the 'books and tapes of famous motivational get-rich-and-famous experts.'

He would also attempt to use persuasive techniques learned from such books on young women he met in bars. By the time he went to the University of Toronto in Scarborough, he had developed dark fantasies about sex. He enjoyed humiliating women in public and frequently beat up women whom he dated.

Bernardo was always looking for ways to make extra money. He started smuggling cigarettes across the United States–Canadian border with his friend Van Smirnis. He had developed a need for cars, toys and women that required a high level of income and the junior accountancy job that he obtained after graduation did not pay enough to keep him in the lifestyle he so desperately desired.

*   *   *

Beginning in 1987, when he was twenty-two years old, Bernardo began committing multiple sexual assaults, of increasing severity, in the area of Scarborough, Ontario. Most of the assaults were on young women whom he had stalked after they had exited buses late in the evening.

On 4 May 1987, Bernardo raped a twenty-one-year-old woman, in front of her parents' house. He had followed her home. The girl reported the attack to the police, saying that the attack lasted over half an hour. Ten days later, Bernardo committed a second rape. He assaulted a nineteen-year-old girl in the back yard of her parents' house.

On 27 July 1987 he attempted a third rape. This time his intended victim fought back fiercely and while he inflicted some physical injuries on her, he failed to rape her.

At the age of twenty-three, Bernardo met seventeen-year-old Karla Homolka in October 1987, in a Scarborough restaurant. Homolka had been born on 4 May 1970 in Port Credit, Ontario, Canada. She was the eldest of Karel and

Dorothy Homolka's three daughters. The Homolka family, who came from a Czechoslovakian background on the father's side, lived in St Catharines, Ontario.

Karla started to date Bernardo and after completing her diploma in 1989 began work as a veterinary assistant at the Thorold Veterinary Clinic. She had to leave the job after she was suspected of stealing drugs. (This would later be a piece of evidence that would corroborate the role she had played in the sex attacks with Paul Bernardo.)

She moved on to find a similar job at the Martindale Animal Clinic, and continued working at the clinic even though she had two separate offers of a college place.

As soon as they met, Paul and Karla became obsessed with each other, especially with regards to the sexual side of their relationship. On their first evening together they reportedly engaged in sex for several hours while Bernardo's friends were watching a movie in the same room.

Paul apparently asked Karla what she would think if he told her he was a rapist. Her answer was that she would think it was 'cool'. Even though Paul was dating Karla, he continued to rape young girls, and now he had her implicit consent.

On 16 December 1987, Bernardo assaulted a fifteen-year-old schoolgirl. It was a violent, prolonged assault. On the next day, the Metropolitan Toronto Police Department issued a warning to women in the Scarborough area about travelling alone at night, especially taking buses.

The next rape was on the 23 December 1987. During this attack Bernardo raped a seventeen-year-old girl using a knife in an unusually vicious manner. The police began to use the term 'Scarborough Rapist', sure that they were now on the hunt for a serial attacker. Still the assaults continued, on 18 April 1988, Bernardo attacked another seventeen-year-old.

On 25 May 1988, Bernardo came close to being apprehended by a investigator from the Toronto Police who was observing a bus shelter, a practice the police had adopted to try to protect women on their way home. The investigator spotted Bernardo hiding beneath a tree and chased him, but Bernardo managed to escape. Five days later, on 30 May 1988 the sixth rape took place in Clarkson, 25 miles south-west of Scarborough. The victim this time was an eighteen-year-old girl. The violent rapes had now been going on for over a year.

The frequency of the attacks seemed to diminish for a while, but then Bernardo attempted a seventh Scarborough rape on 4 October 1988. His intended victim fought him off but he inflicted two stab wounds to her thigh and buttock that required twelve stitches.

Around six weeks later, he attacked an eighteen-year-old in the backyard of her parents' house on 16 November. Now the police went further and created a special task force for the purpose of hunting down the Scarborough Rapist. A statement was issued declaring: 'We're warning all women to plan the routes they take after dark very carefully. We're pleading with people to be on the lookout for anyone loitering in the area of bus stops or anywhere women are likely to be alone. Any woman who feels threatened should immediately make for a house or place of safety and dial 911.'

*   *   *

At this stage it seemed as though the net was closing in on him. But he continued to evade justice. A neighbour chased Bernardo off on 27 December 1988, after he attempted yet another rape. On 20 June 1989, Bernardo again attempted to rape another young woman but she fought against him and her screams alerted neighbours. He ran away with his face scratched by the intended victim. In August 1989 Bernardo raped again. This time his victim was a twenty-two-year-old woman.

Bernardo committed his ninth rape on 21 November 1989, attacking a fifteen-year-old schoolgirl he spotted in a bus shelter. On the 22 December 1989 a nineteen-year-old became Bernardo's tenth victim. The attack occurred in the stairwell of an underground parking lot. The victim later filed a $10-million law-suit that included Homolka as a defendant. In a letter Homolka wrote from prison, four years later, she wrote 'Wow! I don't know what this woman thinks she's going to get because Paul and I are broke!'

In the midst of all these sex attacks, Bernardo was still carrying on his relationship with Homolka. He proposed to her on Christmas Eve 1989, just a few days after his latest rape. Homolka called it 'the most romantic moment of her life'. Still the rapes continued. Whether or not Homolka knew of them at this point isn't known but it is suspected that she may have done.

Five months later on 26 May 1990, Bernardo committed his eleventh rape. This attack was the one which would eventually contribute to his conviction, although it would take a long time. His nineteen-year-old victim had such a clear recollection of her attacker that police were able to make a fairly accurate computer composite photograph. The image was published in the press within a few days of the attack.

*   *   *

The police received a number of tips that Bernardo fitted the Scarborough Rapist composite, and he was interviewed by detectives. Through the summer of 1990, police submitted more than 130 suspects' samples for DNA testing, but none matched the samples taken from victims. After the composite photograph was published, investigators received

106

two reports that the person they were seeking was Paul Bernardo.

In June, a bank employee called in and gave his name to police. The second call was from Tina Smirnis, who was married to Alex Smirnis, one of the three Smirnis brothers who were friends of Bernardo. She told the detectives that Bernardo had been suspected during a previous rape investigation.

The police interviewed her and concluded that it was Alex Smirnis who had suggested that his wife should call the police. Once the police arrived, Smirnis did all the talking. He told police that Bernardo preferred women who were small and not too bright, and that he had discussed his liking for violent sex with Smirnis.

According to police reports, Smirnis 'spoke in non sequiturs; his phrasing was awkward and stilted'. The detectives weren't sure how seriously to take his evidence. However they decided to interview Bernardo.

They interviewed Bernardo on 20 November 1990. He gave them samples for testing, and admitted that he bore some resemblance to the composite picture that had been published. However, during the interview he remained calm and appeared helpful.

In fact, he was so mild and well-spoken that the detectives concluded, 'It just did not seem possible that such a well-educated, well-adjusted, congenial young man could be responsible for the vicious crimes'.

They decided that he 'was far more credible than . . . Alex Smirnis who, with his awkward, strange way of speaking, might just be trying to collect the reward.' As a result they pretty much rejected the claims of Smirnis. Scarborough police would later become the subjects of an accusation of negligence, as a result of their failures to apprehend Bernardo.

Bernardo married Karla Homolka and moved to St

Catharines in February 1991. The wedding pictures are one of the sources of the epithet they later received: the 'Barbie and Ken Killers'. They do look to be a clean-cut, model couple in the photographs, but this image was covering up some terrible secrets.

The rapes in Scarborough stopped once Bernardo moved away. But he had not stopped attacking women. In April 1991, Bernardo committed his twelfth rape in St Catharines. His victim this time was very young. She was a fourteen-year-old school girl.

However, he was careful to avoid detection by deliberately making the attack dissimilar to the ones in Scarborough. Unlike his previous rapes, this one occurred in the early morning, not at night, and he was not stalking near a bus stop. Homolka probably knew by now that Bernardo was indeed the 'Scarborough Rapist'. However, instead of being horrified by his acts, Homolka was intrigued by them, to the point of being willing to join Bernardo in his sexual assaults on young women. The two began work in earnest as a team.

*   *   *

As his relationship with Karla Homolka developed, Bernardo began spending large amounts of time with the Homolka family, upon whom he had apparently made a favourable impression. He was charming and well educated, engaged to the eldest daughter and flirting constantly with the youngest for laughs. What he hadn't told them was that he had lost his prestigious job at Price Waterhouse and was instead smuggling cigarettes for a living.

During the summer of 1990, Bernardo became increasingly obsessed with Tammy Homolka, Karla's youngest sister. He began peeping into her window and even entering her room to masturbate while she slept. Bizarrely Homolka knew of and even encouraged his behaviour by breaking the blinds in her sister's window to allow Bernardo access for his stalking and sexual fantasy.

In July, Bernardo took Tammy across the border to buy some beer for a Homolka party and while there, Bernardo later told his fiancée, 'They got drunk and began making out'. It is clear that Homolka now knew that while he was going out with her, Bernardo was seeing other women and committing rapes, but the trip across the border with her sister still left her feeling 'outraged and humiliated'. Bernardo had told her that if she really loved him she would let him deflower her sister.

It is hard to know what thought processes went on in Karla's head at this stage. She seems to have chosen to blame her sister rather than her partner for the problem, and thus to have acquiesced with Bernardo's suggestion. She promised that she would allow him to have sex with her sister.

The assault on Tammy thus occurred on 25 July 1990. According to Bernardo's testimony at his trial, Homolka laced spaghetti sauce with crushed valium she had stolen from her employer, the Martindale Animal Clinic. She served dinner to her sister, who soon lost consciousness from the drugged food. Bernardo began to rape her while Homolka watched but after about a minute Tammy awoke and the assault was brought to a halt.

Karla did however, follow through with her promise. At her trial she referred to this as a 'Christmas present'. Six months before their 1991 wedding, Homolka stole the anaesthetic agent Halothane from the clinic where she worked.

On 23 December 1990, Homolka and Bernardo gave sleeping pills to her fifteen-year-old sister, disguised in a rum-and-eggnog drink. Once Tammy was unconscious Homolka and Bernardo undressed her. Homolka applied a Halothane-soaked cloth to her young sister's nose and mouth.

With her parents sleeping upstairs, the pair filmed

109

themselves as they assaulted the young girl in the basement. Once again, we see the horrific interaction of the idea of pornography, and the visual recording of sex, with the violence and coercion that occurs in such cases of murder. One has to wonder to what degree the effect of the modern tolerance of pornography has been to legitimize the sickest ideas of such individuals.

During the assault, Tammy woke up and started to vomit, eventually choking. Homolka and Bernardo tried unsuccessfully to revive her. They did eventually call the emergency number, but not before they hid the evidence by replacing Tammy's clothes and moving her into her bedroom. Within a few hours, Tammy Homolka had been pronounced dead at St Catharines General Hospital without having regained consciousness.

Despite an extraordinary level of incriminating evidence, (the couple had been vacuuming and washing laundry in the middle of the night and Tammy had a large and very severe bright red chemical burn on her face and neck), the police and the Homolka family accepted the pair's version of events. The official verdict on Tammy Homolka was accidental death. She was found to have choked on her vomit after consumption of alcohol.

Clearly without grief or guilt the pair subsequently filmed themselves with Karla wearing Tammy's clothing and pretending to be Tammy in a seduction scene. They also moved out of the Homolka house to a rented Port Dalhousie bungalow apparently 'to let her parents deal with their grief'. The couple agreed that they would have to start looking outside the family for their sexual kicks. Whatever Karla Homolka's degree of knowledge of Bernardo's earlier career of rape might have been, from this stage she was clearly implicated in his crimes.

*   *   *

During the time when she worked in a pet shop whilst still at school, two years earlier, Homolka had befriended a thirteen-year-old girl. On 7 June 1991 Homolka invited the girl, now fifteen, who was subsequently referred to as 'Jane Doe' in the trials, for a night out. After an evening out, Homolka took the girl back to their rented house in Port Dalhousie and plied her with alcohol laced with anaesthetic drugs that she had stolen from her workplace. After 'Jane Doe' lost consciousness, Homolka called Bernardo to tell him his 'surprise wedding gift' was ready.

Together, they undressed the girl, who was a virgin. Bernardo videotaped Homolka as she assaulted the girl before Bernardo sodomized and raped her. When she woke up in the morning, the girl was sick but put it down to having drunk alcohol for the first time. She didn't understand that she had been raped the night before.

Two months later, in August, the same girl was invited back to the house. In a disturbing replay of the rape and murder of Tammy Homolka, 'Jane Doe' (whose identity remains protected by law) stopped breathing after she was drugged and Bernardo began to rape her. Homolka called the emergency services for help but called back a few minutes later to say that the problem had been sorted out. The emergency crew was recalled and there was no follow-up.

'Jane Doe' visited the couple once more, on 22 December 1992. This time the pair tried to pressure her into having sex with Bernardo. She refused, became worried and upset by their demands, and left. Luckily for her, she had survived. However Bernardo and his wife simply decided to find someone else with whom they could indulge their sick fantasies.

In order to avoid detection as they cruised for another victim and to help with the cigarette smuggling scheme he had devised, Beranrdo began to steal licence plates. As he drove through Burlington in the early hours of 15 June 1991, halfway between Toronto and St Catharines, he chanced

111

upon fourteen-year-old schoolgirl Leslie Mahaffy. Mahaffy was standing at the door of her Burlington home. She had missed her curfew and was locked out.

Adopting his seemingly harmless, charming manner, Bernardo approached her and offered her a lift and a place to stay. They spoke for some time and went back to Bernardo's car for a cigarette, Once Bernardo had got her to the car he blindfolded her, forced her into the vehicle and drove her to Port Dalhousie, where he told Homolka that they had a new playmate.

Bernardo and Homolka videotaped the subsequent evil torture, rape and sodomy of Leslie Mahaffy, while music by Bob Marley and David Bowie played in the background. At one point in the tapes, which would be played in the trial, Homolka adjusts her make-up for the camera before raping the girl. Bernardo was recorded saying, 'You're doing a good job, Leslie, a damned good job.' He then said, 'The next two hours are going to determine what I do to you. Right now, you're scoring perfect.'

On another part of the tape Leslie Mahaffy cried out in pain and begged Bernardo to stop. He was anally raping her while her hands were bound with twine. It is still unclear which of the two actually killed Leslie Mahaffey. At the trial Bernardo claimed that the following day, Homolka fed the girl a lethal dose of Halcion and that tht she died while he was out of the room.

Homolka claimed that Bernardo had strangled the heavily drugged Leslie Mahaffey with an electrical cord. Whoever the actual murderer was, the couple put her body into the basement until they could decide how to get rid of it. The following day Mr and Mrs Homolka and Lori visited for Father's Day dinner. While the body of Leslie Mahaffey was lying in their basement the family ate upstairs.

*   *   *

Once the Homolkas and their remaining daughter, Lori, had left, Bernardo and Homolka decided that the best way to dispose of the evidence would be to dismember Leslie Mahaffy's body. They decided to cut the corpse into small pieces and encase each piece in cement. Bernardo purchased a dozen bags of cement and a large sheet of plastic at a hardware store. Unwisely he kept the receipts, which would later be produced as evidence at his trial. He used his grandfather's circular saw to cut up the body in a rapidly constructed plastic tent in the cellar. Then they encased the body parts in concrete.

Bernardo and Homolka made a number of trips to dump the cement blocks in Lake Gibson, which lies south of Port Dalhousie. One of the blocks weighed 200 pounds and proved too heavy for them to manhandle into the lake. Undeterred they just left it near the shore.

Ironically, it was on Bernardo and Homolka's wedding day, 29 June 1991, that a father and son found the badly prepared cement block. They had been on a fishing expedition when they made their horrifying discovery. Because of the summer heat, the block had split, revealing its contents. Leslie Mahaffy's orthodontic appliance proved definitive in identifying her body – she had been reported missing as soon as she had disappeared. This discovery would have been at about the time when Homolka and Bernardo, having been married in a grand wedding, were riding together in a horse-drawn carriage at Niagara.

Ten months after they abducted Leslie Mahaffy, on the afternoon of 16 April 1992, Bernardo and Homolka were driving through St Catharines, looking for another potential victim. It was after school hours on the day before Good Friday. Students were still going home but for the most part the streets were empty.

They went past the Holy Cross Secondary School, a Catholic high school in the city, when they passed a fifteen-year-old, Kristen French, who was heading towards her nearby home. The couple pulled into a parking lot and Karla got out of the car, holding a map, pretending she needed directions. Kristen had been brought up to be wary on the streets and was considered by everyone who knew her to be a responsible, mature and helpful person. Karla Homolka was pretty and polite and Kirsten would have had no reason to think that the couple were anything other than lost travellers.

Sadly, this was a mistake that would cost her her life. As the two girls looked at the map, Bernardo attacked her from behind, brandishing a knife and forcing her into the front seat of the car. From the back seat, Homolka kept Kristen under control by pulling down her hair and holding onto it.

Kristen took the same route home each day, taking about fifteen minutes to get home. Soon after the time when she should have arrived, her parents became convinced that something had happened to her and called the police. From the start, Kristen French's disappearance was treated as a criminal matter. Unlike Leslie Mahaffy, she did not have disagreements at home and had a dog that required regular walks and feeding. It was regarded as highly unlikely that she had run away from home.

Within the day, the Niagara Regional Police (NRP) had put together a team and searched the area along her route home. There were several witnesses, who unfortunately did not realise at the time what they had seen. However they were able to tell police what they had seen of the abduction from different points of view and police gained a fairly clear picture of what had happened. They also found one of Kristen's shoes in the parking lot of the church. All of this evidence suggested that this was probably a serious abduction. Later, a piece of Homolka's map and some of Kristen's hair were also found at the scene of the crime.

Homolka and Bernardo took French to Port Dalhousie,

where for the two days of the Easter weekend, they systematically assaulted, sexually abused, and tortured her.

They videotaped themselves doing this, while also forcing her to drink large quantities of alcohol, and to behave in a submissive manner to Bernardo. On Easter Sunday, the couple were due at the Homolkas' for dinner. The couple knew that she had to be murdered before they left.

Once again at their trial the couple would each accuse the other of having been the one who killed Kristen. Homolka would state that Bernardo had strangled Kristen for exactly seven minutes while she watched. Bernardo would claim that Homolka beat her with a rubber mallet because she had tried to escape, and that Kristen ended up being strangled by a noose tied around her neck secured to a chest. In Bernardo's version Homolka then went to fix her hair.

What was not in doubt was Kristen's murder and the couple's intention to murder. Indeed, at Bernardo's trial, Crown prosecutor Ray Houlahan pointed out that Bernardo had always intended to kill her since she was never blindfolded and would have been able to identify her captors.

After returning from the Easter dinner, Bernardo and Homolka washed and cut off Kristen French's hair and the couple washed the body. This was in the hope of making the body harder to identify. They then dumped the corpse in a ditch in Burlington. Her naked body was discovered on 30 April 1992, less than a mile from the cemetery that contained Leslie Mahaffy's remains.

*   *   *

Fingers were already beginning to point to Paul Bernardo. Police had questioned Homolka and Bernardo several times before in relation to numerous incidents, long before the death of Kristen French. They were interviewed first in connection with the Scarborough Rapist investigation, then Tammy Homolka's death and subsequently other related crimes.

Shortly after the discovery of French's body Bernardo's long-time friend, Van Smirnis, told a family friend who was an Ontario Provincial Police officer, that Bernardo would 'make a good suspect in the Kristen French murder'.

Among other factors, he mentioned a time when Bernardo raped a girl in his basement while Homolka was upstairs. The officer filed a report and on 12 May 1992, shortly after the discovery of Kristen's body, an NRP sergeant and constable interviewed Bernardo briefly. The officers decided that he was an unlikely suspect though Bernardo admitted having been questioned in connection with the Scarborough rapes. Towards the end of May, John Motile, an acquaintance of Smirnis and Bernardo, also reported Bernardo as a possible murder suspect.

Finally, the net was beginning to close in. In December 1992, the Centre of Forensic Sciences at last began testing the DNA samples that Bernardo had provided three years earlier. The lab work had unfortunately been caught in a backlog since well before their suspects' first killing. Toronto police were informed that Bernardo's DNA matched that of the Scarborough Rapist and immediately placed him under twenty-four-hour surveillance. Why they didn't immediately arrest him isn't known. It may be that they were trying to link him to the murders as well, although it is a surprising move to merely observe a suspect who is possibly responsible for such serious crimes.

*   *   *

Paul's violence was not limited to the vicitms he raped and murdered. On 27 December 1992, Bernardo beat Homolka severely with a flashlight about the head, face, arms and legs.

Reluctant to implicate him, she claimed that she had been in an automobile accident when she returned to work severely bruised in the new year. Her sceptical co-workers called Homolka's parents. They decided to physically remove their daughter from the house she shared with Bernardo. It was this assault that led Homolka finally to lose her loyalty to her evil husband.

Before leaving, Homolka apparently went back in, frantically searching for something (she was looking for the video-tapes of their crimes). Her parents took her to St Catharines' General Hospital where her injuries were documented and she gave a statement the police, to the effect that she had been a battered spouse. She even filed charges against Bernardo. He was arrested but later released. Once again he had escaped the net, for the time being at least. Homolka moved in with relatives in nearby Brampton.

Investigators from the Toronto Sexual Assault Squad interviewed Homolka on 9 February 1993. They told her their suspicions about Bernardo, but Homolka focused solely on his alleged abuse of her.

However, later that night she told her aunt and uncle that Bernardo was the Scarborough Rapist, that they had been involved in the rapes and murders of Leslie Mahaffy and Kristen French, and that the rapes were recorded on video-tape. She subsequently made her confession to the police, at the urging of her family. The police also reopened the investigation into Tammy Lyn Homolka's death.

Homolka met with Niagara-Falls lawyer George Walker, who appealed for full immunity from St Catharines' Crown Attorney Ray Houlahan in exchange for her co-operation in the investigations of the murders.

Unknown to her, Homolka was then placed under twenty-four-hour surveillance. On 14 February George Walker met with Murray Segal, Director of the Crown Criminal Law Office. They discussed the videotapes of the rapes and Segal told Walker that Homolka's involvement in the crimes meant that full immunity was not a possibility.

It is worth remembering at this point that neither the police nor Homolka's lawyer nor the Crown Attorney had seen the tapes and knew their full content. On 5 May 1993, Walker was told that the government would offer Homolka a twelve-year sentence plea bargain and that she had one week to accept. If she refused to co-operate, the government would charge her with two counts of first-degree murder, one count of second-degree murder and other crimes.

Walker accepted the offer and Homolka later agreed to testify against her husband. The plea bargain meant that she would escape the maximum penalty for her crimes. On 14 May 1993, the deal between Homolka and the Crown was finalized.

A publicity ban was imposed on her plea bargain and subsequent court appearance, which lasted until Bernardo's trial was due to begin. During the interrogation, Homolka told police that Bernardo had once boasted to her of raping as many as thirty women, twice as many as the police suspected him of having done. She described him as 'the happy rapist'.

Weirdly, even though they knew she was going to prison for such horrific crimes, Homolka was given a 'going away' pool party at her parents' house on 27 June 1993.

Bernardo was finally arrested on numerous charges on 17 February 1993, and obtained search warrants. Since Bernardo's link to the murders was weak, however, the warrant contained limitations which made the job of the police far more difficult than it might have been. No evidence that was not documented in the warrant was permitted to be removed from the house.

All videotapes the police found had to be viewed in the house. Damage to the house had to be kept to a minimum; police could not tear down walls looking for the videotapes.

The search of the house, including updated warrants, lasted seventy-one days and the only tape found by the police had a short segment which showed Bernardo, Homolka and an unnamed American prostitute having oral sex with an unconscious, unidentified young woman believed at first to have been Kristen French.

The unidentified girl would later be identified as 'Jane Doe' after the discovery of the full tapes, in which she was revealed to be a minor. Her identity remains covered by the publication ban.

Officials agreed not to prosecute Homolka for the 'Jane Doe' incidents. Legally, that decision was final. The search warrants expired on 30 April 1993. On 6 May 1993, Bernardo instructed his lawyers, Ken Murray and Carolyn MacDonald to enter the house and remove, but crucially, not to watch, six eight-millimetre videotapes hidden behind a ceramic light in the bathroom. If the police had been given sufficient powers they would have found these tapes during the original search. Sometimes one has to wonder whether the law tries too hard to protect suspected criminals, and not hard enough to protect their potential victims. Murray and MacDonald would eventually hand the tapes over, but it is extraordinary that there was any need for delay over this issue.

Later in court, the tapes would cause a sensation when their content became known. They contained the videotaped rapes and torture of Tammy Homolka, 'Jane Doe', Leslie Mahaffy and Kristen French, and proved beyond any doubt that Homolka, far from having been any sort of victim, was a willing, active participant in the crimes. Bernardo's lawyers didn't watch the tapes until 18 May 1993, the day when Homolka was charged.

Since Homolka's confession pointed to many more victims than the police had originally assumed, speculation was rife about other potential vicitms. In addition to the confirmed murders of Tammy Homolka, Leslie Mahaffy and Kristen French, suspicions remain about other possible or intended victims.

In the weeks after Tammy Homolka's funeral her parents went out of town and Lori visited her grandparents in Mississauga, leaving the Homolka house empty. According to one author Bernardo abducted a girl on the weekend of 12 January 1991, took her to the Homolka house and raped her with Homolka watching. Afterwards she was released on a deserted road near Lake Gibson.

He is also suspected of having abducted a fourteen-year-old girl who was practising for her duties as coxswain on a local rowing team. She informed police that a blonde woman waved at her from a car. While she was distracted, a man dragged her into the shrubbery. There, he sexually assaulted her, then made her remove all her clothes and wait five minutes while he disappeared.

On 28 July 1991, a man matching the description of Bernardo stalked a twenty-one-year old called Sydney Kershen, in a gold Nissan. She saw him following her again two weeks later, and hurriedly made her way to her boyfriend's house to escape him. The boyfriend apparently gave chase, saw Bernardo's gold Nissan and noted the licence plate. They reported the incident to the police, who would check that the car belonged to Paul Bernardo. Incredibly, an officer visited the Bernardo house, where the car was parked, but failed to follow up on the incident or submit a report. The number of times that Bernardo could have been apprehended, and the number of separate incidents in which he was involved make the police failure to catch him sooner particularly shocking.

There were yet more incidents to follow. Fourteen-year-old Terri Anderson disappeared, from an area close to the parking lot from which Kristen French would later be abducted, and never returned. Terri was a student at Lakeport

Secondary School, next to Kristen French's Catholic school. In April 1992, police said they could not find evidence for a link. However in May 1992 Terri Anderson's body was discovered in the lake at Port Dalhousie. The autopsy saw no proof of foul play, although it is hard to be certain when a body has been in the water for six months. The coroner ruled that her death was by drowning, after she had been drinking beer and taking LSD. This is questionable in light of Leslie Mahaffy's and Kristen French's murders, and there are many who believe to this day that Bernardo and Homolka were responsible.

A newspaper clipping was found during the police search of the Bernardo house with the story of a violent rape that occurred in Hawaii while the couple were honeymooning there. Extradition issues mean that there has never been a trial for this rape, but the timing and modus operandi suggest that Bernardo would be a strong suspect.

Evidence has also been published tying Bernardo to Elizabeth Bain, who disappeared on 19 June 1990, after leaving the house to make a short trip to the local campus Her car was later discovered with a large bloodstain in the back seat.

Her boyfriend Robert Baltovich, who denied the crime, was convicted of second-degree murder in the death of Elizabeth. At the trial, his lawyers suggested that the 'Scarborough Rapist' was the true guilty party. He served eight years of a life sentence, but was eventually released on appeal, with the possibility of Bernardo's guilt being once again a central part of the case for the defence.

During March 1992, Bernardo had stalked and videotaped two sisters, Shanna and Kerry Patrich, from his car and followed them to their house. They reported the incident and were told to follow up with police if there were any further developments. On 18 April 1992, while Kristen French was still alive, and being guarded by Homolka, Bernardo went out to fetch a pizza and a video. He was spotted by Kerry Patrich, who attempted to follow him to his house. She lost him but took down the details of his car and licence plate, and called the police.

Tragically this information would also be ignored. In the Campbell Report of 1996, Judge Campbell talked about a 'black hole' of evidence, referring to the repeated opportunities the police had to link Bernardo to one crime or another. Ignoring Kerry Patrich's information was particularly atrocious as there is a chance that Kristen French might have been rescued if the police had merely bothered to go round to Bernardo's home to follow up on the stalking allegation.

*   *   *

Bernardo's trial for the murders of French and Mahaffy was in 1995. He faced detailed testimony from Karla Homolka and videotapes of the rapes. The trial came under a publication ban because of the existence of the tapes and Karla's plea bargain and the venue was moved to Toronto from St Catharines, where the murders occurred.

Bernardo tried to claim that the deaths were accidental, and as noted already, he would go on to claim that his wife was the actual killer in each murder. On 1 September 1995, he was convicted of a number of offences, including the two first-degree murders and two aggravated sexual assaults, and sentenced to life in prison. Bernardo was also declared a 'Dangerous Offender', making it unlikely he will ever be released. It is unfortunate for his many victims that he was not apprehended sooner. For that, the police must take some blame, but the most obviously guilty party was his wife Karla Homolka, the one person who could have put an end to the rapes and murders at a far earlier date.

Much has been made of her trial and plea bargain.

Homolka's trial started on 28 June 1993. The judge's orders on the open court issues were very unusual. A non-publication order was applied to the transcript of the trial proceedings. Beyond the families of the accused and the victims and court personnel, only the Canadian press was allowed into the courtroom.

This merely strengthened the public's belief that Homolka did not receive a sufficiently severe punishment for her crimes. Jamie Cameron, Professor of Law at Osgoode Hall, has written that 'at the time of the Homolka trial, three features of the case worried and concerned the public. First, because the videos were never shown, little was known about the sexual captivity and offences the victims endured before being murdered, except that their treatment was rumoured to be sadistic, horrific, and unimaginable. Little was known about the respective roles Homolka and Bernardo played in committing those offences and then killing their victims. And by spring, 1993, it was clear that the Crown's case against Bernardo depended on Homolka's evidence. In simple terms, to secure a conviction against him, her story had to be believed. Yet on no view of the facts then known could she be exculpated, by casting her as a victim of his predatory behaviour, her responsibility for the crimes that were committed could be diminished and her credibility as a witness preserved.'

Homolka's lawyer George Walker, made the case for Homolka having been 'abused' although the prosecution argued that no amount of abuse could account for, or justify, her direct participation in the murders.

The province at the time was governed by the New Democratic Party. The party had a strongly feminist slant, and had a female Attorney-General in Marion Boyd. Boyd, who was not a lawyer, had been given responsibilities for Women's Issues, and had launched a high-profile campaign against domestic abuse in the same year. Homolka's asser-

123

tions that she was a 'battered spouse' played strongly to these sensibilities. The gradual revelation of the degree to which she had been involved in the murders thus made an especially strong impact.

Prior to the plea bargain, Walker had his client assessed by psychiatrists and a clinical psychologist, who reported that Homolka's mental state was 'comparable to that of a survivor of a Nazi concentration camp'. This fed into the Crown's belief that she was a 'compliant victim'. This term was taken from a much-disputed FBI document entitled 'Compliant Victims of the Sexual Sadist'.

On 18 May 1993, Homolka was arraigned on two counts of manslaughter. Ken Murray and Carolyn MacDonald decided to hold onto the tapes and use them to impeach Homolka on the stand during Bernardo's trial. During Homolka's plea bargain trial neither the police nor the prosecution had seen the tapes. The revelation that a key piece of evidence had been kept from the police for such a long time created a scandal.

The public now realised that Homolka, far from having been a 'victim' of the violent Bernardo, had been a willing partner. When the tapes were played in open court at Bernardo's trial it was obvious even to the audience that Homolka had clearly enjoyed herself in the process.

Due to the graphic content of the murder tapes, they were deemed too dreadful to be seen by the gallery, who were only allowed to listen while the prosecution, defence, judge, and jury watched. It should also be remembered that Bernardo has always claimed that, while he raped and tortured Leslie Mahaffy and Kristen French, it was Homolka who actually killed them.

The public now became angry as the extent of Homolka's role was finally revealed. It was generally felt that the plea bargain had been unnecessary and that Homolka was getting away with her crimes.

The official line was that Homolka had already disclosed sufficient information to the police and the Crown did not see good reason to break the agreement and re-open the case. In December 2001, the authorities decided that there was no possible future use of the videos. The six tapes depicting the torture and rape of Bernardo and Homolka's victims were destroyed.

It was claimed both by Bernardo's appeal judge, Michael Moldaver, and during the Campbell inquiry that Homolka would have been convicted of two counts of first-degree murder along with Bernardo, had the videotapes been available at the time her plea bargain was struck.

Homolka pled guilty to manslaughter, as arranged, and served twelve years in Kingston Penitentiary. She seemed to thrive in the prison environment. She underwent a number of psychiatric examinations and was believed to show some symptoms of spousal abuse, although there is a theory that she might have been adopting these as a self-defence mechanism, having read up on the subject in books.

In 2001, the parole board referred to Homolka as a psychopath – a cold-blooded, manipulative offender who showed no remorse. It has been noted that Homolka displays different behaviours according to whom she is talking to and the subject matter. In fact, in a letter of apology to her family, she went on blaming Bernardo for all her misdeeds. She has never admitted to her share of the guilt or blame for the rapes and murders. Neither has she given any real explanation as to why she was involved in them. She has also never apologised to the victims' families.

Whilst in prison, she completed a diploma and took a correspondence course in sociology from nearby Queen's University. News of these self-improvement courses was greeted disdainfully in the media: 'Nothing has changed. Concepts of remorse, repentance, shame, responsibility and atonement have no place in the universe of Karla. Perhaps she simply lacks the moral gene,' wrote one writer, Margaret Wente.

Homolka took part in every treatment programme recommended by the prison authorities, up until the point when she was asked to participate in a programme that had been created for male sex offenders. She refused to do this, arguing that she was neither male nor a convicted sex offender. It was reported that her manner could be 'indifferent, haughty and irritable'.

In June 2005, a two-day hearing was held before Judge Jean R. Beaulieu. He ruled that Karla Homolka, upon her forthcoming release, would still be a risk to the public. As a result, certain restrictions were placed on Homolka as a condition of her release:

- She was to tell police her home address, work address and with whom she was living.
- She was required to notify police as soon as any of the above changed.
- She was likewise required to notify police of any change to her name.
- If she planned to be away from her home for more than forty-eight hours, she had to give seventy-two hours' notice.
- She could not contact Paul Bernardo, the families of Leslie Mahaffy and Kristen French or that of the woman known as 'Jane Doe' or any violent criminals.
- She was forbidden from being with people under the age of sixteen and from consuming drugs other than prescription medicine.
- She was required to continue therapy and counselling.
- She was required to provide police with a DNA sample to be kept on record.

There was a penalty of a maximum two-year prison term for

violating such an order. While this may have reassured the public that Homolka would find it difficult to offend again, the court stated that it might be helpful to her as well, because public hostility and her high profile might put her at risk from public attacks after she was released.

Because of this, she filed a request in the Quebec Superior Court for an injunction aimed at preventing the press from reporting about her following her release. The request was not granted.

On 4 July 2005, Homolka was released from prison. She gave an interview to Radio-Canada television, speaking in French. She told the interviewer Joyce Napier that she chose Radio Canada because it was be less sensational than the English-language media. She said that she had also found Quebec to be more accepting of her than her home province of Ontario. She confirmed that she would be living in the province but unsurprisingly did not give full details.

She accepted the point that she had paid her debt to society in a legal sense, but not yet in an emotional or social one. On 5 July national media reported that she had moved to the Island of Montreal. On 21 August, the newspaper *Le Courier du Sud* reported a sighting of her in the South Shore community of Longueuil, across the St Lawrence River from Montreal.

By this stage Homolka was desperate to escape the constant press hunt and exposure. She tried to overturn the restrictions placed on her by Judge Beaulieu.

The Société Elizabeth Fry du Québec (The Canadian Association of Elizabeth Fry Societies) which works on behalf of women who are in the justice system, offered its services to her. On 30 November 2005, Quebec Superior Court judge James Brunton lifted all restrictions imposed on Homolka, saying there was not enough evidence to justify them. On 6 December 2005, the Quebec Court of Appeal upheld his decision.

Karla Homolka now lives in an undisclosed location in the Antilles, in the French Caribbean with a son and her current husband. Bernardo remains in prison for his terrible crimes, and will never be released.

Love and Murder

Introduction

None of the murderous couples in this section could be called serial killers, with the possible exception of Trevor Hardy. We have included here a miscellany of cases in which couples murdered, separately or together and it is interesting to see how varied the motives can be for such killings, from the grinding poverty that inspired Jessie King and Thomas Pearson, to the satanic fantasy world that underpinned the Rudas' murder case.

Most of these stories do raise questions about what love is. It can be hard to distinguish love and passion. Any kind of love can, and perhaps should, have a passionate aspect to it. But there can be a fine line between passion and irrationality.

Indeed some might argue that love itself is a kind of madness. When we study the behaviour of Martha Beck, or Pauline Parker and Juliet Hulme, we see individuals who had such a strong attachment to a romantic ideal that they allowed it to overcome all moral and social obstacles. In each case they became involved in murder in pursuit of their vision of love, even though one doubts that they would in other circumstances have become killers.

In other cases here, such as that of Teri Depew and Carole Hargis, and Holly Harvey and Sandra Ketchum, we see the way that love can be twisted into a selfishness so extreme that it seems to the killer to justify atrocious behavior.

The case of Leopold and Loeb is eternally fascinating. In some ways one can see it as the first truly modern murder, in that the couple were clearly treating murder as simply another amusement. Loeb was fascinated by crime stories, and this was his motivation for trying to come up with a series of perfect crimes. The decision to kill a boy merely to act out a kidnap scenario was a psychotic one, but it demonstrates the way in which treating murder as a story can lead to a moral degeneration in which murder does not get treated with the seriousness it deserves.

Possibly the most disturbing of these accounts to consider is that of Trevor Hardy and Sheilagh Farrow. In this case, Sheilagh Farrow was innocent of any actual killing. However her assistance in covering up her lover's crimes clearly left him free to kill again. There is a degree to which, as with other cases here, one could argue that she was acting out of love. But what kind of love can lead one to knowingly allow a human being to die?

These are the kinds of questions that force us to examine the idea of love and passion, and to wonder if the madness of love is innate to the romantic ideal, or if true love should only be defined as something that could never be besmirched in this way.

Raymond Fernandez and Martha Beck

Lonely Hearts Killers

Few of the murder cases in this book contain anything which can be described, even tangentially, as 'romance'. In many cases couples who kill turn upon one another as soon as they are discovered and attempt to blame one another. In other cases the love they once felt turns to hate. And in many cases the bleakness and nihilism of the relationship in the first place defeats any attempt to view it as a love story.

The case of Raymond Fernandez and Martha Beck, who became known as the 'Lonely Hearts Killers' certainly isn't a standard love story. They were guilty of some heinous crimes. But at moments in their baffling relationship and downfall there are nonetheless weird moments of pathos. At their trial for murder, they acted like a pair of teenage lovers, and while there were many twists and turns in their relationship, Fernandez's last words were a declaration of love for Martha.

Perhaps love is always a kind of madness and it is only when a couple turns to murder or crime that this madness can fully be understood. Or perhaps Fernandez and Beck were in the end only a cruel parody of the condition of love. Either way their story is an interesting one, and one that has provoked a number of Hollywood films, albeit none that tell the true story in its original weirdness.

Between 1947 and 1949 Raymond and Martha are between them suspected of killing up to twenty people, although they confessed to only a fraction of these crimes, and it is probable that the tabloid newspapers accused them of far worse crimes than they were actually guilty of. What is certain is that Fernandez was a prolific swindler, who targeted women that he attracted through lonely hearts advertisements. Raymond would flatter and seduce the women, while Martha posed as his sister. They would often con these women out of their savings and in several cases, murder was the end result. But how did their homicidal story start?

* * *

Raymond Fernandez was born in Hawaii in 1914. His parents were Spanish and while he was a child the family moved to Connecticut. Raymond was a handsome young man, although he had an awkward demeanour and didn't get on well with his family. At the age of twenty he decided to move to the Spanish countryside, where he worked on a relative's farm near the village of Orgiva.

There he met and married Encarnacion Robles, a local girl. He would have four children with her. During the Second World War, Raymond was at sea, firstly with the Spanish merchant marine fleet. Subsequently he was recruited to the British intelligence services, and by all accounts he worked to the best of his ability, carrying out duties that were at times dangerous.

In his early life there was nothing to suggest the turn his life was to take. The event that changed his life appears to have been a head injury in late 1945. There have been numerous cases where the trauma suffered in a head injury has brought about a change of personality. The serial killer Fred West suffered two separate head wounds early in life, although in his case there was some evidence of a violent personality prior to his injury.

However for Raymond Fernandez, it seems rather likely that the trauma to his head changed his personality in significant ways. He was on his way to the United States, where he planned to find work, and then send for his wife and family. He had managed to get passage on a freighter that was headed for Curaçao in the Dutch West Indies.

Whilst he was climbing out onto the deck, an unsecured metal hatch fell onto his skull, concussing him and causing a serious wound. He spent three months in hospital on the island after it landed. The effect on his behaviour was immediately apparent. He became more emotionally erratic and prone to bizarre conversations. He lost a considerable amount of his previously healthy head of hair, leaving a plainly visible scar, which he would later take to covering up with hairpieces. He was also prone to severe headaches and became more introspective than he had previously been.

When he subsequently sailed to the United States, landing at the port of Mobile, he was arrested at the port for stealing an unreasonable number of clothes and other items from the ship's storeroom. His explanations for his behaviour were incoherent and he was jailed for a year, a sentence he served in Tallahassee, Florida.

This led to a second life-changing event. He was the cellmate of a Haitian, and, as a result of their friendship, he became fascinated by voodoo.

Vodun is an ancient historical religion that was brought to the Caribbean area by slaves who had their origins in the Yoruba people of the Dahomey area of west Africa in the eighteenth and nineteenth century. Since the slaves of African descent who practised this religion were doing so in secret rather than accepting the Christianity that was imposed upon them, it became demonised. It is a religion that recognises many spirits and that acknowledges black and white versions of magic, but it is nonetheless a long way removed from the modern conception of 'voodoo'.

However, Fernandez was strongly influenced by his reading of *Haiti: the Black Republic,* an absurdly sensationalised account of voodoo, which is one of the sources of the myth of Vodun as an evil religion in which the practice of zombification and devil dolls is widespread. This book would later be a source for the early Hollywood movies that established the zombie genre in its modern form.

Fernandez took a different message from the book and from his cellmate. He decided that he was a *houngan,* a male priest of Vodun, who could obtain sexual power over women from a distance. He believed that by obtaining a lock of a woman's hair he could force her to bend to his will and become sexually attracted to him.

Fernandez had always been a reasonably handsome, superficially charming man, and was able to make an impression on the women he met. The combination of this and his new, deranged ideas about his magical virility, led to a new pattern of behaviour on his release from prison in 1946. He moved to Brooklyn in New York, where he lived initially with his sister.

He immediately began to attempt to use his imaginary new powers over women. He became a devotee of the lonely hearts columns in magazines and newspapers. Through them he would target lonely women and develop relationships with them from a distance.

He started to seduce these women, often obtaining a lock of hair to fuel his 'magical powers'. Once he had gained their trust, he would swindle them out of money in a variety of ways. He was able to get away with this because his victims were too ashamed to report him to the police, knowing that they would become the subject of mockery for the desperation of using the lonely hearts columns in the first place, and for being so gullible as to fall for his schtick.

It is likely that Fernandez's first murder victim was Jane Lucilla Thompson. She had separated from her husband and fell for his 'Latin Lover' persona. Using her money, they bought cruise tickets to Spain. This was a wholly selfish act on the part of Fernandez, who, in spite of his sexual misadventures in America, wanted to visit his wife.

After a few weeks of sight-seeing, he guided them to La Linea where Encarnacion was still caring for his children. The exact train of events that led up to Jane's death is unknown. He had introduced her to his wife and the three had even eaten together. But it seems that an argument got out of hand. Jane Thompson was found dead in her hotel room, from unknown causes. Raymond left town, abandoning his wife once again, and returned to America. On his return he presented a faked will for Jane Thompson, of which he was the beneficiary. By this means he managed to acquire her apartment, even though her elderly mother was still living there (he allowed her to remain).

He also returned to his lonely hearts pursuits One of the women he corresponded with was Martha Beck.

*   *   *

Martha Seabrook was born in Florida in 1919. She had a glandular problem which caused her to put on weight and to go through premature puberty. It is likely that her brother sexually abused her at a young age (as she would later claim) and it is certain that her relationship with her mother was a fraught one. Either way she had a fairly miserable childhood as she was teased and bullied remorselessly at school.

She trained as a nurse, but was unable to get a job in her chosen vocation, so instead ended up working in a mortuary.

137

In the early 1940s she moved to California, hoping to find a new life. She was sexually promiscuous and became pregnant. She returned to her home town, knowing that as an unmarried mother she would be treated with further derision, so she pretended to have met and married an officer in the navy. Later on she would send herself a telegram announcing the death of her husband, and go through a performance of grief at the news that won her considerable sympathy in the town.

At this stage of her life Martha does not seem to have been a cruel woman, but she was clearly someone who was used to retreating into a fantasy world. She always loved romance comics and films and fantasised about meeting a man who would truly love her rather than just treating her as a passing sexual opportunity.

Her first child, Willa, was born in early 1944. Within a few months she had become pregnant again, this time by a local man called Alfred Beck. He showed slightly more responsibility than the father of her first child as he at least offered to marry her. However the marriage quickly ended in divorce, leaving her with two children to look after. Martha retained the surname of Beck.

In 1946 she finally managed to get a job as a nurse in Pensacola. She was apparently a caring, conscientious nurse, who was quickly promoted. But her romantic longings for a soulmate were still evident. After someone jokingly sent her a lonely hearts advertisement (something she would later describe as a cuttingly cruel joke), she decided to advertise for a man. As fate would have it, her advertisement was answered by one man alone, Raymond Fernandez.

Fernandez wrote a charming letter in which he depicted himself as a suave, wealthy bachelor, new to New York from his native Spain, who respected her as a caring nurse. She was immediately enchanted by his ploys. She worried about sending him her photograph, as she was close to twenty stone. She was not to know that he didn't care in the slightest what she looked like, as to him she was merely the next name on his list of marks and victims.

They had a rapid correspondence, which seemed intense to Martha, while for Fernandez, he was merely going through motions that he had deployed with numerous previous women. Eventually he asked Martha for a lock of her hair. For her this was a romantic request. For him it was a tool which would allow him to assert his magical power over her.

The next stage of Fernandez's scheme was to visit his intended victim. He travelled to Florida by train and visited Martha. She introduced him to her two children, and during the few days they spent together they became lovers. Fernandez attempted to discover how much money she had and whether or not she would be a profitable mark. Concluding that she wasn't, he returned to New York for 'business reasons' at short notice.

Martha believed that he was in love with her and declared to her friends and family that they would be married. He eventually wrote to her to disabuse her of this notion, at which point she became hysterical and attempted suicide. At this stage, Fernandez allowed her to visit him for two weeks in New York, possibly feeling guilty, in spite of his moral vacuity in other respects.

When she returned to Florida, Martha discovered that she had lost her job, possibly because her behaviour over her imagined relationship with Fernandez had exposed her to ridicule and scandal. She decided that her only option was to return to the man that she now loved.

She arrived on his doorstep on 18 January 1948. It is unclear what his feelings towards her were at this point. Clearly at some point between his first visit to Florida and their final relationship, he had started to see her as different to his usual victims. It's possible that her submissiveness to

139

his desires, and her slavish devotion to him had made him see other possibilities in her, or perhaps he simply warmed to her over the time they had spent together.

Either way, he was now willing to allow her to stay with him, but not with her two children. Shamefully, she abandoned the two children at the Salvation Army and would have nothing more to do with them until she was in prison awaiting execution. Clearly her devotion to Fernandez was approaching monomaniacal dimensions, and she was prepared to push aside all other ties and moral restraints in order to be with him.

Can we regard this as a form of love, or is it merely sexual or romantic obsession? In some ways, it is hard to pass judgment on Martha Beck, as she was clearly a victim of her own delusions in some respects. However, from the moment when she gave up her children to be with Fernandez, she had crossed a moral line and it is perhaps this transgression that led her on into increasingly desperate and evil acts over her remaining time in this world.

*   *   *

At this stage of their relationship Fernandez made a crucial decision. He told Martha the truth about his pursuit of women through the lonely hearts columns. He confessed that he had a wife in Spain, that he was a swindler who preyed on widows and lonely women. Instead of treating her as his next victim, he co-opted her as a potential accomplice. And since she was besotted with him and prepared to do whatever he told her to do, she went along with this, and enthusiastically joined in with his schemes.

From this point forwards, he would continue with his activities, but now Martha worked with him, even pretending to be his sister when he found a new victim to swindle. However this did introduce a new complication to his

140

schemes, one that would eventually become deadly. Martha Beck was a jealous woman and she was in love with him in her own strange way. His schemes often meant that a new woman would stay with them in his apartment, or that they would stay in her home.

Martha went to extraordinary lengths in these situations to try to stop Fernandez sleeping with the women he was swindling, and when he did sleep with them she would fly into a jealous rage. She might have been submissive within their relationship, but she believed that they belonged together and she couldn't bear the idea of him with another woman.

She soon had to confront this possibility when he decided to marry one of his penpals, Miss Esther Henne, who lived in Pennsylvania. Esther started out believing he was a decent man who had fallen in love with her through their correspondence. However after their marriage in Virginia, things quickly became difficult. At the trial of Beck and Fernandez, details would emerge of a salacious game of cards in which Fernandez chose whether to sleep with Beck or Esther. He also demanded that she sign over her pension and insurance policies to him and she refused. He became furious and shouted and raged at her as a result.

She left the apartment before things became too ugly, although he managed to relieve her of her car and a few hundred dollars.

The movements of Beck and Fernandez in the subsequent months are not fully known. Fernandez had been corresponding with women across the country and it is likely that they travelled extensively to meet some of them. It is also possible that they were responsible for some murders in this period that were undiscovered or unproven. In the furore that surrounded the later trial of the couple, any death of a single woman in the previous two years would be pinned on Beck and Fernandez by journalists eager for a scoop. But it may be that they only killed those victims to whom they confessed at the trial and that the numerous other 'victims' were associated with them through the imagination of salacious journalists exploiting an easy story.

Fernandez was not too bothered about the sanctity of the marriage vows. Already a serial bigamist, he went on to marry another women, Myrtle Young, in Illinois. She would die as a direct result of her involvement with Fernandez.

They were married in August, but Beck was determined not to let them consummate their wedding vows. She was now posing as Fernandez's sister, and insisted on sharing a bed with Myrtle.

Myrtle became disturbed by this weird behaviour and argued with Fernandez. At this point he gave her a strong dose of drugs. The couple robbed her of several thousand dollars, and then physically manhandled her onto a bus, still heavily drugged. The bus took her back to Little Rock in Arkansas, where she was discovered insensible in her seat and removed by the emergency services. She died in hospital the next day as a result of her ordeal.

Martha Beck's jealousy was becoming a problem for Fernandez. He had made an easy living for a while by tricking women but now she would object to any that seemed too young or too pretty. While they travelled the country to meet some of his potential victims, none of them seemed to be suitable either, because they were insufficiently rich or because Martha objected.

It was this jealousy that seems to have been the cause for the next death with which the couple were associated.

*   *   *

One of the women with whom Fernandez had been corresponding was a sixty-six-year-old widow from Albany in New York State, called Janet Fay. She was reasonably well-

142

off, a devout Catholic lady who had acquired the habit of writing to lonely hearts clubs. Fernandez was always able to adapt his writing style to different women he encountered, and to Janet, he pretended he was a religious man himself.

Fernandez arrived in Albany with Beck in tow as his 'sister' on 30 December 1948. The two of them got to know Janet and stayed over at her apartment, though as guests. Soon Fernandez proposed marriage to the widow, and she accepted, taking him at face value as a decent, upstanding man.

Beck had arranged for an apartment in Long Island to be rented and the couple planned to move there. The trusting Janet took out all her life savings, over $6,000, before they all drove down to Long Island together.

Janet Fay died on the very first night she spent in that apartment. The stories that Beck and Fernandez gave later were not entirely coherent, but it seems that Fernandez became tired after dinner and went to bed. Beck claimed to have found Janet naked with Fernandez, but it may have been simply that her jealousy became uncontrollable. A screaming row developed, waking Fernandez. He told Beck to 'keep this woman quiet'.

In court Beck would claim that she had blacked out during the actual murder and had no recollection of it. The wound that rendered Janet unconscious was caused by a hammer blow, during a sustained attack which left her with serious head wounds.

Fernandez seems to have intervened in Beck's attack, shaking her out of her frenzy, before killing Janet by strangling her with a scarf. One of the many unpleasant details that came out at the trial was Beck's statement that Janet's false teeth had popped out while she was being garroted, and that the murderers had disposed of them, reasoning that they might assist in a later identification.

The body was wrapped in linen and towels and shut in the

cupboard. Next day they went out and returned to the house with a trunk big enough to conceal the body. They stored this at Fernandez's sister's house in Astoria (without her knowing the contents). Then, on 15 January, the trunk was moved to a house rented by Fernandez in Queens – here they buried the trunk and covered the grave with concrete

The pair took Janet Fay's money, cashing several cheques, and wrote a note to her family, in an attempt to gain their assistance in obtaining more of her belongings. The typed note read:

Dear Mary,

I am all excited and having the time of my life. I never felt so happy before. I soon will be Mrs Martin*, and go to Florida. Mary, I am about to ask you a great favour. I would like you to call on the American Express Agency and have them ship my trunks and boxes that I have there to me. The address is on the various stickers I am enclosing in the letter.

I would like to sort out many things before I leave for Florida. I am so happy and contented, for Charles is so good and nice to me and also his family. They have done everything to make me feel comfortable and at home. I will close with my best wishes for you both and love and kisses for the children. I really do miss you all, but I am sure that my prayers are granted to me by sending me this wonderful man.

God bless you all.

Janet J. Fay

*'Mrs Martin' was a reference to the false name, Charles Martin, that Fernandez had used.

144

This whole letter was an obvious fake, firstly because Janet didn't type, and secondly because of the unnatural formality of the signature. It only served to make her family concerned enough to call the police. However for the time being the trail was cold and the two killers would not be apprehended until after they had killed again.

*　　*　　*

Fernandez and Beck moved on from Long Island to Grand Rapids in Michigan. This was the home of another of Fernandez's correspondents, Delphine Downing, a forty-one-year-old widow with a two-year-old daughter Rainelle. Delphine had been writing to the lonely hearts club in the hope of finding a man to remarry, someone who would not object to her already having a child. As usual, Fernandez had said whatever he felt she wanted to hear and had won her trust.

The couple arrived in Grand Rapids about ten days after disposing of Janet Fay's corpse in Queens. Fernandez won Delphine's trust and the two of them moved in to stay with her. For a few weeks there were no problems with this arrangement. The crisis seems to have been triggered by an incident where Delphine walked in on Fernandez in the bathroom and saw him without his toupee. Suddenly, instead of the debonair, charming gentleman she thought she knew, she saw him as an impostor, an old man. She started yelling at him to get out of the house.

Fernandez was morally vacuous but still a weirdly vain man, who lost his temper at the suggestion that he was no longer young and handsome. He appealed to Martha for support, which was of course forthcoming, and the scene became ugly.

Once again, the accounts that Beck and Fernandez gave in later evidence don't fully settle the chronology of how

Delphine and her daughter died. According to one account, Fernandez shot Delphine during the argument that ensued. Alternatively, it may have been that he drugged her to calm her down. If the latter account is the correct one, her daughter Rainelle wouldn't stop crying when she found her mother in a drug-induced torpor, and Beck half-choked her in an attempt to shut her up.

They then panicked, thinking that Delphine might awake and see what had happened, and Fernandez shot her through the head to prevent this from happening.

Subsequently Fernandez asked Beck to finish the job and kill the two-year-old Rainelle, after which he planned to bury the mother and daughter in the cellar of the house. Beck was initially unwilling, but she would do anything that Fernandez asked of her, so eventually she filled a bathtub with water and drowned the poor infant. Then Fernandez carried out his plan to bury the two dead bodies.

At this stage the story once again takes a surreal turn that makes one wonder as to how mentally unstable or competent the pair really were. Rather than flee the scene of the crime or attend to other details, they chose to spend the night at a local cinema, canoodling and treating themselves to popcorn and soda. There are times when their behaviour was truly callous and preconceived, but at times like this the couple could act like senseless children who had done no more than pull the wings off a fly.

They returned to the house late that night, but they were soon disturbed by police at the door. The neighbours had become suspicious after overhearing various strange noises and had called the emergency number.

The police asked if he was Raymond Fernandez, and if they knew Janet Fay. It immediately became obvious that their problems were deeper than trying to cover up Delphine and Rainelle's absence.

Beck tried to attack the police to make them leave her

beloved Fernandez alone, but she was easily overpowered and the two were arrested. The date was 28 February 1949. Less than two months after meeting Janet Fay for the first time, the couple stood accused of three murders over a two-month period.

* * *

From the day when they were arrested up until their eventual executions, the couple became the most notorious criminals in the country. The tabloid press had a field day, finding them guilty by association with an outlandish variety of murders, and vilifying Martha Beck in particular. While she was in prison awaiting execution, she would end up writing impassioned letters to the newspapers protesting about her treatment, but it was to no avail. She was called the 'Obese Ogress', 'Big Martha', 'Fernandez's Sex Slave' and so on. The trial itself would turn into a circus, but from the start the couple seemed almost as concerned with their reputations and with how the other was coping as they were with addressing their crimes.

When he was first arrested, Beck boasted to the investigators, saying: 'I'm no average killer. I have a way with women, a power over them.' From the point of view of strict procedure, the couple were not well served by the legal system. The district attorney in Michigan convinced them that he would help them to avoid the death penalty by trying them in Kent County, rather than extraditing them to New York.

He used this reassurance to coax them into giving and signing a seventy-three-page confession to the three murders that they had confessed to. Martha Beck in particular was terrified of the electric chair, and was happy to give a full confession in return for her life. However the district attorney had lied to them and they were duly extradited to

147

New York, where the death penalty would apply. The details in their confession would become both the central piece of evidence in their trial, and the fuel that fed the media's greed for salacious detail.

From the start, headlines such as 'Hearts Killer Explodes at Attorney', and 'Fernandez Tells Strange Love Story' presumed the lovers' guilt and built the story of the 'Lonely Hearts Killers' into a soap opera of gripping immorality.

The trial took place in a blistering heat wave in the summer of 1949. The trial had been due to take place in Long Island, but it was relocated to the Bronx Supreme Court, near to the Yankee Stadium. Seats at the trial were highly sought after, and scandal-loving crowds attended in the searing heat to hear the details of the crimes, and in particular to catch up with sex, lies and swindling that had marked the pair's criminal career.

Beck and Fernandez shared a defence lawyer, Herbert Rosenberg – once again, this is not the standard legal procedure, although no number of lawyers would have been able to turn the momentum of the trial away from the inevitable convictions.

The trial started with a parade of friends and family of the deceased, and witnesses who, for the most part, confirmed the details of the confession statement. When Fernandez came to the stand, he started out by claiming his confession had merely been an attempt to protect Beck. He had apparently been chivalrously protecting his lover, although now that he might die for that behaviour, his chivalry had reached its limits. He tried to retract his previous statements, but the sheer level of detail the pair had given made it difficult for him to do so.

Martha watched without criticism, not seeming to notice that this was something of a betrayal on his behalf. When the prosecuting lawyer, Edward Robinson, hectored Fernandez about the details of his statement and the inconsistencies in

148

his revised version, she tried to intervene on several occasions to protect her lover, before being silenced by the judge.

Fernandez was also presented with extensive evidence regarding the suspicious deaths of Janet Thompson and Myrtle Young, although he refused to confess to either murder.

Beck took to the stand herself on 25 July, several weeks into the lengthy court case. When questioned about her first victim, Janet Fay, she reiterated her claim that she had no recollection of the exact events, saying only that she remembered Fernandez shaking her shoulders, saying, 'My God, Martha, what have you done?'

She didn't attempt to blame Fernandez for her crimes and restated her love for him at any opportunity. At one stage she said 'a request from Mr Fernandez to me is a command. I loved him enough to do anything he asked me to.' She also objected to the questioning at one point, saying, 'You referred to the love-making as abnormal but for the love I had for Fernandez, nothing is abnormal.'

The defence lawyer drew Martha Beck into telling the court about her difficult childhood and adolescence. She talked about her controlling mother and the incestuous assault that she claimed left her pregnant at thirteen. She also spoke of her failed relationships and the way that being left divorced with two children had left her suicidal. She said she had thought about killing herself on a daily basis, and that the idea of being rescued by someone who loved her was a daydream that she believed would never come true.

She also claimed to have been heartbroken when she abandoned her children, although this evidence seemed somewhat self-serving given her willingness to do so in the first place.

This kind of background information may not have made

the jury pity her, but it certainly cast some light on her devotion to Fernandez and the way that she idealised him, both romantically and sexually.

The trial was notable for the lurid sexual detail that emerged concerning Fernandez and Beck's relationship. Fernandez's testimony included information about their sex life and the game of strip poker that the couple had played with Esther Henne. Meanwhile Beck gave details about their 'voodoo sexual practices'. Such was the level of public interest in the case, the *New York Times* reported that in spite of the heat, 'many of the would-be spectators, predominantly women, did without lunch in order not to lose their places'. In an era when such things were at best hinted at in the trashier pulp magazines, the trial was a rare opportunity to hear such bizarre and intimate stories.

The jury retreated on 18 August. To no one's great surprise, the verdict that came back was that both Beck and Fernandez were guilty of first-degree murder, and the jury made no recommendation of mercy (which might have meant that they would be spared execution).

*   *   *

The guilty verdicts were far from being the end of the story. It would be another twenty months before Beck and Fernandez faced the electric chair, and through that period they were rarely out of the media.

They were held on death row at Sing Sing, in New York, on the Hudson River. The press reported on every detail of the process, including the fact that Martha gave the guards a list of acceptable visitors which included her ex-husband Alfred Beck and her two children.

The two convicted killers were held while their appeals for clemency were heard and in the meantime, the press filled

150

their pages with any scrap of gossip on the Lonely Hearts Killers that they could discover, or indeed invent. At one stage they reported that the sexually deprived Martha was having an affair with a guard. She responded with a published letter protesting her innocence.

She was also moved to complain about the press coverage of herself, and the way that she was demonised. 'I'm still a human being,' she wrote, 'feeling every blow inside, even though I have the ability to hide my feelings and laugh. But that doesn't say my heart isn't breaking from the insults and humiliation of being talked about as I am.'

The couple's feelings towards each other seemed to vary. They didn't turn on each other as so many couples who kill do when their crimes are exposed. But over the months of imprisonment, their long-distance relationship was a stormy one. Fernandez believed the rumours about Martha's affair and responded by demanding his appeal be dropped so that he could die and be released from the mental torture.

For her part, Martha sometimes criticized Fernandez for cowardice or for letting her down. But for the most part they continued to play out their love affair from their separate cells. At one stage, Beck sent Fernandez a love poem, which inevitably reached the public domain via the press:

Memo to Ray

Remember, sweetheart, the night that you and I
Side by side were sitting.
Watching o'er the moonlit sky
Fleecy clouds were flitting,
How close our hands were linked then,

151

When, my darling, when will they be linked again?
What to me the starlight still
Or the moonbeam's splendour,
If I do not feel the thrill
Of your fingers tender?

It was reported that Fernandez was so moved by the poem, he cried and sent a note back: 'I would like to shout my love for you to the world.'

However, in yet another bizarre twist in this tangled tale, it became apparent that old habits died hard. Fernandez was also involved in a loving correspondence with another woman. But this time, the other woman was his wife, Encarnacion, who knew he was involved with Martha, but still wrote to him.

In January 1951 he wrote: 'Kisses and hugs to the children and you receive a million kisses and hugs from the one who always will have you until the last second of my life.'

Encarnacion wrote back: 'Do you prefer me to fly to you and spank you for not writing, just as if you were a little child? Kisses from the children. All my love to you, from your wife, Encarna.'

It seems that Fernandez retained his ability to charm and to make himself an object of love to several women at once. The love he professed appears genuine in some respects, but so did the love he professed to many of his victims, both those who died and those he swindled. The truth about his state of mind will never be known, but it has to be remembered how his personality was affected by the head injury he had suffered. He seems to have ended up with a psychopathic personality, and a strangely childish need to be loved and supported, even by those he was cheating.

*   *   *

Even the execution of this couple turned into a circus. The press would avidly report every detail of the final preparations, their final meals, the way that their last hours were spent, and their final words. There were fifty-two witnesses booked for the actual execution, an unusually high number which reflected the obsessive press interest in the case.

Executions in New York had become increasingly rare, and only five women had been executed there before Martha Beck in the entire twentieth century. The execution of a woman was always a major event for the media, and Martha's complex character made her someone who could excite both pity and contempt in the reading public, and thus an ideal icon of fallen womanhood for the press to exploit.

Every newspaper from the various areas in which the couple had lived and operated was granted a pass for a journalist to observe the deaths. Fernandez stood up to the ordeal less well than Beck. He had to be carried to the chair. His last words were a declaration of love: 'I want to shout it out. I love Martha! What do the public know about love?'

Meanwhile Martha had been disappointed by being let down by her favourite matron, who had not spent her last evening with her because of the staff rotas, but after writing a last letter complaining of this slight, she went to the electric chair with considerable courage.

Her final statement was released to the press:

> What does it matter who is to blame? My story is a love story, but only those tortured with love can understand what I mean. I was pictured as a fat unfeeling woman . . . I am not unfeeling, stupid or moronic . . . in the history of the world how many crimes have been attributed to love?

*　　*　　*

153

The story of Raymond Fernandez and Martha Beck has lived on in popular culture through various re-enactments. The 1970s' movie *The Honeymoon Killers* is a fairly faithful, slightly lurid depiction of their crimes. *Deep Crimson* in 1996 and *Lonely Hearts* in 2006 revisited the same story, as did an episode of the television series *Cold Case*.

It is not surprising that the case has excited ongoing interest. Whereas many murder stories are grubby, depressing affairs, there is a certain nobility and tragedy in the story of these two lovers, in spite of all the salacious and distressing detail of their murders.

It seems clear that Fernandez was affected badly by his head injury, though we will never know whether or not that was the catalyst for his transformation into a killer.

Meanwhile there is something deeply affecting about the character of Martha Beck. Her desperate need to be loved strikes a chord with many people who read about her, and the fact that she found a man who operated by making women love him seems horrifically ironic.

One also can't help but suspect that if she had fallen in love with someone who had a different personality she would never have become a murderer. If she had met a missionary, or businessman, or preacher she might have become a fanatical supporter of his message. But as it was she became a fanatical supporter of a swindler with murderous tendencies, and the fate that ensued was almost inevitable once her terrible jealousy was added into the mix.

In the final analysis, both were deeply damaged individuals. This doesn't vindicate their terrible crimes, but it does lead us to have some understanding or empathy with them as people. And whilst they were vicious in their behaviour, they are distinguished from many couples who kill by the fact that we can really believe that, on some level, each genuinely was devoted to the other. There is a real passion in their behaviour and it is this that exercises such a strong but distressing hold on our imaginations.

We like to be able to distinguish love stories from murder tales, but in this case it is surprisingly hard to know where to draw the line.

Trevor Hardy and Sheilagh Farrow

The Complicity of Lovers

The case of Trevor Hardy raises a difficult and disturbing question. How far would someone who is in a relationship go to protect the person they love? We all know that our moral limits would be tested by a case in which someone we love asked for our protection. Luckily, most of us will never be put in a situation where lives are at stake as a result.

This is a case where the second partner had nothing to do with the original crimes. However she did provide him with alibis for the occasions on which he had murdered young girls. Sheilagh Farrow's evidence did, eventually, help to convict her partner, Trevor Hardy, of three murders. However, her initial delay in reporting the crimes and her complicity in covering up the evidence meant that Hardy remained free to kill again.

*   *   *

Like so many perpetrators of violent crime, Trevor Hardy had a disturbed childhood in which he was treated with casual violence. He was born in 1947 in Manchester, in the

156

United Kingdom. At a young age he was placed in a special school, and he showed a stereotypical pattern of bullying behaviour. He was known as the scourge of the neighbourhood, a violent, difficult youth who would be involved in any trouble that was going on. He became a burglar as a teenager, and served time in a prison when he was apprehended.

He apparently had a close relationship with his mother, with whom he lived. But he was violent in his relationships with others and in those intervals that he spent out of institutions in his teenage years, he became a heavy drinker who was unstable in his behaviour.

He was sentenced to two years in jail in 1972 after a drunken fight in which he injured a man. He was released in November 1974. At the age of twenty-seven, he was a dangerous, angry man, who had had few successful relationships with women other than his mother, and it would not be long before he killed for the first time.

On New Year's Day 1975, Hardy was out and about in Manchester in the small hours when he saw a girl getting out of a taxi. Fifteen-year-old Janet Lesley Stewart was a complete stranger to him, although he would later claim that he mistook her for a girl who had rejected his advances.

Without warning, he attacked the innocent young girl, beating her to the ground, before cutting her throat and watching her bleed to death. He later commented that he wasn't affected by her suffering after the bad things he had been through.

This infantile explanation gives a hint as to why he was such a dangerous man. Content to complacently blame all his problems on the world, he had rejected any sense of morality on the basis that if he had bad experiences he could take them out on the world.

He buried the poor girl in a shallow grave at Newton Heath in Manchester late that night. However he returned to the body on several occasions over the next few weeks.

157

Digging it back up, he removed the hands, feet and head, in an attempt to make the body impossible to identify. The head was thrown into a nearby lake.

The cold-blooded mutilation of the victim may have been a simple attempt at covering his tracks, but it also suggests a deeply disturbed mind that found some kind of catharsis in these horrific acts. He even removed one of the thigh bones, which clearly can't have been for mere self-protection, and suggests that he shared the tendency of some killers to take trophies from their victims.

*   *   *

It was shortly after this that Hardy started living with Sheilagh Farrow. She was ten years older than him, a divorcée. Farrow was not especially intelligent or attractive, and it seems that he partially transferred the connection he had previously had with his mother on to her, as an older woman. She seems to have been willing to take his side in his belief that the world was against him, and to have encouraged him in his victim mentality.

Hardy was still returning to the body of his first victim when he started seeing Farrow. He gave her some jewellery that had been removed from the body of the young girl, although Farrow would not have known where it originated. Hardy was still a heavy drinker and there were fights between the two, so she would have been familiar with his violent tendencies.

It was in July that Hardy committed his next murder. He had argued with Farrow while he was drunk and he went out alone in the early hours. A seventeen-year-old girl called Wanda Skala was on her way home after working as a barmaid at the local Lightbowne Hotel. Wanda was known as a smart, athletic girl, who was interested in judo. But she had no chance to defend herself against Hardy.

He pounced on her and assaulted her with the utmost brutality. He battered her with a paving stone, kicked and beat her, attempted to strangle her with a sock and finally killed her by hitting her in the face with a stone. In a horrifying twist he also bit off her nipple. Her body was discovered on a bit of derelict ground on Lightbowne Road close to its junction with Thorpe Road in Moston.

After this vicious, depraved assault, he returned to the home he shared with Farrow covered in blood. She washed his clothes, although at this stage she would not have known where the blood came from.

However the police visited their home, checking on a list of known violent criminals in the area, and Farrow lied to them, assuring them that Hardy had been with her all evening. This was the moment at which she became clearly involved in Hardy's crimes, as she must have at least wondered if he was the murderer.

One of Hardy's brothers subsequently heard him drunkenly boast that he had killed the girl, and reported this to the police, so they arrested Hardy on suspicion of the crime. While Hardy was in prison, under investigation, he became concerned that he could be identified by the teeth marks that he had left on Skala's breast during his assault on her.

He asked Farrow to smuggle a file into the prison. Again, the fact that she went along with this request strongly suggests that she was knowingly helping him to evade justice.

Hardy filed his teeth down to narrower points, making it impossible for the medical expert to identify the pattern of his teeth as being the same as those left on the corpse, As a result it was not possible to prove conclusively that he was the murderer.

The police were convinced he was the killer, but they had no alternative, but to let him go. Farrow had now knowingly helped the vicious murderer regain his freedom, and inevitably this led to a further death.

* * *

Hardy was involved in a vicious assault on a girl in the toilet of a pub in March 1976, but luckily patrons of the establishment heard the noise and came to the rescue – Hardy was able to escape without being apprehended. After an eight-month hiatus, he was now running out of control once more, and it was only three days before he killed his third victim.

He was actually attempting to break into a shopping centre at the time. Seventeen-year-old Sandra Mossoph unfortunately passed by on her way home. She was a popular, well-liked girl in the local area. Hardy attacked her, and killed her after a violent struggle as she tried to get away from him.

She was stabbed in the stomach, then strangled with her own tights. Once again he mutilated the body by biting off a nipple. It is unclear whether this was a fetishistic action, or an attempt to mislead the police into treating the assaults as primarily sexual assaults, rather than the result of the drunken, incoherent rage of a man full of hatred. He dumped the young girl's body into the Rochdale Canal.

The police recognised this murder as being the work of the same person who had killed Wanda Skala, so they re-arrested Hardy, the most obvious suspect. This time they interrogated Farrow at greater length, and she finally confessed to providing him with false alibis.

Hardy now confessed to the crimes, but he claimed that Farrow had been with him for one of them – he stated that she had been present when he killed Skala, that it had been an attempted mugging that went wrong when the victim recognised them.

Farrow finally stopped protecting her lover at this stage.

160

The police recognised that their best chance of convicting the violent Hardy rested on her evidence, so they granted her immunity for her complicity in covering up evidence and providing false alibis in return for her being a witness in the trial of Hardy.

He was tried in 1977, and attempted to plead guilty to the lesser charge of manslaughter on the grounds of diminished responsibility. But the jury recognised that this was not an insane man, just a violent monster who had made rational attempts to cover his own tracks. He was evil but not insane, in their view, and they accordingly found him guilty of murder.

*　　*　　*

Friends and relatives of the victims were appalled that Farrow was granted immunity. It was widely believed that she must have been complicit to a greater degree and that she may even have been involved in the murders. However it does seem to be a case where her role was limited to protecting the man she was living with.

This is morally debased in itself, and it can be said with almost total certainty that Hardy would not have been free to kill his third victim if it weren't for Farrow's false alibi and the file she smuggled into the prison where he was detained.

It is interesting to note that, while this case occurred only ten years after the far more notorious Moors Murders, which had also happened in Manchester, it has received far less attention in the tabloid press and television in the UK. There are a number of reasons for this.

The Moors Murders grabbed the public attention while the murderers were still free, as the pattern of killings was clear, and the public were warned to be on their guard, whereas Hardy's serial killing only became evident at the stage when he was finally arrested and tried. It was only the fact that he volun-

161

tarily confessed to killing Janet Lesley Stewart that meant that the police knew he had killed three times rather than twice. In fact Hardy hinted at other deaths, though in her fascinating book *Couples Who Kill,* the writer Carol Anne Davis suggests that this was merely an attempt to gain notoriety by claiming to be a more prolific killer than he actually was.

The Moors Murders were also notorious because of Myra Hindley's clear involvement in the crimes of Ian Brady. While Sheilagh Farrow had helped to cover up the deaths of young girls, she was not demonised by the press to the same degree, and she had certainly not been guilty of the same level of depravity as Hindley. And the Hardy case did not furnish the press with the same level of detailed evidence, photographs, and heartbreaking detail that had been the hallmark of the earlier murders.

Nonetheless, Hardy was clearly one of the more disturbed, evil murderers that had been apprehended in the UK. He may have killed in a drunken rage, but the cold-blooded mutilation of his victims makes it clear that he was a monstrous killer and someone who was an extreme danger to the public.

Farrow shared some of the blame for his crimes, but it should also be remembered that the police did well to capture him rapidly enough to prevent further deaths. It seems certain he would have killed again if he had remained free.

In 2008, when Trevor Hardy had been in prison for over twenty years, it emerged that he was on a list of less than fifty prisoners in the country whose life sentences were to be full life sentences. In other words, the British home secretary had identified him as someone who would never be released from prison.

*   *   *

Sheilagh Farrow's whereabouts are unknown. She was free to go after the trial. It is possible that she voluntarily went into hiding, or that the police helped her to disappear. This is a strategy that is sometimes invoked where there is significant danger to the safety of an individual.

In another well-known case, the killer Mary Bell (who had killed two children while she was under the age of twelve herself) was given anonymity and a new identity when she was released from prison.

Clearly, there was a threat to Farrow, as many people in Manchester and elsewhere regarded her behaviour as unforgivable. If she was forced into hiding in one way or another she would have effectively lost a great deal of her freedom. Manchester is a town with tight-knit working-class communities, and it would have been impossible for her to live a normal life there after the events of 1975 and 1976.

Whatever has happened to her since the trial of Trevor Hardy, she will have had to live the rest of her life with the guilt of knowing that she could have prevented the death of an innocent young girl, that she could have saved a third family from suffering the misery of losing a loved one. Whether that is sufficient punishment for her actions, only she (and God) can know.

Teri Depew and Carole Hargis

The Inconvenient Husband

Many crimes of passion are committed on the spur of the moment, in a jealous rage, or a moment when the attacker loses his or her self-control. Others are acts of madness committed by people who are clearly incapable of restraining their most savage urges. The two things that mark out the murder committed by Teri Depew and Carol Hargis as an unusual one are the cold-blooded way in which the two murderesses pursued their goal, and the fact that they made so many attempts on the life of the same man.

David Hargis was Carole's husband. He was a member of the Marine Corps, having re-enlisted to try to pay off some debts. He acted as father to the two children that Carole had from a previous marriage. They lived together as a family in San Diego. He also, unfortunately for him, had a double indemnity life insurance policy which would pay out $40,000 to Carole if he died.

This didn't become a problem until Carole, a good-looking blonde woman, fell in love with their neighbour Teri Depew, who was twenty-seven years old. Teri, an unemployed physical therapist, was a butch-acting lesbian.

The two women had hoped that David would be sent away on military service (the Vietnam War had recently finished) but this didn't happen. Neither of the women had any way of supporting themselves, so they were unable simply to set up home together. So they decided that they would kill David in order to gain the money from his life insurance policy.

This was the start of a truly bizarre train of events.

*　　*　　*

The first attempt to kill David was motivated by the desire to make his death appear to be an accident. Carole waited until he was in the shower one day before starting to dry her hair. Pretending to trip, she threw the hair-dryer, still plugged in, into the shower. David was unharmed and assumed that this incident was indeed a mere accident. So the lesbian couple were forced to come up with a new plan.

The second attempt was a poisoning plot. Over a period of weeks, Carole laced David's food with poison. He did become ill, but not fatally. He thought he had influenza, and sought medical treatment. The pair decided that a more direct approach would speed up the poisoning.

Teri kept spiders, including a tarantula, as pets in her house. They took the poison sac from this tarantula and Carole inserted it into David's food. However, David noticed that there was something strange in the food, and simply placed it on the side of the plate. Once again he had survived.

Once again the couple tried to come up with a new plan. They decided to try and make it look as though he had died from a misadventure with drugs. They drugged him and then, while he was asleep, they used a hypodermic needle on him. They had intentionally allowed air into the hypodermic, hoping that by injecting an air bubble into his bloodstream, they could kill him.

This attempt failed when the needle broke off in David's

arm. They fetched a pair of forceps to remove the needle and abandoned their plan. When David woke from his sleep he thought that he had been bitten by a particularly vicious insect while he slept.

The innocent failures of David to realise the murderous intent of the couple seem particularly tragic given his final fate. He was in love with Carole, and simply didn't imagine that she might be trying to kill him, even given the strange events which kept occurring.

*   *   *

The two lovers finally succeeded in killing David on 20 July 1977. The children were at a Boy Scout event, so the Hargis's house was empty, apart from the married couple. Teri came round to the house and the three played cards together. David became tired and retreated to the bedroom, where he fell asleep in bed.

The two women stayed downstairs discussing their plan quietly, before Teri crept upstairs to the bedroom. David was asleep when Teri smashed a heavy object into his skull. He wasn't killed but he was badly injured, and bleeding profusely.

He started calling for Carole, not knowing what had happened to him. Teri had gone back downstairs to be with Carole, but Carole urged her to go back and finish David off. She did as Carole asked and David was finally killed when she returned and hit him again.

They decided to remove the corpse in David's own truck. They started dragging him to it, but the bleeding was still copious and they were getting blood everywhere. So they paused to apply bandages to his head and ears to try and staunch the flow of blood.

The lifeless body was finally hoisted into the truck, and Teri drove to a nearby bridge, where she dumped him over the side. Carole spent this time washing the sheets and bedding to try to remove the evidence. The next day she cleaned some more and where she couldn't remove the bloodstains in the bedroom, she calmly painted over them.

The couple knew they had to report David missing, so while Teri waited in the background, Carole placed a call to the police. She pretended to be crying as she reported him missing. She claimed that he had gone out snake-hunting, clearly hoping that the body wouldn't be found soon.

During the call, the operator put Carole on hold. At this point she immediately stopped her pretence of sobbing and talked in measured tones to Teri. Then, when the operator came back onto the line, she resumed her charade of sorrow and worry.

What Carole hadn't realised was that the police recording of emergency calls keeps running all the time, so she had been caught on tape breaking off from her performance to speak to her lover. Even worse, David's body was discovered rapidly, and there were still bandages sticking to his head.

This made it very obvious that he had been subjected to something more than a random attack, and that his body had probably been transported to the place where it was found.

The police searched the house and found significant traces of blood in the truck, in the bedroom under the fresh paint, and on the bed and floor. They questioned the couple. Teri realised that they were in trouble and attempted to concoct a story which they could use a defence.

She stated that David had tried to assault her in his truck. She admitted killing him, but claimed that it had been in self-defence, and she had acted from panic when she disposed of the body.

The police knew that she was lying and she was taken into custody. They were convinced that David had been killed in the house and that Carole must know something about it.

They continued their investigations, and under prolonged

interrogation, Teri changed her story and admitted Carole's complicity. Carole reacted with fury, regarding this as a betrayal, and in return she claimed that Teri had forced her to help kill David, saying that the younger woman had been obsessed with her and had threatened to hurt her children if she didn't go along with the plan.

Teri pleaded guilty to murder and was sentenced to life imprisonment in November 1977. At Carole's trial, which was a month after Teri's, the real story became undeniable, as Carole's deeply incriminating emergency phone call to the police was played.

Carole followed Teri to jail, once again for a life sentence. The couple's attempts to evade guilt had only delayed the revelation of their cold, vicious attempts on the life of a husband whose only crime was to love his wife too much.

Holly Harvey and Sandra Ketchum

Teen Killers

Parents and grandparents the world over know how much of a worry teenagers can be. They often go through phases where they become nihilistic and hostile. They may take drugs or get into trouble of various sorts, and at best they are prone to being uncommunicative. But most of these teenagers come through these difficult phases and grow up into perfectly decent adults.

However, in a few cases parental fears are justified, and what appears to be malignant rebellion can turn into violence, abuse or even murder. One such case was that of Holly Harvey and Sandra Ketchum, teenage lesbian lovers who callously murdered the grandparents of Holly Harvey, Carl and Sarah Collier.

Their case bears an obvious resemblance to the notorious 1954 New Zealand murder case in which Pauline Parker and Juliet Hulme killed Pauline's mother. Both took place in genteel locations where the two teenagers felt themselves to be outsiders who could not live as they wanted to. And in both cases the measures they resorted to in their angst were an outrage to society.

*   *   *

Carl and Sarah Collier lived in Fayette County, about fifteen miles south of Atlanta. They weren't able to have children, so they chose to adopt. Their adoptive son Kevin gave them no problems at all, but they also adopted Carla Harvey as a daughter, and this led to far more difficulties. Carla was known as a troublesome teenager herself. She had two children herself by different fathers and was eventually charged with a drugs felony and sent to the State prison in the spring of 2004.

At this stage Carl and Sarah chose to take in their adoptive grand-daughter Holly Harvey, whose father was unable to care for her because he was confined to a wheelchair after an automobile accident. She was fifteen at the time, while her grandparents were both in their seventies.

What started as an act of charity soon turned into a trial as Holly was already known to the police as a troublemaker, who had run away from home on a number of occasions. The problem was compounded by the fact that Carl and Sarah were relatively conservative people who hoped to be able to persuade Holly to go to church. She immediately reacted against their authority.

Holly was in love with sixteen-year-old Sandra Ketchum, who was generally known as Sandy. She had been banned from seeing Sandy and her grandparents continued to impose this ban.

Holly was probably clinically depressed. During investigations into the crime, a poem she had written came to light describing how she cried herself to sleep at night, and only wanted to kill.

She became increasingly abusive towards the Colliers, at one point screaming death threats at them. Carl Collier was concerned enough to speak to his son Kevin about her behaviour. He told Kevin that Holly wanted him dead. But he couldn't have known how true that statement was.

* * *

170

Sandy Ketchum had also had a troubled childhood. Her birth mother had left while she was still a baby, and she had been with a string of stepmothers. At least one of these had been accused of abusing her physically. Her relative isolation may be a partial explanation of the intensity with which she attached herself to Holly Harvey when they fell in love.

The two had been banned from seeing each other, but continued to meet in secret . They had conversations about how to escape from what they saw as the injustice of their situations, and they decided to run away together. They wanted to be free to be together forever. But increasingly they decided that the only way to achieve this was to kill the Colliers.

It is hard to say how definite the murder plan was at this stage. The fact that they boasted to friends at school that they planned to kill the Colliers and openly asked around for a gun suggests that there may have been an element of bravado to it, although they may simply have been too stupid to realise the harm this would do to their plans.

On 1 August 2004 Holly and Sandy spent the evening together at the home of Calvin Lawson, a forty-one-year-old friend of Holly's mother. He supplied them with crack cocaine and marijuana. The murder would be committed by the girls the next day while they were still under the influence of these drugs. As a result Lawson was at one point arrested by the police – Georgia law allowed him in theory to be charged with felony murder as his felony of drug dealing had contributed to the murders. However these charges can rarely be made to stick as it is hard to prove the degree to which the felony actually caused the ensuing crime.

The girls were back at the Colliers' house in the early hours of the morning before Carl and Sarah had woken up. While they were listening to music, they discussed the idea of taking Carl's truck and running away. Harvey later told the judge that she had been joking when she said 'We'd have to kill him to do that.' Whether it was initially serious or not, they were soon discussing exactly how this could be achieved.

They even broke the plan down into stages so they wouldn't forget. Holly wrote this down as a terse 'things to do' list in pen on her arm: 'Kill, keys, money and jewellery.' They needed the money and jewellery to sustain them after they ran away.

Ketchum suggested hitting Carl with a heavy object, but instead they decided to find a knife. They took the largest blade they could find in the house, which was between eight and ten inches long.

They proceeded to practise using the knife, stabbing a mattress in the room and a picture of some puppies that happened to be there. They continued to smoke marijuana through the morning, hoping that the smell would bring the grandparents down and provoke an argument.

In the event, it was the afternoon before Carl and Sarah came to the basement, in search of a suitcase for Sarah's forthcoming vacation in Hawaii. When they heard them coming, Ketchum hid behind the bed, and Harvey concealed her knife in her jeans.

While Carl was looking in the closet for the bag, Sarah stood with her back to Harvey. She took her chance and stabbed her in the back three times. At the trial she said that she had closed her eyes while she struck at her grandmother.

Carl came to the rescue of his wife, and together they tried to fight off their grand-daughter, pinning her briefly to the bed. But at this stage Ketchum came out from her hiding place and joined in the struggle. Sarah was stabbed at least twenty times in the struggle and Carl also received stab wounds.

He managed to get out of the room and run upstairs. He found a knife to defend himself and tried to call the police.

However Harvey ran after him, wrestled the knife off him, cut the phone wire and continued the attack.

At her trial she would describe his final moments saying that '[I] closed my eyes and stabbed my grandpa real fast,' and that when it was over, 'I had blood all over my face and on the right side of my body.' The judge at the trial, Judge Paschal English, was appalled by this description, commenting that it was like she had gutted a deer.

Carl died face-down on the kitchen floor in a pool of his own blood. He had been stabbed fifteen times in his chest and neck.

*　　*　　*

The two girls now moved on to the next stage of their plan. They took the car keys for Carl's pick-up truck, and searched the house for money and jewellery, although there was no cash to be found so they had to make do with Sarah's jewellery. They were both covered in blood, but they made no attempt at this stage to clean themselves or conceal their crime.

They drove to the nearby town of Griffin and called a sixteen-year-old friend (identified only as Sara P.) They initially claimed that they had been mugged and that this was the reason for their blood-spattered clothes. They washed and changed their clothes at the girl's house, but while they were doing so Holly told her the real story.

Again they seem to have been so solipsistically convinced that they were the victims in the story that they naïvely confessed the murder to the first person they spoke to. One has to assume that for whatever reason they had failed to achieve an understanding of their moral responsibility for their situation. But even that is an unsatisfactory statement as it comes too close to saying they didn't understand what they had done. They understood it well enough and Sandy Ketchum would later show some remorse. But as the crime

developed they showed little understanding of the seriousness of the situation they had created.

Sara threw the girls out of her house once Holly made her
confession and immediately told her parents. She then
called the police, who went straight to the Collier house.
Sheriff Randall Johnson discovered a scene of terrible
bloodshed and tragedy and an arrest warrant was issued
immediately. Fayette County is a relatively sedate backwa-
ter and it was unheard of for a crime of this viciousness to
occur there.

After they left the house of Sara P., the two girls drove to
Tybee Island which is a resort on the coast near Savannah,
Georgia. Calling themselves Jessica and Casey, they met two
brothers. They asked the elder brother to help them pawn the
jewellery they had stolen. He refused to help them with this,
but the brothers believed the girls' story that their grandmother had recently died, leaving them with nowhere to go.
They allowed Harvey and Ketchum to stay the night at their
house, with the agreement of the family.

In the morning the family was shocked to find the house
surrounded by armed police. The teenage girls had been
naïve enough to use their mobile phones, not realising that
this allowed their location to be pinpointed using satellite
technology.

As a result the police had been able to track them down
within twenty-four hours of their disappearance. This may
have been extremely lucky for the family concerned. Some
accounts suggest that Ketchum and Harvey had discussed
killing the mother in order to steal her car, having abandoned
Carl Collier's pick-up truck a few miles away.

*   *   *

From the time they were arrested, some differences between
the two girls became apparent. Holly Harvey seemed uncon-

cerned and uncaring, even laughing as she was arrested. Whereas Sandy Ketchum was nervous from the start and was apparently beginning to regret what had happened.

It is always interesting to consider the dynamics of a couple who kill together. In many cases there is a dominant partner, who is the one who would have been more likely to kill if left to his or her own devices. But within a relationship a mutually reinforcing feedback cycle can develop whereby one partner legitimises and encourages the other partne's ideas and decisions. One can't know what would have happened if a couple had not been together, whether either would have been either capable of or likely to murder on their own. There are too many contingent events that lead up to the line being crossed that leads to murder.

However it does seem that in the relationship between Harvey and Ketchum, it was Harvey who was the dominating force. She was the one who hated her grand-parents, whereas Ketchum was motivated more by the desire to be with Harvey. And after they were apprehended it was Ketchum who showed greater comprehension of what had happened and a higher level of empathy.

At her trial Ketchum would say, 'If there was any way I could take their place and give my life, I wouldn't think twice . . . I'm real sorry.' An alternative interpretation would be that she had a clearer understanding of the fact that penitence was expected, but most observers felt that she did show some real contrition after the event, once she was no longer under the direct influence of Harvey. Ketchum also co-operated with the police during the investigation and would give evidence against Harvey at her trial.

Carl Collier's truck had been quickly found. The police found the girls' belongings which included bloodied clothes and the bloodstained knives which had been used in the fatal attack. From the start there was no doubt that the girls had carried out the attack. But friends and relatives were nonetheless deeply shocked at the events and bewildered as to what had driven the girls to such a vicious act.

*   *   *

The two girls had separate trials in March and April 2005. Both were found guilty of the charges. The trial of Holly Harvey was especially dramatic. She had refused to talk about the crime up until this stage, but while he was considering the sentence, Judge English (who was well-known after making an appearance on the reality show, *Suvivor*) insisted on questioning her to elicit more information about her motives and attitudes.

The transcript of the questioning makes for fascinating, if unsettling reading. Holly Harvey sounds like a typical recalcitrant teenager, while Judge English could be mistaken for a weary teacher trying to get some information from a student.

At one point he asked why they had tested out the knife on a mattress.

'To see if the knife was sharp enough,' was her reply.

'Sharp enough for what?' asked English.

'I guess . . .' started Harvey, before pausing.

'Don't guess, tell me,' said the judge. 'You know. You did it.'

'To see if it would be sharp enough to stab them wherever the knife went.'

Harvey insisted she had killed the Colliers 'for Sandy', so that they could be together, and made Ketchum out to be an equal partner in the crime.

However Harvey was judged to be the leader of the two in the planning of the murder and consequently received a longer sentence. (The death sentence wasn't available because the girls were underage.) She was sentenced to a life term with the possibility of parole after twenty years, whereas Ketchum could hope for parole after fourteen years.

Later in the judge's questioning he asked Harvey:

'Do you think twenty years is a pretty good exchange for killing your grandparents? What do you think ought to be done with you?'

'I think I should be dead,' she said.

'Well, we both agree on that,' said Judge English.

After the verdict, Harvey's mother Carla was interviewed about her daughter. She said, 'All I ever did was love her and try to teach her right from wrong. It was her actions. It was her doings. I can't hold myself responsible for that.'

Should any parent blame him- or herself for the crimes of their children? It is hard to completely deny the role of upbringing in the development of criminality. Time after time, in reading about killers, one finds that they had deprivations, abuse or unhappiness in their childhoods. One can't help but feel that if all children could be guaranteed a happy, loving childhood there would be a great deal less murder in the world.

However even those with every excuse for unhappiness can learn moral responsibility and to distinguish right from wrong. Not every child from a miserable or abused background turns to crime. The vast majority rise beyond their backgrounds and become decent responsible adults.

When, as with Holly Harvey, an individual turns to crime, and when that choice comes in the form of a vicious, selfish murder then the only person who can be asked to take the moral responsibility is the killer herself.

Jessie King and Thomas Pearson

Crimes of Poverty

In modern times, the public in Britain has been outraged by
two cases in which women were involved in the murder of
children or young women. It is often assumed that Myra
Hindley and Rosemary West are unusual in the fact that they
were found guilty of such heinous murders. However there
are cases going back into history in which women have been
found guilty of murder. One case which gives an interesting
historical perspective is the case of Jessie West.

In the late 1880s, West lived with her lover Thomas
Pearson in a lodging house in Edinburgh, Scotland. They
were a poor couple who drank heavily at times. In her early
twenties, Jessie was not very intelligent, and known for her
mendacity. Pearson was a labourer who was in his fifties, so
considerably older than Jessie West.

It was a grim economic period. From the early 1870s to
the mid 1890s the global economy went through the 'great
sag' or the 'long depression'. This was a period of deflation,
in which economies and investment almost ground to a halt.
In America, the Populist Party grew out of the Farmer's
Alliance, a movement that opposed the power of Eastern

bankers and the gold standard, believing that they were responsible for the harmful effects of the deflation. In the United Kingdom, the industrial revolution hit a period of unprecedented stagnation in which the working classes were subject to reduced real wages, with high levels of bankruptcy and unemployment.

It was also a time when it was regarded as unacceptable for young women to have illegitimate children (in other words children born outside of marriage). If a girl were to get herself in trouble she had to make a difficult choice. She could go home to her parents in shame, or she could appeal to the charity of the parish, in a time when the undeserving poor were heavily stigmatised. As a result, unmarried women who became pregnant often resorted to desperate measures.

The risky procedure of an illegal abortion was one option. Dubious doctors would also provide a range of drugs that might help to induce a miscarriage, although many of these were alarmingly risky.

The final alternative was to arrange a private adoption. Prior to the twentieth-century reform of social work, there were no formal, state-sanctioned arrangements for adoptions, but unwilling parents could advertise in newspapers to find someone who would adopt their child in return for a payment.

*   *   *

This was the situation in which King and Pearson realised that money could be made from the adoption of babies. When Jessie first adopted a child is unknown. All that is certain is that at least three children she adopted in return for a payment ended up dead.

The couple's landlady was away when her daughter saw Jessie with a young baby. However the baby had disappeared by the time the landlady returned. Jessie explained that she

179

had adopted a child for a payment, but had made a profit by passing the child on to another adoptive mother for a smaller payment. The landlady noticed that there were still baby clothes in the house, but Jessie explained this away with another lie, that she was planning on having a child herself.

In October 1888 some children who were playing in the street in the Stockbridge area of Edinburgh made a gruesome discovery. The found a parcel wrapped in old cloth tied in string. On opening it they found the dead body of an infant child. There were marks on its neck, which suggested that the baby had been strangled.

When King and Pearson's landlady heard of this discovery she went to the police with her suspicions. They took Jessie in for questioning and searched the lodging house. A second corpse was rapidly discovered. This time it was in the basement of the building, again wrapped in cloth. It was a girl of about six weeks old, with string around its neck, again suggesting that the death had been a result of strangulation.

It came to light that a third child had died whilst in the care of Jessie King. She had been seen giving the child whisky, and when questioned on this death she claimed that the child had choked to death accidentally.

The case against Jessie was not that strong from a prosecution point of view. It seemed likely that she had accepted money to adopt the children and had then not wanted to look after them so had killed them. However this was a period in which the casual death of children was not unknown and poor people often disposed of bodies in unorthodox ways to avoid funeral costs. Jessie might have been able to escape justice.

However Thomas Pearson did not want to risk being tried as an accomplice to the murders, so he chose to give evidence against Jessie to save his own life. Jessie subsequently admitted to the murder of the first two infants discovered, although she continued to deny the third death was her fault.

This case raises an interesting moral dilemma that the police sometimes face. Pearson's role in the deaths seemed at best to have been turning a blind eye, and at worst complicity in the crimes. Just as in the case of Sheilagh Farrow and Trevor Hardy, there was an argument for prosecuting both parties. But just as in that case, a decision was made to use the evidence of one party to secure a conviction of the person who seemed to be the prime mover.

Sheilagh Farrow had not participated in any murders, merely helped to cover them up, leaving Trevor Hardy free to commit a further assaults and murders. Thomas Pearson's role in the death of the three children is unknown. He may have been entirely innocent, but it seems more likely that he was at least aware that Jessie had taken the money for the children and then disposed of them in some way. His claim in court that he believed Jessie had sent the children to orphanages seems unlikely given that she kept the first baby's clothes in the house.

This in itself would be something he should be held morally culpable for. But the police concluded that their case was best served by using Pearson as a witness for the prosecution and granting him immunity.

The court case was in fact a model of decent justice. Jessie was tried for only the two deaths which she had admitted to. The counsel for the defence focused on the possibility of reasonable doubt and asked the jury to consider carefully the role they believed Pearson might have played. Jessie herself defended Pearson, saying he had known nothing. She claimed to have killed the first child because she couldn't afford to pay for its care any more, and to have accidentally strangled the second child while Pearson was out of the house.

The Lord Justice Clerk who was in charge of the case also spoke to the jury about the conditions of poverty that existed in the city of Edinburgh, and asked the jury to bear in mind

181

the moral responsibility that the original parents of the dead children shared for giving up their children in the care of a stranger.

However for all the mitigating circumstances, it was abundantly clear that King was guilty of at least one murder, probably more, and the jury took only four minutes to reach a guilty verdict. The death sentence was still in force in the nineteenth century and King was sentenced to death by hanging.

While she was in Calton prison awaiting execution she made a number of attempts to take her own life by tearing strips from her own clothes to create makeshift nooses. However these attempts failed.

Jessie King was a Catholic, and priests and nuns went into the prison in order to speak with her and hear her confessions in the days before the execution. She was hanged on 11 March 1889 holding her crucifix. Thomas Pearson remained a free man.

The story of Jessie King is a deeply sad one. She was sufficiently morally corrupt to kill children and there is no adequate excuse for that. But it is depressing to contemplate the depths of poverty that meant that the children were given to her in the first place, and that she accepted the money out of desperation in spite of not having the capacity or desire to carry through on her promises.

Unlike some of the killers in this book, it seems unlikely that she would have been a killer if she had had better circumstances and a greater dignity of life in the first place. However in the end, the killing of a baby is an act so morally repugnant that it is hard to retain any pity for her.

Susan and Michael Bear

The Hippy Witch Hunters

Never trust anyone who changes their name or 'gets religion'.

Perhaps that's a bit of a sweeping statement, but the case of Susan Barnes Carson and James Clifford Carson is an example of the fact that murderers come in all shapes and sizes. And perhaps it's also evidence for the idea that people often change their name as a result of deep-seated insecurity and are therefore more likely to be of an impressionable personality type. When insecure, impressionable people take to a new fanatical idea, they can often take it to unreasonable extremes.

The Carsons appeared to be regular hippies, harmless members of the counterculture that still flourished in San Francisco in the 1970s. Each of them had come from relatively affluent families, but had chosen to 'drop out' and to seek out radical and alternative ways of life.

They managed to acquire some land in Humboldt County, California and set up a pot farm, from the proceeds of which they were able to live a fairly secluded and comfortable life. However they were also consuming an increasing quantity of psycho-active chemicals and hallucinogenic drugs and the results were explosive.

On one of their many trips, Susan had a series of visions which persuaded her that the pair should convert to Islam, and change their names. The fact that they chose the rather silly names Susan and Michael Bear gives the story a moment of weird childishness. Just as Charles Manson had chosen the cosy name of 'The Family' for his cultish clan, the Bears chose a name that sounded innocent and playful. The names sound like characters from a children's story.

However the couple behaved nothing like characters in a children's story. In the wake of Susan's increasingly bizarre hallucinations, they declared themselves to be missionaries of the Muslim faith (of which they don't seem to have had a particularly profound understanding).

Susan had become convinced that the world was being populated by malign witches, and that missionaries of Islam such as herself and Michael were duty-bound to stop them. The couple kept a list of claimed witches in the public eye, which apparently included such esteemed figures as Ronald Reagan and Johnny Carson.

Up to this stage this might have been merely one of the many forms of schizophrenic breakdowns that affect people who have taken too many drugs, in the grip of the rather nonsensical association of drug-taking and freedom that was the main legacy of the hippy movement to the 1970s and 1980s. However the Bears soon moved on to murder.

As well as public figures, they had decided that some of their friends and acquaintances were witches, who had to be stopped. Susan had decided that Allah was speaking to her, and that he was telling her to kill.

In some respect Susan Bear's behaviour resembles that of a typical cult leader. By declaring herself to be seeing through the pretences and inanities of the world, and to be perceiving true good and evil, she also acted out her personal likes and hatreds. Where she differed from a cult leader was that she had only one devotee, her partner in crime Michael Bear.

184

The couple killed at least three people in California between 1981 and 1983. Karen Barnes was stabbed to death at her home in the hippy capital Haight-Ashbury. Clark Stephens was murdered and suffered mutilations in Humboldt County. And John Hillyar was murdered after the Bears picked him up while he was hitch-hiking in the Napa Valley area.

There was no pattern to the murders. The Bears used blunt weapons, knives or guns indiscriminately. They seem to have been genuinely convinced that they had to carry out these terrible acts in order to prevent evil spells from being enacted.

After they had been arrested in 1983 they held a news conference at which they blankly confessed to their crimes, but any sign of real contrition was hard to detect.

Each received a penalty of twenty-five years to life.

One could almost find a story such as that of Susan and Michael Bear comical in a dark way. But that would be to forget that behind the story of hippies gone wrong, there were real people, real victims who suffered senseless violence and death.

The bizarre circumstances that led up to these murders does not make them any less tragic, or the Carsons any less culpable for their acts.

Leopold and Loeb

The 'Perfect Crime'

Nathan Freudenthal Leopold Jr and Richard A. Loeb were two wealthy and highly intelligent students who gained notoriety when they kidnapped and murdered fourteen-year-old Bobby Franks in 1924. Their trial made history not only because of the wealth and privilege of the boys involved, but also for being a trial that was used as a campaign against the death penalty by their attorney Clarence Darrow who promised to save the boys from execution.

The murder that captivated a nation in 1924 began as a fantasy in the mind of eighteen-year-old Richard Loeb, the handsome and privileged son of a retired Sears Roebuck vice-president. Leopold himself was a mere nineteen years old. Both Leopold and Loeb lived in Kenwood, an extremely affluent Jewish neighborhood on the South Side of Chicago.

Besides owning an impressive mansion in Kenwood, two blocks away from the Leopold home, the Loeb family also had a summer estate in Charlevoix, Michigan. Like Loeb, Leopold was a child of wealth and opportunity, the son of a millionaire box manufacturer. The Leopolds were a highly respected family of German Jews who had arrived in the

United States in the mid-1800s. The family had initially made its fortune transporting grain, minerals and other freight on the Great Lakes.

Leopold had studied philosophy and was attracted to the writing of Friedrich Nietzsche. Nietzsche's influence on early twentieth-century academics was powerful, and the meaning of ideas contained in books like *Beyond Good and Evil* were frequently debated in places of learning like the University of Chicago. Nathan Leopold agreed with Nietzsche's criticism of moral codes, and believed that legal obligations did not apply to those who approached the status of the 'superman'. For Leopold, his friend and lover, Richard Loeb, embodied his personal idea of the 'superman'.

Despite a level of wealth that meant he could have afforded anything he wanted, Loeb was obsessed with crime. He loved reading detective stories. He spent his time reading about crime and planning and carrying out crimes although none involved actual physical harm to another person until the 1924 murder. (Defence Attorney Clarence Darrow and Nathan Leopold later saw Loeb's fascination with crime as a form of rebellion against the well-meaning, but strict and controlling governess who raised him.)

For Loeb, crime became a sort of game. Based on Nietzsche's ideas, the boys dreamed of committing the 'perfect crime' just to prove that it could be done.

The friendship between Leopold and Loeb began at university in the spring of 1920. Both boys were exceptionally intelligent. Leopold had already completed college and was attending law school at the University of Chicago. He studied fifteen languages and spoke five fluently. By the time of the murder, at the age of nineteen, he was already a well-respected expert in ornithology (he was known as the nation's leading authority on the Kirtland warbler).

Loeb was the youngest graduate in the history of the University of Michigan and planned to enter the University of Chicago Law School after taking some post-graduate courses. It is clear that the pair were more than close friends but because of social attitudes at the time, they were constantly forced to deny accusations of homosexuality.

It would later come out at the trial that the two were indeed involved in some form of a sexual relationship and were to all intents and purposes a couple at the time of their crime. Faced with his friend's insatiable desire for crime, Leopold had agreed to act as Loeb's accomplice as long as Loeb agreed to have sex with him. The couple began with petty theft, but as time went on committed a series of more and more serious crimes, eventually culminating in murder.

*   *   *

Murder was a necessary element in the boys' plan to commit the 'perfect crime'. The two teenagers spent hours discussing and refining a plan that included kidnapping the child of a wealthy parents, demanding a ransom, and collecting the ransom after it was thrown off a moving train as it passed a designated point. Neither Loeb nor Leopold relished the idea of murdering their kidnap victim, but they thought it critical in minimising the likelihood of their being identified as the kidnappers.

Leopold and Loeb spent a few months planning the murder, working out the perfect way to get ransom money with little risk of being caught. They finally put their plan into action on Wednesday 21 May 1924. After driving around in a rented grey Winton automobile, the boys waited outside the Harvard School after classes had finished. They considered taking many of the boys who were on their way home but rejected them for various reasons. Eventually they spotted fourteen-year-old Bobby Franks, a neighbour and distant relative of Loeb's. Unfortunately for him, Franks was simply in the wrong place at the wrong time.

Franks already knew the boys because he lived next door to Loeb and had played tennis at the Loeb's house. However, although the Franks were residents of Kenwood, they had not been completely accepted socially for several reasons. The area at the time was primarily Jewish and elitist. The Franks had renounced their Jewish faith to become Christians and Jacob had made much of his money running a pawn shop, which didn't recommend them socially to the powerful Jewish executives, bankers and attorneys in the neighbourhood. Still, Bobby would have had no hesitation in approaching the car since its occupants were familiar to him.

Bobby was hit over the head with a chisel and then, after a struggle, was gagged with a sock. He died as a result of this treatment.

Some have suggested that Franks was sexually molested, then killed later but there has never been any concrete evidence that this was the case. The killers covered the body of the boy with a rug and drove to a remote marshland area near Wolf Lake in Hammond, Indiana. There they stripped Franks naked.

They poured hydrochloric acid over his face and genitals in order to make identification more difficult. Without showing any emotion about what they had just done, Leopold and Loeb then had dinner at a hot dog stand. After finishing their meal they waited until dark to drive towards Wolf Lake. This remote area was only accessible along a dirt road and they passed no one as they drove. They concealed Frank's body in a drainage culvert north of Wolf Lake.

On returning to Chicago, Leopold telephoned Bobby Franks' mother Flora, calling himself George Johnson and told her that her son had been kidnapped. They then mailed the ransom note to the Franks and threw away the chisel used to strike Bobby on his head.

At Loeb's house they burned their clothes to prevent the

189

bloodstains from incriminating them and cleaned the seats of the rental car. The two then spent the rest of the evening playing cards.

Meanwhile, worried that he had not come home for dinner, Bobby's mother Flora had been telephoning Bobby's school friends to try to find out where he was. His father Jacob had gone to inspect the school buildings with his friend, prominent lawyer Samuel Ettelson. While they were gone, Flora received Leopold's phone call. She was told, 'Your son has been kidnapped. He is all right. There will be further news in the morning.'

The next morning the Franks family received a special delivery letter asking that they immediately obtain $10,000 in old, unmarked bills and telling them to expect further instructions that afternoon.

The boys placed the note telling Jacob Franks where to throw the money, in a telegraph box on the last car of a train going to Michigan City, Indiana. Leopold (as George Johnson) then telephoned Jacob Franks, Bobby's father, to tell him that a taxi cab was about to arrive at his home and that he should take it to a specified drugstore in South Chicago. The ransom letter read:

> Dear Sir,
>
> As you no doubt know by this time, your son has been kidnapped. Allow us to assure you that he is at present well and safe. You need fear no physical harm for him, provided you live up carefully to the following instructions and to such others as you will receive by future communications. Should you, however, disobey any of our instructions, even slightly, his death will be the penalty.

1. For obvious reasons make absolutely no attempt to communicate with either police authorities or any private agency. Should you already have communicated with the police, allow them to continue their investigations, but do not mention this letter.

2. Secure before noon today $10,000. This money must be composed entirely of old bills of the following denominations: $2,000 in $20 bills, $8,000 in $50 bills. The money must be old. Any attempt to include new or marked bills will render the entire venture futile.

3. The money should be placed in a large cigar box, or, if this is impossible, in a heavy cardboard box, securely closed and wrapped in white paper. The wrapping paper should be sealed at all openings with sealing wax.

4. Have the money with you, prepared as directed above, and remain at home after one o'clock. See that the telephone is not in use.

The letter was signed George Johnson and guaranteed that if the money were delivered according to his instructions that Bobby would be returned unharmed.

However, before Jacob could begin to comply with the kidnapper's demands, a second telephone call came in, this one from the police. Tony Minke, a Polish immigrant and labourer, had discovered the body of a boy under shrubbery covering the open culvert near Wolf Lake. The body was soon identified as that of Bobby Franks. The 'perfect crime' had been ruined. It wasn't perfect after all. When Leopold and Loeb learned that the body had been found, they

191

destroyed the typewriter used to write the ransom note and burned the robe used to move the body.

*   *   *

The police were now investigating a murder. One initial problem was that Jacob Franks and Samuel Ettelson couldn't remember the address of the downtown drugstore where they were supposed to go to receive instruction from the kidnapper. A yellow cab arrived as promised but hadn't been given a destination address.

Across town at the Van de Bogert & Ross drugstore on East Sixty-Third Street a phone call came in for 'Mr Franks'. The store manager later informed the police that he had told the caller that there was no Mr Franks there, the caller hung up but called again a few minutes later, this time giving a description of Mr Franks. Again the store manager told the caller that there was no man in the store matching his description.

The man in charge of the investigation was State's Attorney Robert E. Crowe. Crowe took on Bert Cronson, a nephew of Samuel Ettelson, as his assistant along with two other policemen. At the time Crowe was trying to establish himself as the top Republican in the Chicago area. If he could solve the Franks' case it would help him his political ambitions. He was forty-five years old and known for being incredibly stubborn. He was determined to make a name for himself with this crime.

Bobby Franks' body was found close to railway tracks. In fact, it was members of a railroad crew who had helped out by lifting his naked body from the water. None of Bobby's clothes were found close to the body but police did find a pair of horn-rimmed glasses in the undergrowth by the culvert that didn't belong to Bobby.

From their analysis, police scientists were certain that the ransom note had been written on an Underwood portable typewriter. Coroner Oscar Wolff told the press that he believed that only an educated person could have drafted it. 'That would signify intelligence, a dangerous attribute in a criminal . . . Greed would be the controlling passion, and, dead or alive, they intended to cash in on Robert Franks, the millionaire's son.'

Initially, the police focused on three teachers at the Harvard School where Bobby Franks had been a pupil. They were taken to the police station and questioned for hours while their apartments were thoroughly searched. One of the teachers was eventually released, but the other two were kept in custody.

It was confirmed that the small, horn-rimmed glasses found near the body did not belong to Bobby Franks. The frames, which were made of xylonite, were chewed at the ends. The prescription was very common. The chances of finding the owner of the glasses seemed slim, but every attempt was made. The Franks family were after all, very wealthy. The daily newspapers carried photos of the glasses and the police contacted optical companies in the area hoping to get a lead on finding the murderer(s).

Newspaper reporters began turning detective themselves and started to ask questions around the city. On Friday 23 May, Loeb was at his Zeta Beta Tau fraternity house at the University of Chicago, with Howard Mayer who was the campus liaison to the *Evening American* newspaper. Mayer was speculating about the murder when Loeb suggested that they try to locate the drugstore that the kidnapper had instructed Jacob Franks to go to with the ransom money.

Just as the two of them were about to check the various drugstores, two *Daily News* reporters, one of whom was a ZBT member, came into the fraternity house and decided to go with them. The small team of investigators travelled the city calling at drugstores until eventually, they found the Van de Bogert & Ross drugstore and confirmed that there had been two calls the previous day for Mr Franks.

According to reports, Loeb appeared animatedly excited about finding the right drugstore. Mulroy, one of the reporters, asked Loeb if he had known the murdered boy. Loeb replied that he had and then said, 'If I were going to murder anybody, I would murder just such a cocky little son of a bitch as Bobby Franks.'

At the same time as Loeb and his acquaintances were looking for the drugstore, the coroner's inquest was being held. Dr Joseph Springer who conducted the autopsy, concluded that Bobby Franks had died of suffocation, perhaps when his kidnapper held his hand over the boy's mouth or when he had shoved something down the boy's throat. There were a number of small wounds on the boy's body, which suggested that he had fought with his captor. He had been struck on the head with a blunt object causing bruising and bleeding on his forehead.

An acid-type chemical had been poured on his face and his genital area. While there was some dilation of the rectum, Springer said that he didn't believe that Bobby had been sexually abused, although given the nature of society at the time and the Franks' wealth and social standing he could have simply been trying to spare the family any more anguish.

The game warden for the Wolf Lake area told police that a young ornithologist called Nathan Leopold was a frequent visitor to the area. Police went to his house and asked a servant to awaken Leopold so that he could come down to the police station for questioning. The police soon let him go. Leopold was polite and well-spoken and his stories about his bird-watching expeditions were very credible.

The investigation seemed to be leading nowhere. But, just as the police were running out of suspects they had an amazing lucky break. Eight days after the murder, police discovered that the hinges on the pair of eyeglasses were very uncommon. Only three pairs of that particular design had ever been sold in the Chicago area. One of those three pairs of glasses belonged to Nathan Leopold. On 29 May Police moved in again to question him further.

By now the press had heard about the glasses and news reporters swarmed the police station. State's Attorney Crowe was sensitive to questioning the son of a prominent family under the eyes of the press and instead arranged for him to be questioned in a room at the LaSalle Hotel.

When police arrived at his house and asked him if he had lost a pair of glasses, Leopold said that he hadn't. When a police search of the house did not produce any glasses Leopold changed his story and said that he must have lost them whilst bird watching a few days earlier on 17 and 18 May. He told police that he had tripped and the glasses must have fallen out of his jacket pocket. Crowe was immediately suspicious. One of Crowe's assistants had Leopold put the glasses in his breast pocket and re-create the fall. Although Leopold re-created the fall several times, the glasses did not once fall out of the pocket.

Crowe's interrogation became more intense. Leopold was initially vague about his activities on the day of the murder. Under more intense questioning, he changed his story once again and told police that he had been with his friend Richard Loeb, eating, drinking and looking for birds in Lincoln Park. He told police that later that day, after dinner, they picked up two teenage girls and drove around in Leopold's car eventually returning to Leopold's house where his aunt and uncle were waiting to be driven home. They had never learned the women's last names. Leopold remained calm under questioning and answered all questions as politely as he could.

The questions began to lean more towards his personal life. He was clearly highly intelligent. By 1923, he had

195

graduated from the University of Chicago and had been attending law school. He planned to attend Harvard Law School later that year. He was very accomplished in the study of languages, was fluent in five and familiar with fifteen foreign languages. He was certainly educated enough to have written the ransom note which had included some legal knowhow. Police confiscated his Hammond Multiplex typewriter but were disappointed to learn that it was not the typewriter used to write the ransom note.

Leopold maintained his innocence. He told police that he had not known the Franks family and his knowledge of the crime came from following the case just like everyone else in Chicago. The police confiscated some of his private letters that contained some allusions to homosexuality.

Leopold said that he was planning to translate the work of an Italian writer on the subject of sexual perversion but denied any sexual relationship with Richard Loeb. At 4 a.m. he was taken to the police station and allowed to sleep. What he didn't know was that Richard Loeb had also been picked up for questioning and was also at the LaSalle Hotel being interrogated in another room.

Police were beginning to get suspicious. Loeb's story differed significantly from Leopold's. He said that he was with Leopold during the afternoon, but insisted that they had parted at dinnertime and hadn't seen each other again that night.

He couldn't remember what he was doing on the night of the murder. Later, he would change his story to match Leopold's saying that he had simply been too drunk to accurately remember the events of the evening. Police at least considered believing their story. They were polite, well-educated and wealthy and to the police didn't fit the usual profile of murderers

Feeling apologetic, State's Attorney Crowe took the boys out for a lavish supper. Afterward, the boys talked amicably and openly with the attending journalists. 'I don't blame the police for holding me,' Leopold told the *Tribune*. 'I was at the culvert the Saturday and Sunday before the glasses were found and it is quite possible I lost my glasses there.'

However, Leopold's and Loeb's luck was running out. Two reporters who knew that Leopold belonged to a law student study group went to question their study group members. The law students told them that Leopold usually typed up the study sheets on his Hammond, but that at least once, he had used a different portable typewriter. A few of the students still had the typed notes written on the portable and gave them to the newsmen. When they compared them with the typing on the ransom note, they could see that the type was identical.

Needing to think fast, Leopold admitted to police that he may have used a portable typewriter but said that he didn't own it. Police searched his house again but of course no typewriter was found. Just as police were beginning to give up, it was the Leopolds' staff who betrayed the young rich boys.

The maid remembered seeing a portable typewriter in the house several weeks earlier and told police that it belonged to Nathan Leopold. Crowe and his assistants decided to interview all the Leopold staff. On 31 May they interviewed the chauffeur who told police that on the day of the murder, he had worked on Leopold's car all day long. The chauffeur also maintained that the car had remained in the garage until late that night when he went home. The plot was beginning to unravel. The boys had told the police that they had used Leopold's car to drive around on the afternoon and evening of Bobby Franks' death.

The police decided to interview them again in separate rooms. When Loeb was finally confronted with the lie about Nathan Leopold's car, he asked who told them that. When he learned that it had been the chauffeur he asked to see Crowe and began to tell him a new story.

*　　*　　*

197

In their confession, the boys made the kidnap and murder seem as if it had been a sort of intellectual challenge to two very clever but spoilt and bored young students. Crowe maintained that the boys seemed to enjoy the telling of how they plotted 'the perfect crime'. They admitted that collecting the ransom money without being caught was a more difficult problem for them than the kidnapping and murder.

They had put together several different plans for the ransom collection, researching each plan diligently. They finally agreed on the drugstore version where they would tell Mr Franks over the telephone, to get on a train that was leaving almost immediately so that the police could not be notified. They would place a note on the train that told him an exact point at which he must throw the ransom money from the train. The boys would be waiting to pick it up.

Leopold and Loeb confessed that they had been planning the kidnapping for a number of months, although they told police that they eventually decided that they would select their victim on the day of the kidnapping. They just had to be sure that he had a rich father to pay the ransom. They had also discussed the fact that it would be useful if he was acquainted with the two boys so that it would be easy to persuade him to get into the car.

They planned to murder him with or without the ransom money so that they could never be identified. They picked the prestigious Harvard School because it was close to their homes and as former pupils they were known to many of the boys there. Their plan was to randomly select a boy.

It was important to them that the victim was killed quickly to avoid him escaping or the three of them being discovered. Once dead, the body had to be disposed of immediately. Leopold chose the culvert at Wolf Lake because it was so well concealed that even Leopold, who was familiar with the area, was not initially aware of its existence. It also provided them with a ready grave for their victim without any digging. They couldn't use one of their own cars for fear of being spotted and identified so they came up with an elaborate scheme to rent a car in a false name. They even covered the licence plate so that it couldn't be traced back to them.

The boys told police that they realised that their plans had failed when Mr Franks didn't go to the drugstore. Loeb apparently ended his confession with the words, 'I just want to say that I offer no excuse, but that I am fully convinced that neither the idea nor the act would have occurred to me had it not been for the suggestion and stimulus of Leopold. Furthermore, I do not believe that I would have been capable of having killed Franks.'

When he heard of Loeb's confession, Leopold confessed himself. Although their confessions were in agreement as regards most major facts in the case, each blamed the other for the actual killing. Initially, the police and the press decided to believe Loeb and treat Leopold as the 'evil genius' who had dominated his affable friend with his superior intellect and complicated philosophical reasoning. Crowe is said to have told the boys that it didn't matter which of them had killed the boy. The charge of premeditated kidnapping and murder meant that they would both hang anyway.

Later, Crowe made the boys accompany him on a search for evidence. Leopold led him to the clerk who had sold him the hydrochloric acid to disguise Bobby Franks' face and also conceal the fact that he had been circumcised, to further hamper identification. They also found Bobby's shoes discarded on the side of the road. A man handed in the chisel that was used to kill Bobby Franks after he picked it up when he saw it thrown from a car. A cabdriver told the story of two well-dressed, affluent young men who had hired him to drive them to the home of Jacob Franks. Crowe was satisfied with the evidence they found that day. He announced to the press that, 'We have the most conclusive evidence I've ever seen in a criminal case.' The two boys needed to find an attorney.

* * *

Once the boys' confessions became known, the story dominated the news both in Chicago and nationally, focusing on the wealth and social prominence of their families.

A typical report in the *Tribune* read: 'In view of the fact that the solving of the Franks kidnapping and death brings to notice a crime that is unique in Chicago's annals, and perhaps unprecedented in American criminal history, the *Tribune* this morning gives to the report of the case many columns of space for news, comment, and pictures.

'The diabolical spirit evinced in the planned kidnapping and murder; the wealth and prominence of the families whose sons are involved; the high mental attainments of the youths, the suggestions of perversion; the strange quirks indicated in the confession that the child was slain for a ransom, for experience, for the satisfaction of a desire for "deep plotting", combined to set the case in a class by itself.'

The general public was horrified at the crime and the newspapers mirrored them in calling for swift retribution. According to the *Herald and Examiner*, 'It should not be allowed to hang on, poisoning our thoughts and feelings. Every consideration of public interest demands that it be carried through to its end at once.'

The Jewish community was also reeling from the shocking news. It was unheard of that the intelligent and cultured children of Kenwood's Jewish elite could commit such a crime. The fathers of both boys were millionaires and respected members of the local community.

Novelist Meyer Levin wrote of the scandal, 'There was one gruesome note of relief in this affair. One heard it uttered only amongst ourselves – a relief that the victim, too, had

200

been Jewish. Though racial aspects were never overtly raised in the case, being perhaps eclipsed by the sensational suggestions of perversion, we were never free of the thought that the murderers were Jews.'

Terrified that he would lose his son to capital punishment, Loeb's father hired sixty-seven-year-old Clarence Darrow, a well-known opponent of the death penalty, to defend the two boys against the capital charges of murder and kidnapping. He begged Darrow to, 'get them a life sentence instead of death. That's all we ask. We'll pay anything, only for God's sake, don't let them hang.'

Clarence Darrow accepted the challenge as an opportunity to fight the death penalty. The case had now gathered so much national media attention that Darrow knew that his arguments against capital punishment would be widely heard.

By confessing without an attorney present, showing police where the evidence was hidden and chatting to the press, Darrow decided that the boys had done irreparable damage to their defence.

Leopold had told one reporter, 'Why, we even rehearsed the kidnapping at least three times, carrying it through in all details, lacking only the boy we were to kidnap and kill . . . It was just an experiment. It is as easy for us to justify as an entomologist in impaling a beetle on a pin.' Loeb told the police, 'This thing will be the making of me. I'll spend a few years in jail and I'll be released. I'll come out to a new life.' Every word had been splashed across the nation's newspapers.

Knowing that the media expected Leopold and Loeb to plead not guilty (by reason of insanity), Darrow told them both to plead guilty. This was Darrow's way of avoiding trial by jury which, given the publicity of the case would most certainly not be a sympathetic hearing and was more likely to result in the death penalty. Without a jury Darrow could present the case against capital punishment and leave the decision in the hands of one man, Cook County Circuit Court Judge John R. Caverly.

Believing that the defence would make a case for insanity, Crowe had gathered three traditional psychiatrists to interview the boys to pronounce them fit for trial. He would not allow Darrow to talk with the boys until the psychiatrists had declared them sane.

Meanwhile, leaks about the treatment of the boys in prison were outraging the general public even more. Tales about good food, cigarettes and alcohol being smuggled into prison from Stein's Restaurant in addition to the rumour that their wealthy families were going to pay millions of dollars to save their sons from the gallows incensed people. The news media reported every last detail including the boys' full confessions.

Anxious not to inflame people's feeling any further, the two families constructed a joint statement with Darrow's help, which insisted that no large sums of money were going to be paid either for medical assessment or legal costs.

On 5 June 1924, the grand jury indicted the two boys on eleven counts of murder and sixteen counts of kidnapping. To counteract Crowe's traditonal psychiatrists, the defence recruited what were then known as 'progressive' psychiatrists from the American Psychiatric Association. They hired Dr William A. White, president of the American Psychological Association (APA) and superintendent of St Elizabeth's Hospital in Washington, DC, Dr William Healy, an expert in juvenile criminal psychiatry; and Dr Bernard Glueck, head of the psychiatric clinic at Sing Sing Prison in New York State. These experts were innovative Freudians who believed in subconscious motives and compulsions stemming from childhood history. For balance the team also hired two other psychiatrists, Dr Harold Hulbert and Dr Carl Bowman.

Most accounts state that Leopold thoroughly enjoyed his sessions with the psychiatrists. He loved to talk about himself and was more than willing to let the 'experts' examine his personality and motivations. Loeb on the other hand is said to have been bored by the sessions and sometimes actually fell asleep during their conversations.

Neither boy showed any guilt or remorse for their appalling crime, though both of them were concerned about the effects of their actions on their families. What was gained however, was a much more detailed account of the personal relationship between the boys and their sexual preferences, in particular, the sexual relationship between the two of them.

*   *   *

The psychiatrists noted that Leopold 'does not make friends very easily and he has especial difficulty in getting along with the opposite sex.' Leopold mentioned the names of two boys with whom he first had sexual relations, as being Joe and Henry. The only sexual experience he had with women was with prostitutes. He told doctors that he had never really been attracted to women and considered them to be inferior intellectually. He also clearly implicated Loeb in references to his early sexual encounters. 'His acquaintance with Dick Loeb dates from the spring of 1920. When he was fifteen years old he [Leopold] was a member of a group of seven or eight boys. The patient went around with one of these boys a good deal and they practised mutual masturbation a number of times.'

In Loeb's psychiatric personal history, Leopold is alluded to but not named in a similar fashion. 'When he was fifteen-and-a-half years old he had, for the first time, sexual relations with a woman. It was the custom among the boys of his group, who had automobiles, to take a friend and drive out and pick up two girls and then endeavour to have sexual relations with them. He had been out on a number of such parties but the girls they had secured would never permit anything more than fondling or caressing. That night he and his friend picked up two girls who at once, in a business-like way, offered sexual relations in the car for three dollars or at their homes for five dollars. The patient sat in the back seat caressing and petting the girl who was with him. He was doing this rather perfunctorily and he had no erection. However, he did have an extreme desire to urinate, and he got out of the car and did urinate. When he returned the girl raised her skirts and said, "Let's go." The patient found himself quite impotent and was greatly chagrined at this. He was so embarrassed at this that he made his comrade solemnly swear he would never reveal his secret.'

Their intense and stormy relationship came to a head in the Fall of 1921, when Loeb transferred to the University of Michigan. Leopold had followed him to Michigan but his admittance was delayed by illness. He eventually entered the university in October and roomed with Richard Loeb, with whom he expected to continue a relationship on the same terms as before.

However, he found that Loeb was suffering some personal inner difficulty with the entire situation and was cold to him in public. Loeb finally explained the situation. There were apparently rumours that the two of them had engaged in homosexual relations, and were a 'couple of cocksuckers.' Richard was desperately trying to get into Zeta Beta Tau and they had informed him that although they didn't believe the rumours, Loeb should try not to be seen with Leopold too much. Loeb's brother, Allen, also encouraged Loeb not to be seen alone with Leopold.

The couple formed an agreement. They agreed to remain friends, but not to be seen alone together in public, or in any way that could be misunderstood. They decided to take along another friend as a third party rather than go anywhere alone together. Richard became very involved with his fraternity and kept Nathan at bay.

Zeta Beta Tau had accepted Richard on the understanding that he behaved in such a way as to quash rumours of homosexuality. After his arrest, Nathan Leopold, still bitter at the memory, told the psychiatrists that Loeb was not popular when they met. He also confessed to police that he had once contemplated killing Loeb over a perceived breach of confidentiality.

The confidentiality incident happened around New Year's Eve, at the University of Michigan. Richard Loeb and his friend from the fraternity house Dick Rubel, had made plans behind Nathan's back to go out on a double date with some girls. Leopold found out about the arrangement and was furious. Amidst heated words, Loeb became convinced that Leopold had said something to Rubel about their relationship to spoil the New Year's date and his [Loeb's] acceptance within the fraternity house.

Loeb accused Leopold of betraying a confidence by telling Rubel things he shouldn't have. The couple brought Rubel into the argument to resolve it. Leopold asked Rubel, 'Dick, when we were together yesterday, did I tell you that Dick Loeb had told me the things which I then told you, or that it was merely my opinion that I believed them to be so?' Rubel replied, 'No, you did not tell me that Dick told you these things, but said that they were in your opinion true.' The incident prompted Leopold to write a letter to Loeb that was read out in court at their trial years later:

October 9th, 1923

Dear Dick:

In view or our former relations, I take it for granted that it is unnecessary to make any excuse for writing to you at this time, and still am going to

205

state my reasons for doing so, as this may turn out to be a long letter, and I don't want to cause you the inconvenience of reading it all to find out what it contains if you are not interested in the subjects dealt with.

First, I am enclosing the document which I mentioned to you today, and which I will explain later. Second, I am going to tell you of a new fact which has come up since our discussion. And third, I am going to put in writing what my attitude is toward our present relations, with a view of avoiding future misunderstandings, and in the hope (which I think is rather vain) that possibly we may have misunderstood each other, and can yet clear this matter up.

Now, as to the first, I wanted you this afternoon, and still want you, to feel that we are on equal footing legally, and, therefore, I purposely committed the same tort of which you were guilty, the only difference being that in your case the facts would be harder to prove than in mine, should I deny them. The enclosed document should secure you against changing my mind in admitting the facts, if the matter should come up, as it would prove to any court that they were true.

As to the second. On your suggestion I immediately phoned Dick Rubel, and speaking from a paper prepared beforehand (to be sure of exact wording) said: 'Dick, when we were together yesterday, did I tell you that Dick (Loeb) had told me the things which I then told you, or that it was merely my opinion that I believed them to be so?' I asked this twice to be sure he understood and on the same answer both times (which I took down as he spoke) felt that he did understand. He replied:

'No, you did not tell me that Dick told you these things, but said that they were in your opinion true.'

He further denied telling you subsequently that I had said that they were gleaned from conversation with you, and I then told him that he was quite right, that you never had told me. I further told him that this was merely your suggestion of how to settle a question of fact, that he was in no way implicated, and that neither of us would be angry with him at his reply. (I imply your assent to this.) This of course proves that you were mistaken this afternoon in the question of my having actually and technically broken confidence, and voids my apology, which I made contingent on proof of this matter.

Now, as to the third, last, and most important question. When you came to my home this afternoon I expected either to break friendship with you or attempt to kill you unless you told me why you acted as you did yesterday. You did, however, tell me, and hence the question shifted to the fact that I would act as before if you persisted in thinking me treacherous, either in act (which you waived if Dick's opinion went with mine) or in intention.

Now, I apprehend, though here I am not quite sure, that you said that you did not think me treacherous in intent, nor ever have, but that you considered me in the wrong and expected such a statement from me. This statement I unconditionally refused to make until such time as I may have become convinced of its truth.

I never did. But you shouldn't have said those things and you should apologise. You acted hastily

However, the question of our relation I think

must be in your hands (unless the above conceptions are mistaken) inasmuch as you have satisfied first one and then the other requirement, upon which I agreed to refrain from attempting to kill you or refusing to continue our friendship. Hence I have no reason not to continue to be on friendly terms with you, and would under ordinary conditions continue as before.

The only question, then, is with you. You demand me to perform an act, namely, state that I acted wrongly. This I refuse. Now it is up to you to inflict the penalty for this refusal – at your discretion, to break friendship, inflict physical punishment, or anything else you like, or on the other hand, continue as before. The decision therefore, must rest with you. This is all of my opinion on the right and wrong of the matter.

Now comes a practical question. I think that I would ordinarily be expected to, and in fact do expect to continue my attitude toward you, as before, until I learn either by direct words or by conduct on your part which way your decision has been formed. This I shall do.

Now a word of advice. I do not wish to influence your decision either way, but I do want to warn you that in case you deem it advisable to discontinue our friendship, that in both our interests extreme care must be had. The motif of 'a falling out of a pair of cocksuckers' would be sure to be popular, which is patently undesirable and forms an irksome but unavoidable bond between us. Therefore, it is, in my humble opinion, expedient, though our breech need be no less real in fact, yet to observe the conventionalities, such as salutation on the street and a general appearance of at least not unfriendly relations on all occasions when we may be thrown together in public.

Now, Dick, I am going to make a request to which I have perhaps no right, and yet which I dare to make also for 'Auld Lang Syne'. Will you, if not too inconvenient, let me know your answer (before I leave tomorrow) on the last count? This, to which I have no right, would greatly help my peace of mind in the next few days when it is most neccessary to me. You can if you will merely call up my home before 12 noon and leave a message saying 'Dick says yes,' if you wish our relations to continue as before, and 'Dick says no,' if not.

It is unnecessary to add that your decision will of course have no effect on my keeping to myself our confidences of the past, and that I regret the whole affair more than I can say.

Hoping not to have caused you too much trouble in reading this, I am (for the present) as ever,

Babe

The following letter was also read into the official trial record:

I, Nathan F. Leopold Jr, being under no duress or compulsion, do hereby affirm and declare that on this, the 9th day of October 1923, I for reasons of my own locked the door of the room in which I was with one Richard A. Loeb, with the intent of blocking his only feasible mode of egress, and that I further indicated my intention of applying physical force upon the person of said Richard A. Loeb if necessary to carry out my design, to-wit, to block his only feasible mode of egress.

There was little doubt that the boys were involved in a sexual relationship. After his eventual release from prison, Leopold would write, 'Loeb's friendship was necessary to me – terribly necessary' and that his motive, 'to the extent that I had one, was to please Dick.'

The era prevented the boy's relationship from being seen as anything other than deviant behaviour. Homosexuality wasn't seen as 'normal' and as such Clarence Darrow at the trial focused on what he called their 'weird and almost impossible' relationship that led the two boys to commit an act together that neither would ever have done alone.

* * *

The case of The People against Nathan Leopold, Jr, and Richard Loeb opened in Chief Justice of the Criminal Court John R. Caverly's courtroom on 21 July 1924. Judge John R. Caverly was sixty-seven years old. He was almost at the end of his career when this trial began and he had imposed the death sentence only five times on the bench, each time fixed by a jury.

The courtroom held only 300 people, 200 of which were representatives of the news media. A mere seventy places were given for the general public. In his opening statement Darrow told the court, 'We want to state frankly here that no one in this case believes that these defendants should be released or are competent to be. We believe that they should be permanently isolated from society . . . After long reflection and thorough discussion, we have determined to make a motion in this court for each of the defendants in each of the cases to withdraw our pleas of not guilty and enter a plea of guilty.'

There was a sharp intake of breath in the courtroom. People had expected Darrow to defend the accused with pleas of not guilty by order of insanity. For his part, Darrow knew that a guilty plea would avoid trial by jury and was his best chance of avoiding the death penalty in what had become an emotive and famous case. Because of the public outcry a jury would have no trouble making a collective decision for the death penalty whereas a judge would have the decision as his and his alone. Darrow intended to rely on this and emphasise the young ages of the two boys when giving his defence.

The prosecution was led by State's Attorney Robert E. Crowe who opened his argument with the proclamation that the boys had committed the murder in order to obtain the ransom money:

> The evidence in this case will show that Nathan Leopold, Jr, is a young man nineteen years old, that the other defendant, Richard Loeb, is a young man of nineteen years; that they are both sons of highly respected and prominent citizens of this community; that their parents gave them every advantage wealth and indulgence could give to boys. They have attended the best schools in this community and have, from time to time, had private tutors. These young men behaved as a majority of young men in their social set behaved, with the exception that they developed a desire to gamble, and gambled, for large stakes, the size of the stakes being such that even their wealthy companions could not sit with them.
>
> The evidence will further show that along in October or November of last year these two defendants entered into a conspiracy, the purpose of which was to gain money, and in order to gain it they were ready and willing to commit a cold-blooded murder.

After speaking for an hour, he concluded his statement with, 'in the name of the people of the State of Illinois, in the name of the womanhood and the fatherhood, and in the name of the children of the State of Illinois, we are going to demand the death penalty for both of these cold-blooded, cruel, and vicious murderers.'

The strategy employed by the prosecution was to emphasise the horror of the crime by stressing how long it was in the planning and how cold-bloodedly it was carried out. There was little cross-examination by the defence to avoid further dwelling on the gruesome details.

Crowe took a week to make his case and called eighty-one witnesses. He had proven the boys' guilt beyond a doubt but the boys had already made a guilty plea and therefore rendered most of his argument irrelevant. This was to the boy's advantage because their statements already verified what he said. Their own defence argument would take a different slant on things.

Finally, one week into the trial it was Darrow's chance to save the boys from the gallows. He responded to the prosecution:

'We shall insist in this case, Your Honour, that, terrible as this is, terrible as any killing is, it would be without precedent if two boys of this age should be hanged by the neck until dead, and it would in no way bring back Robert Franks or add to the peace and security of this community.'

The strategy employed by Clarence Darrow was to extensively use the testimony of the psychiatrists to convince the court that the reason for the killing lay more in the minds and personal history of the accused rather than in any conscious desire to murder. It was a Freudian argument unprecedented in a courtroom at the time.

Doctors Hulbert and Bowman had studied every single detail of the lives of Leopold and Loeb and compiled it into an exhaustive report of around 300 pages. The report clearly showed that Richard Loeb's criminal tendencies first became apparent when he was eight or nine years old.

They told the court that Loeb stole money and objects with 'absolutely no compunction of guilt or fear connected with this theft . . . but felt ashamed [when] his lack of skill caused him to be caught.' He was stealing and shoplifting for the excitement of it, not desire for whatever he stole. He continued stealing throughout his teenage years.

When Leopold came on the scene his role was that of accomplice to Loeb's criminal pursuits. In exchange for limited homosexual favours (Leopold was first allowed to insert his penis between Loeb's legs), Loeb drew Leopold into criminal acts that began to grow in their seriousness. Instead of stealing from shops they began stealing cars and breaking into houses. They moved from setting off fire alarms to starting fires. They also began to commit their crimes armed with a revolver determined to shoot anyone who got in their way.

Initially, Crowe objected to psychiatric information being used in the defence's argument on the grounds that measuring state of mind rather than insanity was irrelevant to the case in hand.

'You do not take a microscope and look into a murderer's head to see what state of mind he was in, because if he is insane he is not responsible, and if he is sane, he is responsible. You look not to his mental condition, but to the facts surrounding the case – did he kill the man because the man debauched his wife? If that is so, then there is mitigation here . . . But here is cold-blooded murder, without a defence in fact, and the attempt on a plea of guilty to introduce an insanity defence before your honour is unprecedented. The statute says that is a matter that must be tried by a jury.'

Judge Caverly overruled the objection and allowed Darrow to make his defence. The report written by Doctors Hulbert and Bowman was put into the court record. This was important because although only some of the report was used in the trial testimony, the whole 300 pages would now be read by Judge Caverly who needed to make the decision as to whether or not the psychiatric analyses counted.

The psychiatrist's reports give valuable insight into the family lives and social environment in which these two boys lived. They also provided an appreciation of the boys' values and morals, and showed them to be at odds with those of their families and friends. It was to Darrow's advantage that the judge had allowed these findings to be part of the defence testimony. They would play a key role in the outcome of the trial.

The defence proceeded with an in-depth psychological evaluation of each boy in an attempt to convince the court that although they were 'sane' their state of mind had been affected by their background and upbringing to the extent that their relationship could not be considered 'normal'. Whether this was simply expressing an attitude at the time towards homosexuality or something deeper is not clear. As regards Richard Loeb, the psychiatrists concentrated on inter-personal relationships within his family as well as his early education.

When it came to Richard Loeb's parents, the evaluation was largely positive, 'Albert H. Loeb is fair and just. He is opposed to the boys' drinking and often spoke of it; he is not strict, although the boys may have thought he was. He never used corporal punishment. In early childhood, he was not a play-fellow with the boys . . . Dick and his brothers loved and worshipped their father and did not want to lose their father's love and respect.'

The doctors told the court that his mother Ann Bohnen Loeb was from a Catholic family and her marriage to a Jew had not been welcomed, regardless of the wealth and social status of her husband. They did add though that Albert's friends regarded her highly. The couple had four sons altogether, Allan, Ernest, Richard and Thomas. Ann was described as 'poised, keen, alert and interested.'

Much was made of Loeb's governess Miss Struthers who taught him from the age of four. Struthers devoted an enormous amount of time to coaching, tutoring and encouraging him to study. Richard was a very clever boy whose IQ was 160 and she was very successful in getting Richard promoted rapidly through school.

He finished grade school at age twelve, graduated from high school at fourteen and entered the University of Chicago the same year. Miss Struthers left the household after an argument with Mrs Loeb. The psychiatrists traced Canadian-born Struthers, interviewed her and decided that she was 'too anxious to have him become an ideal boy . . . She would not overlook some of his faults and was too quick in her punishment and therefore he built up the habit of lying without compunction and with increasing skill. She was quite unaware of the fact that he had become a petty thief and a play detective.'

Richard later transferred to the University of Michigan in a bid to get away from home. He was one of their youngest graduates at age seventeen. However, he was considered lazy and unmotivated, so his grades were not outstanding, despite his high level of intelligence.

The psychiatrists dwelled on the fact that Loeb's extensive and expensive education did not include sex. Apparently, Richard Loeb learned the basics from talking to the family's chauffeur.

Sex did not become important to him and he believed himself less sexually driven than his friends. They told the court that although his good looks, sophistication, wealth and social graces allowed him many opportunities with the opposite sex, neither sex nor a long-term relationship with a woman was a high priority for him.

What Richard did excel at was lying and while he

admitted that lying was wrong, he felt no guilt about doing it. He loved detective stories and fantasised about how to commit the perfect undetectable crime. Dr White's summary attempted to concentrate on the fact that Richard Loeb was confused and immature, periodically becoming nihilistic and suicidal.

'All of Dickie's life, from the beginning of his antisocial activities, has been in the direction of his own self-destruction. He himself has definitely and seriously considered suicide. He told me that he was satisfied with his life and that so far as he could see, life had nothing more to offer, because he had run the gamut. He was at the end of the situation. He had lived his life out.' Dr White thought that infantilism was Loeb's outstanding characteristic and firmly believed that it must have been Loeb who murdered Bobby.

Dr Glueck thought that Loeb was cold and psychopathic. 'I was amazed at the absolute absence of any signs of normal feelings, such as one would expect under the circumstances. He showed no remorse, no regret, no compassion for the people involved in this situation . . . He told me the details of the crime, including the fact that he struck the blow.'

The psychiatrists were much more sympathetic to Nathan Leopold. Nicknamed 'Babe' he was the youngest of four sons. As a young boy he was frequently sick, suffering from many gland-related problems including hyperthyroidism, a calcified pineal gland and related complications. He had not been expected to reach an old age.

When he was seventeen, his mother died from nephritis. She had never recovered her health after his birth, a fact for which Nathan felt to blame. After his mother's death the household was managed by his maternal aunt, Mrs Birdie Schwab. Unable to accept what had happened to his mother Leopold became an atheist after her death.

Nathan was a genius with an IQ of 210. It has been reported that he started to speak at the age of four months.

The boys were taught by a succession of governesses and their father Nathan Leopold Sr more or less left the raising of the children to Aunt Birdie.

Compared to Richard Loeb, Leopold was considered truthful and honest. 'The patient makes no effort to shift the blame for the crime to his companion, although he insists that he did not desire to commit the crime and derived no special pleasure from it. He feels that his only reason for going into it was his pact of friendship with his companion, and his companion's desire to do it . . . Since he had a marked sex drive, and has not been able to satisfy it in the normal heterosexual relations, this has undoubtedly been a profound upsetting condition on his whole emotional life . . . he endeavoured to compensate for [his physical inferiority] by a world of fantasy in which his desire for physical perfection could be satisfied. We see him therefore fantasising himself as a slave, who is the strongest man in the world.' The slave fantasies began at the age of five and continued throughout his youth: 'In some way or other [in these fantasies] . . . he saved the life of the king. The king was grateful and wanted to give him his liberty, but the slave refused.'

Leopold loved to discuss his philosophy with the psychiatrists, and they were quite familiar with it when they wrote their report. His leanings towards Nietzsche's philosophy of the superman, where a man governed by intellect is above moral constraints went a long way to explaining the planning of the murder of Bobby Franks.

'In such a philosophy, without any place for emotions and feelings, the intelligence reigns supreme. The only crime that he can commit is a crime of intelligence, a mistake of intelligence, and for that he is fully responsible . . . In the scheme of the perfect man which he drew up, he gave Dickie a scoring of 90, himself a scoring of 63, and various other of their mutual acquaintances various marks ranging from 30 to 40.'

Dr White viewed the Franks murder as the result of the boys' abnormal personalities and fantasies. In their eyes, Richard needed an audience to his crimes and Nathan became that audience. In general the psychiatrists thought that Leopold's tendencies were towards the king/slave fantasy.

> [Leopold] is the slave who makes Dickie the king, maintains him in his kingdom . . . I cannot see how Babe would have entered into it at all alone because he had no criminalistic tendencies in any sense as Dickie did, and I don't think Dickie would have ever functioned to this extent all by himself. So these two boys, with their peculiarly inter-digited personalities, came into this emotional compact with the Franks homicide as a result.

Dr Healy elaborated on this tense emotional relationship between the boys: 'Leopold was to have the privilege of inserting his penis between Loeb's legs on particular occasions. At one time it was to be three times in two months, if they continued their criminalistic activities together.'

When Crowe asked for Dr Glueck's opinion on the motivation for the crime, the response was that they seemed to have no real motivation. It was just something that they had done. Although clinically sane the boys were described as being far from 'normal' and healthy.

On 22 August 1924 Clarence Darrow began his final speech. He spoke for two hours in what many regard as his finest speech. He stressed to the court that there had never been a case in Chicago where such young boys had been condemned to death and pointed out that in the last ten years, around 450 people had pleaded guilty to murder and only one was ever hanged.

He also argued against the use of the term 'cold-blooded murder' telling the judge that to sentence the boys to death was more 'cold-blooded' than committing the murder itself. He stressed that Bobby Franks did not suffer and said there was no malice in the crime, although one has to wonder whether a jury or indeed Bobby's parents would agree with that.

Darrow dismissed the argument made by Crowe that the ransom money was the prime motive for the crime. He pointed out to the court that at the time of the murder, Loeb had $3,000 in his bank and he could get money from his father any time he wanted it. Leopold's father was paying thousands of dollars for a trip to Europe that summer. The huge gambling debts that Crowe had mentioned amounted to no more than $90.

> We are talking of placing a blot upon the escutcheon of two houses that do not deserve it. And all that [the State] can get out of their imagination is that there was a game of bridge and one lost ninety dollars to the other, and therefore they went out and committed murder.

He placed a lot of emphasis on the relationship between the two boys. 'They had a weird, almost impossible relationship. Leopold, with his obsession of the superman, had repeatedly said that Loeb was his idea of the superman. He had the attitude toward him that one has to his most devoted friend, or that a man has to a lover. Without the combination of these two, nothing of this sort probably would have happened . . .'

His famous final speech was a heartfelt plea for the boys' lives:

> I do not know how much salvage there is in these two boys. I hate to say it in their presence, but what is there to look forward to? I do not know but that

219

Your Honour would be merciful if you tied a rope around their necks and let them die; merciful to them, but not merciful to civilisation, and not merciful to those who would be left behind. To spend the balance of their lives in prison is mighty little to look forward to, if anything ... So far as I am concerned, it is over ... And I think here of the stanza of Housman:

> Now hollow fires burn out to black,
> And lights are fluttering low:
> Square your shoulders, lift your pack
> And leave your friends and go.
> O never fear, lads, naught's to dread,
> Look not left nor right:
> In all the endless road you tread
> There's nothing but the night.

I care not, Your Honour, whether the march begins at the gallows or when the gates of Joliet close upon them, there is nothing but the night, and that is little for any human being to expect ...

None of us are unmindful of the public; courts are not, and juries are not. We placed our fate in the hands of a trained court, thinking that he would be more mindful and considerate than a jury. I cannot say how people feel. I have stood here for three months as one might stand at the ocean trying to sweep back the tide. I hope the seas are subsiding and the wind is falling, and I believe they are, but I wish to make no false pretence to this court.

The easy thing and the popular thing to do is to hang my clients. I know it. Men and women who do not think will applaud. The cruel and thoughtless will approve. It will be easy today; but in Chicago, and reaching out over the length and breadth of the land, more and more fathers and mothers, the humane, the kind and the hopeful, who are gaining an understanding and asking questions not only about these poor boys, but their own – these will join in no acclaim at the death of my clients. They would ask that the shedding of blood be stopped, and that the normal feelings of man resume their sway. And as the days and the months and the years go on, they will ask it more and more.

But, Your Honour, what they shall ask may not count. I know the easy way. I know Your Honour stands between the future and the past. I know the future is with me, and what I stand for here; not merely for the lives of these two unfortunate lads, but for all boys and girls; for all of the young, and as far as possible, for all of the old. I am pleading for life, understanding, charity, kindness, and the infinite mercy that considers all. I am pleading that we overcome cruelty with kindness, and hatred with love. I know the future is on my side . . .

I feel that I should apologise for the length of time I have taken. This case may not be as important as I think it is, and I am sure I do not need to tell this court, or to tell my friends that I would fight just as hard for the poor as for the rich. If I should succeed in saving these boys' lives and do nothing for the progress of the law, I should feel sad, indeed. If I can succeed, my greatest reward and my greatest hope will be that I have done something for the tens of thousands of other boys, for the countless unfortunates who must tread the same road in blind childhood that these boys have trod; that I have done something to help human understanding, to temper justice with mercy, to overcome hate with love.

Judge Caverly passed sentence on 19 September 1924. The boys' lives would be spared but they would face a sentence of life imprisonment that would probably be harder for them to cope with.

> It would have been the path of least resistance to impose the extreme penalty of the law. In choosing imprisonment instead of death, the court is moved chiefly by the consideration of the age of the defendants . . . Life imprisonment may not, at the moment, strike the public imagination as forcibly as would death by hanging; but to the offenders, particularly of the type they are, the prolonged suffering of years of confinement may well be the severer form of retribution and expiation.

For the murder of Bobby Franks, Leopold and Loeb would be sentenced to life imprisonment at Joliet penitentiary. There would never be any parole. For the crime of kidnapping they were sentenced to ninety-nine years each.

*   *   *

Leopold and Loeb were initially kept apart in prison but they did eventually end up back together. The two put their intellects and education to good use and opened a school for prisoners. There were reports that their rehabilitation was going well and they enjoyed their work. Unfortunately, this state of equilibrium wouldn't last.

On 28 January 1936, Loeb was attacked by his cellmate James Day in the showers. Day slashed Loeb with a straight razor causing over fifty wounds. Although doctors battled to save him he died aged thirty-two from loss of blood with Leopold by his bedside.

James Day accused Loeb of homosexual advances to him and even though Loeb's throat was slashed from behind, Day was believed. Day himself was unharmed despite his plea that he had killed Loeb in self-defense. It has been reported that many years later Day's cellmate at the time said that the killing had been planned.

Leopold continued to study and learn in prison. He mastered twelve more languages and studied mathematics. In 1944, Leopold participated in the Stateville Penitentiary Malaria Study, in which he volunteered to be infected with malaria. Eventually he decided to cultivate the press to rehabilitate his image with the public. He was granted a parole hearing in 1953 but was turned down and he was told that must wait another five years for another hearing.

He was finally released on parole in March 1958, after thirty-three years in prison. The same year he wrote his autobiography titled *Life Plus Ninety-Nine Years*. To avoid media intrusion he went to live in Puerto Rico. There he published *The Birds of Puerto Rico* and obtained a Masters degree from the University of Puerto Rico. In 1961, Leopold married Trudi Feldman Garcia de Queveda, a former social worker from Baltimore and widow of a Puerto Rican physician. He died of a heart attack 30 August 1971 at the age of 66.

Leopold described his feelings towards Loeb in his book *Life Plus Ninety-Nine Years*.

We covered him at last with a sheet, but after a moment, I folded the sheet back from his face and sat down on a stool by the table where he lay. I wanted a long last look at him.

For, strange as it may sound, he had been my best pal.

223

In one sense, he was also the greatest enemy I have ever had. For my friendship with him had cost me – my life. It was he who had originated the idea of committing the crime, he who had planned it, he who had largely carried it out. It was he who had insisted on doing what we eventually did . . . Dick was a living contradiction.

As I sat now by his cooling, bleeding corpse, the strangeness of that contradiction, that basic, fundamental ambivalence of his character, was borne in on me.

For Dick possessed more of the truly fine qualities than almost anyone else I have ever known. Not just the superficial social graces. Those, of course, he possessed to the nth degree . . . But the more fundamental, more important qualities of character, too, he possessed in full measure. He was loyal to a fault. He could be sincere; he could be honestly and selflessly dedicated. His devotion to the school proves that. He truly, deeply wanted to help his fellow man.

How, I mused, could these personality traits coexist with the other side of Dick's character? It didn't make sense! For there was another side. Dick just didn't have the faintest trace of conventional morality. Not just before our incarceration. Afterward too. I don't believe he ever, to the day of his death, felt truly remorseful for what we had done. Sorry that we had been caught, of course . . . But remorse for the murder itself? I honestly don't think so.

Pauline Parker and Juliet Hulme

'Heaven beyond Heaven'

There are living amongst two dutiful daughters
Of a man possesses two beautiful daughters
The most glorious beings in creation . . .
And above us these goddesses reign on high.
I worship the power of these lovely two
With that adoring love known to so few.
'Tis indeed a miracle, one must feel
That two such heavenly creatures are real.
. . . And these two wonderful people are you and I.

Pauline Yvonne Parker

In Christchurch, New Zealand, on 22 June 1954, the body of Honora Rieper was discovered in local beauty spot, Victoria Park. Shortly before, her daughter Pauline, aged sixteen, and her daughter's best friend Juliet Hulme, aged fifteen, had run from the scene to a small tea kiosk in the park. They were covered in blood, clearly distressed and shouted to the owner of the kiosk, 'Please, help us! Mummy's been hurt.'

Their explanation was that Honora Rieper had fallen and

struck her head on a rock. Her body was found by Kenneth Ritchie, still lying where she'd been killed. She had suffered major lacerations to her head, neck, and face, and minor injuries to her fingers. It did not take long for police to discover the murder weapon in the nearby woods, and the girls' story that Honora was killed by a fall began to fall apart.

It turned out that the two young girls had carefully plotted Honora's death. They had savagely killed Pauline's mother with a brick wrapped in a sock. When details of the crime became public they shocked the then very conservative city of Christchurch.

More than fifty years have passed since Parker and Hulme were convicted and sentenced to prison for the death of Honora, a solid, honourable woman well known to most of the local community. It's been more than forty-five years since the two killers were released from prison, yet their story lives on in fictional portrayals such as the French film *Mais ne nous délivrez pas du mal* (*Don't Deliver us from Evil*) and Peter Jackson's Academy Award-nominated film, *Heavenly Creatures*.

The girls' backgrounds could not have been more different. Juliet's parents Hilda and Henry Hulme moved to New Zealand from England in 1948 after Dr Hulme accepted the post as rector at Canterbury University College. Juliet's mother Hilda Hulme was a poised and dignified woman who spent much of her free time working with the local Marriage Guidance Council.

Part of the reason Dr Hulme accepted the post was because Juliet, his eldest child, had had many respiratory illnesses as a child, eventually resulting in tuberculosis. He thought that the climate in New Zealand would be beneficial to her condition.

Initially it looked like the move had been a good choice. By 1950, the university had given the professor a large mansion named Ilam with beautiful gardens. The family also owned a country cottage in Port Levy, thirty-five miles from Christchurch. Outwardly, the family's life in Christchurch seemed idyllic, in reality it was beginning to unravel.

During and after the trial much was made of Juliet's fear of abandonment, supposedly brought about by remedies for her illnesses. On at least one occasion, when she was about six, a serious case of bronchitis nearly killed her and her parents were constantly worrying about her health.

When she was eight, she survived a bout of pneumonia so severe that her family arranged to have her shipped to the Bahamas where she lived for more than a year. There was another separation for Juliet and her family when, not long after arriving in New Zealand, Juliet's parents again became worried about her health and sent her to a boarding school on the more tropical North Island of New Zealand.

She remained there for a few months but became so severely homesick that she was eventually sent home to Christchurch where she was privately tutored at home for the rest of that school year.

* * *

When Juliet was sent to Christchurch Girls' High School the following academic year, she met Pauline Parker and the two girls became very close friends. Pauline was dark and brooding and had few friends before Juliet, while Juliet was bright and intelligent. The pair formed a relationship of mutual support, possibly deriving from the fact that both of them had been severely ill as children. (As a young child, Pauline suffered from osteomyelitis, a serious bone disease for which she underwent painful surgery.)

Parker, then fifteen, was in her own way, an attractive and inventive girl. She kept a diary, wrote poetry and was a talented writer even as a young girl. Juliet was more the more obviously beautiful and graceful of the two, but had an equally vivid imagination.

However, unlike the Hulmes, Pauline's family was lower middle class. Her father Herbert Rieper managed a fish shop, and her mother Honora took on boarders to help make ends meet in their little home at 31 Gloucester Street, Christchurch.

It emerged later at the trial that her mother's surname was not legally Rieper. Although that was the name by which everyone in Christchurch knew her, the couple had never actually married, a fact unknown to everybody except Pauline's parents.

For Pauline Parker, Ilam seemed like some kind of magic kingdom, and the people who lived there seemed like royalty. She lived a sheltered life, but her intelligence and curiosity could be precocious. She lost her virginity to the family's boarder at the age of fifteen, although she would later discard him in favour of her all-consuming relationship with Juliet Hulme.

As their friendship progressed, they formed an elaborate fantasy life together. They would often sneak out and spend the night acting out stories involving fictional characters they had created in their imaginary kingdom that they called 'Borovnia', a 'heaven beyond heaven'.

They began calling this place the 'Fourth World', and considered themselves to be superior to all other people. There is no doubt that Parker and Hulme had no room for anyone else in the world they had created.

The girls' growing attachment to one another worried their parents who were becoming concerned that their relationship was sexual. In New Zealand in the 1950s lesbianism was illegal and thought to be a symptom of mental illness.

The fact that the girls were from different backgrounds was less important than the way in which they were so deeply involved with each other. It is now accepted by many that the relationship between the girls was far more passionate than a simple friendship.

At first their closeness was tolerated. The Hulmes in particular were so welcoming to Pauline that she began to have fantasies about abandoning her own family and joining Juliet's. However, eventually both sets of parents became so uncomfortable with the relationship that they began trying to separate them. This separation would not work. The girls devised a way to stay in contact despite the wishes of their parents.

On 29 May 1953 Pauline wrote in her diary: 'This evening I had a brainwave. That Juliet and I should write to each other as Charles and Deborah. I wrote a six-page letter as Charles and a two-page letter as Pauline. She has entered into the spirit of the thing greatly.' The parents could do little to stop this obsessive friendship. The *Sydney Sun-Herald* wrote about the girls' relationship on 29 August 1954:

> The friendship between the two girls began as any normal one. They walked home from school together, shared their homework and visited each other on weekends.
>
> Each still had a small circle of acquaintances, their notes and diaries were at first the usual schoolgirl scribbles about movies, books, food, outings and occasionally – though very occasionally – boys.
>
> Then something seemed to click suddenly into gear as the friendship progressed. Slowly the two girls seemed to move away from normal family relationships and grew closer together. Other friends dropped out of the picture one after the other. Soon the two became almost as one – living, thinking, even bathing and sleeping together.

Later, Pauline wrote in her diary about the event that was to mark the ending of the girls' dreamy fantasy world. Juliet discovered that her mother was having an affair.

This afternoon I played *Tosca* and wrote before ringing Deborah. Then she told me the stupendous news. Last night she woke at 2 a.m. and for some reason went to her mother's room. It was empty, so she went downstairs to look for her. Deborah could not find her, so she crept as stealthily as she could into Mr Perry's flat and stole upstairs. She heard voices from inside his bedroom, and she stayed outside for a little while, then she opened the door and switched the light on in one movement. Mr Perry and Mrs Hulme were in bed drinking tea. Deborah felt an hysterical tendency to giggle. She said, 'Hello' in a very [illegible] voice. She was shaking with emotion and shock, although she had known what she would find. They goggled at her for a minute and her mother said, 'I suppose you want an explanation?'

'Yes,' Deborah replied, 'I do.'

'Well, you see, we are in love,' Mother explained. Deborah was wonderful. 'But I know THAT,' she exclaimed, her voice seemed to belong to someone else. Her mother explained that Dr Hulme knew all about it, and that they intended to live as a threesome. Anyway, Deborah went as far as telling about our desire to go to America in [illegible], six months, though she could not explain the reason of course. Mr Perry gave her 100 [pounds] to get permits. Everyone is being frightfully decent about everything and I feel wildly happy and rather queer . . . I am going out to Ilam tomorrow as we have so much to talk over.

* * *

Juliet had believed that her parents had the perfect marriage. The reality was very different. By 1954, Dr Hulme's job was not going well and the university decided to end his contract. As Dr Hulme's tenure at Canterbury College came to an end, so did his marriage. Juliet's father decided to return to England. It was decided that Juliet would go to stay with relatives in South Africa as this was seen as a better place for her health.

Pauline asked her mother if she could go with Juliet but permission was refused. The two girls were distraught at the idea that they were to be separated. It was then that the two girls came up with a plan to murder Pauline's mother and leave the country for the United States, where they imagined themselves working as screenplay writers. The girls would do whatever it took to avoid being separated – feelings that perhaps derived from Juliet's separation issues earlier in her life.

There was little question in the girls' minds that the dissolution of Juliet's parents' marriage would mean that Juliet and Pauline would be separated. Determined to stay together Pauline and Juliet decided that their main impediment was Honora Parker, Pauline's mother.

For some time the two girls had had a pact to lose weight. Bonding through anorexia is not uncommon among teenage girls. Pauline's mother often set conditions, sometimes involving the girl's health or behaviour, before allowing her to visit Juliet. Unsurprisingly, Pauline saw these conditions as unreasonable.

She wrote in her diary on 13 February 1954,

There seemed to be no possibility of mother relenting and allowing me to go out to Ilam. This afternoon mother told me I could not go out to Ilam again until I was eight stone and more cheerful. As I am now seven stone there is little hope . . . she is so unreasonable. Why could mother not die? Dozens of people are dying, thousands are dying every day. So why not mother and father too?

By 28 April Pauline had finally come up with a plan, 'Suddenly a means of ridding myself of the obstacle occurred to me. I am trying to think up some way . . . I do not want to go to too much trouble but I want it to appear either a natural or an accidental death,' she wrote on 29 April of that year. She was now determined that the murder would happen.

*   *   *

According to Pauline's diaries she shared her plans with her friend Juliet and by 19 June, the two had come up with what they saw as an infallible plan. According to written accounts of the court proceedings, Parker and Hulme had decided to collect a half-brick from a pile outside the garage at Ilam and wrap it in a stocking. With this weapon they would hit Honora Parker over the head and kill her in the process.

The two girls would get Honora Parker to accompany them to a secluded area of Victoria Park, a lush green area on the side of a mountain, overlooking the city. Their plan was to lead the woman along an isolated path where Juliet would drop a pink stone. When Honora Parker bent down to retrieve it Pauline would strike her over the head with the brick. Pauline's diary entry for that morning read, 'I felt very excited and the night-before-Christmassy last night. I did not have pleasant dreams, though. I am about to rise.'

In the days just before the murder, the girls tried to lull everyone into a false sense of security by pretending that they had come to terms with their impending separation. They had lunch at the Parkers' home before setting off to Victoria Park.

When they arrived at the park they had afternoon tea at the park kiosk before setting off along a remote overgrown path through dense woodland. Pauline had the brick concealed in her bag when Juliet dropped the pink stone. As her mother bent down to pick up the stone Pauline began beating her. Unfortunately, the quick, clean death the girls had imagined in their fantasies was not to be. The murder was gruesome and brutal. Honora Parker was struck about the head a total of fifty-four times before she eventually lay still on the footpath.

In the aftermath of the murder, once police had ascertained that the death was not an accident resulting from a fall, Juliet gave her version of events:

We went to a spot well down one of the paths and Mrs Parker decided to come back. On the way back I was walking in front. I was expecting Mrs Parker to be attacked. I heard noises behind me. It was loud conversation in anger. I saw Mrs Parker in a sort of squatting position. They were quarrelling. I went back. I saw Pauline hit Mrs Parker with the brick in the stocking. I took the stocking and hit her too.

I was terrified. I thought one of them had to die. I wanted to help Pauline. It was terrible. Mrs Parker moved convulsively. We both held her. She was still when we left her. The brick had come out of the stocking with the force of the blows. I cannot remember Mrs Parker saying anything distinctly. I was too frightened to listen.

By saying that she understood that Pauline's mother 'had to die', Juliet was accepting the girls' plan that it was the only way they could stay together, to remain in their imaginary Fourth World, a place that Juliet had described as 'even better than heaven'.

*   *   *

It took police less than a day to unravel the circumstances of Honora Parker's death. Pauline's diaries provided the most critical evidence. At first, Pauline tried to take the blame alone, but Juliet's involvement rapidly became clear and both girls were charged with murder.

The trial caused a sensation. Rumours reached the press about the girls' sexual relationship and the belief that the girls were suffering from a *folie à deux* (shared insanity), a suggestion made by the girls' defence attorneys. The reason was their shared fantasy world.

The defence told the court that it was a world that was accessible only to the two of them, a world where they were above the level of normal human behaviour and morals. Staying together and inhabiting this world was the most important wish that the girls had.

Many people have since been interested in the fantasy world created and inhabited by the two girls. There is something intriguing about the idea of this imaginary utopia, and Peter Jackson created an extraordinary visualisation of their shared dreams in his movie *Heavenly Creatures*, which tells the story of the case in a fairly straightforward manner, fantasy sequences aside.

However, there have been others who have argued that the Fourth World was not a sign of collective insanity but rather the only place where two young girls from such different social backgrounds could have found common ground in the class-conscious city of Christchurch.

234

Pauline's diary was used as evidence during their trial. The court was particularly shocked with Pauline's entry for 22 June, the day of the murder.

> After the murder
> the judge said
> they were not mad,
> but bad.

The page for the day was headed 'The Day of the Happy Event.'

Pauline Parker and Juliet Hulme were convicted of murder on 29 August 1954. They were spared hanging but were sentenced to imprisonment 'at her Majesty's Pleasure', which meant possibly indefinitely.

In his summation, Crown Prosecutor Alan W. Brown told an all-male jury. 'This was a coldly, callously planned and carefully committed murder by two precocious and dirty-minded little girls, they are not incurably insane, but incurably bad.'

Both girls served five years in prison and were released just weeks apart on condition that they never see or try to contact one another again. Parker has remained silent since her release from prison. She has never given interviews or spoken about her crime.

Juliet Hulme on the other hand went to live in the United States. Staying true to her childhood dream she became a writer, publishing crime and mystery books with some success. She became a Mormon in 1968 and now lives in a small Scottish fishing village. She has had no contact with Pauline Parker since their conviction, nearly fifty years ago.

After the film *Heavenly Creatures* was screened in 1994, interest in the crime led Hulme (as Anne Perry) to give an interview to the newspaper the *Press*. She denied that she and Parker had had any overt sexual relationship, explaining that 'Pauline was a really good friend. We had all sorts of romantic dreams. I like women very much as friends but for romance give me men.' She has also disputed published accounts of the crime that state that the girls' relationship was unusually devoted going beyond normal teenage girl affections.

She reiterated in March 2006 that while her friendship with Pauline Parker could be seen as obsessive, they were not and had never been lesbians. Pauline is now rumoured to have converted to Roman Catholicism and is living in England. She has continued to preserve a silence on the subject of the murder for which she became famous.

Daniel and Manuela Ruda

The Work of the Devil

Black-haired vampire seeks princess of darkness who despises everything and everybody and has bidden farewell to life

This was the sinister advertisement that Daniel Ruda placed in a black metal music magazine. It resulted in his meeting the woman he saw as his soul mate, his wife Manuela. The couple shared a fascination with the macabre.

Manuela's infatuation with the Devil had begun in her early teenage years and she shared wholeheartedly Daniel's desire to stand out from the crowd and be different. Daniel and Manuela were both Goths, a term usually relating to nothing more than a youth culture with a focus on music and style. For the Rudas however, it took on an altogether darker theme, involving collusion with the Devil that resulted in the brutal murder of thirty-three-year-old Frank Hackerts in 2001.

This grisly murder case began in 2001 when former car-parts salesman Daniel, twenty-six, claimed to have received a vision of the numbers 6667 in a message from Satan. He was convinced that this vision meant that he and Manuela should be married on 6 June (6/6), and that they should kill themselves on 6 July (6/7), but only after carrying out a ritualistic human sacrifice.

*　　*　　*

Frank Hackerts was the unlucky victim apparently chosen by the Rudas for this Satanic killing because of his love of the Beatles. They also told police that they had decided Hackerts would be their victim because he was 'always so funny' and they thought he would be an ideal 'court jester' as a present for Satan.

Consequently, on 6 July 2001 the couple invited Hackerts to their apartment near the city of Bochum for a drink. According to Manuela, Satan took possession of them as they sat on their sofa. She told the court at their trial that Daniel:

> had terrible, glowing eyes and hit out at Frank with the hammer. Frank stood up and said something, or wanted to say something. The knife was glowing and a voice told me: 'Stab him in the heart' . . . he then sank down. I saw a light flickering around him. That was the sign that his soul was going down. We said a satanic prayer. We were then exhausted, and alone, wanted to die ourselves. But the visitation was too short. We could no longer kill ourselves.

Because Daniel and Manuela planned to kill themselves after the murder, Manuela had made the mistake of writing and sending a farewell note to her parents. Worried by the letter, Manuela's parents contacted police and asked them to go to the Rudas' apartment.

238

When the police entered the building they found a horrific bloodbath, the centre of which was Frank Hackerts' week-old mutilated and decomposing corpse. He had been hit over the head with a hammer and stabbed sixty-six times with a variety of sharp objects, including a small knife, a carpet cutter and a machete.

A pentagram, a symbol of Satan, had been carved on his chest with a scalpel. The scalpel was still protruding from his stomach. Near his body were human skulls, cemetery lights, scalpels, incense and a coffin in which the Rudas claimed to have had sex and then slept after the killing.

They had even drunk Hackerts' blood from a bowl in the belief that they would achieve immortality as vampires. A death list found in the flat contained the names of possible future intended victims.

After the gruesome murder, seemingly not knowing what to do next, Daniel and Manuela drove around Germany by car until they were eventually arrested on 12 July 2001, a week after the murder, in the eastern city of Jena.

After their capture neither Manuela nor Daniel had any hesitation in confessing to the crime. 'We wanted to make sure that the victim suffered well,' Manuela said. Daniel gave a statement read to the court by his lawyer explaining, 'I got the order to sacrifice a human for Satan.'

He also bizarrely compared the murder to a car accident, in which someone was killed, 'The car would not be charged. The driver is the bad guy. I have nothing to regret because I haven't done anything.'

*　　*　　*

The trial of the Rudas was as outlandish as the murder had been brutal. At the start of the trial, the Rudas' defence lawyers asked the court to black out the windows, stating that Manuela lived only at night because sunlight hurt her eyes.

Unsurprisingly, the judge threw out the request but did allow her to wear sunglasses during the trial. Manuela arrived at court on the first day of the trial dressed in black and made Satanic hand signs to the public gallery in the courtroom. She and Daniel held hands and kissed as they entered the court.

In evidence put forward for the defence the Rudas claimed to be vampires driven by the desires of Satan. Manuela, who insisted that she could not cope with sunlight and preferred to sleep in a coffin told the court that she had developed her taste for vampirism in the United Kingdom.

She said that the Devil had first contacted her in 1994 when she was fourteen after which she began to follow the Goth scene. By the age of sixteen, life in the small German town of Witten where she had grown up had begun to bore her and she dropped out of school.

In 1996 she travelled to the Scottish Highlands where she worked in a hotel for five months. She told the court that she had 'enjoyed the emptiness, the cemeteries and gloomy atmosphere of the low clouds'. She is also said to have lived for a short time in a cave on the Isle of Skye with a heavily tattooed sixty-two-year-old man called Tom Leppard.

Manuela left Scotland and moved to London in February 1997, where she worked in a Goth club in Islington and began studying black magic and Satanism. It was during this period that she claimed to have joined a group that attended 'bite parties' where people drank the blood of willing donors and worshipped the Devil.

She told the court that 'We went out at night, to cemeteries, in ruins and woods. We drank blood from living people . . . We slept on graves. One time we dug a grave and I slept in it, just to see what it would feel like.'

On her return to Germany, Manuela had her two canine teeth pulled and animal fangs implanted in their place so that she looked more like the popular image of a vampire.

She answered Daniel Ruda's weird lonely-hearts plea and the two made their home in western Germany, in the Ruhr region. They filled their apartment with knives, axes and skulls along with other black magic paraphernalia, sliding ever deeper into the Devil-worshipping world outside the confines of ordinary humanity.

*   *   *

At the murder trial the Rudas claimed that because they were following the orders of the Devil, they could not be held responsible for murder. Daniel Ruda is said to have repeatedly told the court, 'I have nothing to repent, because I did nothing.' Manuela also insisted to the jury that, 'It was not murder. We are not murderers. It was the execution of an order. Satan ordered us to. We had to comply. It was not something bad. It simply had to be.' Their defence counsel initially argued for their acquittal, insisting that the Rudas were 'mentally unfit to stand trial.'

Judge Arnjo Kerstingtombroke however, said the Rudas were not insane and were able enough to stand trial but acknowledged their apparent underlying psychiatric disorders. Psychiatric experts agreed, testifying that Daniel and Manuela clearly suffered from 'severe narcissistic personality disturbances'.

In addition to these testimonies, several witnesses called to give evidence at the trial told the court that the couple suffered from personality disorders. Indeed, for the duration of the trial the Rudas showed no remorse for the murder, maintaining that they had done Frank Hackerts 'a favour' because he was now 'beside Satan, the best place that he could be'.

They also frequently displayed provocative behaviour such as rude gestures, eye-rolling and sticking their tongues out at prosecutors and witnesses.

One of the trial witnesses, twenty-eight-year-old Frank Lewa, testified that he had first met Daniel Ruda on the local Far Right/skinhead scene. During the 1998 general election campaign in Germany, Daniel had canvassed for the extreme neo-nazi National-Democratic Party of Germany (NPD), a Far-Right party that the government has since tried to outlaw.

Lewa said that after the election Daniel drifted into the Gothic scene where he began listening to 'black metal' music and played in a band called the Bloodsucking Freaks. Daniel, it seemed, loved the attention he got whilst performing on stage. He enjoyed setting himself up as someone apart from and against everybody else, clearly revelling in the belief that he was different and special.

Lewa told the court that Daniel broke off contact with him after a row at a party and the two did not see each other again until the court case. Lewa told the court that he had received a letter from Daniel a few days before the Rudas killed Hackerts. With the letter Daniel enclosed a self-portrait photograph depicting him covered in blood and dangling from hooks in the ceiling. In the picture Daniel was pointing two gas pistols at the camera lens.

The letter written by Daniel called Lewa a Judas. Chillingly, Frank Lewa's name was on the list that police found at the Rudas' apartment after the murder. It was clear that he was to be another, perhaps even the next, victim of Satanic execution.

At the end of the trial Judge Arnjo Kerstingtombroke rejected calls for life sentences – the norm in Germany for pre-meditated murder – arguing that the couple were indeed mentally ill and could not be held wholly responsible for their actions.

In late July 2002, Daniel and Manuela Ruda were sentenced to fifteen and thirteen years respectively in a secure psychiatric institution. Concluding the case, Kerstingtombroke said: 'This case was not about Satanism, but about a crime committed by two people with severe disorders. Nothing mystical or cult-like happened here; just simple, base murder.'

Crime Prosecutor Dieter Justinsky said, 'I have never, ever seen such a picture of cruelty and depravity before. They simply had a lust for murder.' The sentence included the insistence that the Rudas should undergo therapy in prison to 'ensure that they never repeated their crime.'

*　　*　　*

The defendants sat silently as the sentence was read out. Manuela looked bored and chewed gum whilst Daniel stared blankly at Frank Hackerts' mother. The victim's father, Hermann Hackerts had been in court for the duration of the trial.

After the verdict Mr Hackerts said: 'Now I understand that they are bad people, but people, not devils, and absolutely unsound of mind.'

Some time after the trial had ended, Daniel Ruda's lawyer, Hans Reinhardt told a journalist on UK television's Channel 4 News, that he believed that the Rudas' claim that they were possessed by the Devil was a cover. 'I think he [Daniel] pretended to be an instrument of Satan because he is the sort of person who says, "I am the best, I am the greatest,"' Mr Reinhardt said.

He went on to state that he believed that Daniel's motive was quite possibly to attain celebrity status. 'He says, "I want to get on stage, I want that everybody knows me . . . I want to be as famous as Charles Manson and so I have to kill someone."' Unfortunately for Frank Hackerts, he believed that these two severely deluded individuals were his friends.

Spree Killings

Introduction

Spree killing is something that has a weird hold on our imaginations. Two of the cases featured here, those of Charles Starkweather and Caril Fugate and Bonnie and Clyde have been transformed into something approaching mythology through their representations in film and elsewhere.

The case of Bonnie and Clyde is a fascinating study in the way that murderers can be transformed into the heroes of their narratives. Even at the time, there was something ambiguous in the way that the story of this couple was covered by the press. For a period they came close to being popular heroes in the mould of Robin Hood, partly because people were fascinated by their rebellion against authority. But while the public mood turned against the real-life couple after too many callous murders, they would later be resurrected as antiheroes in Arthur Penn's 1967 film *Bonnie and Clyde*.

Meanwhile, the story of Charles Starkweather and Caril Fugate has been referred to in a strange variety of songs and books, and was turned into another classic film, in Terence Malick's *Badlands*. In this case, it is the pure banality of the killings that was the central point of the film.

The idiotic murder spree was depicted as numb and pointless in this film. But gradually, further adaptations of the story have elevated the killers to something that removes this level of banality from the story. And when Oliver Stone attempted to satirise the media's love affair with psychopathic killers in his own spree movie *Natural Born Killers,* he found that he had a hit, but one which seemed to attract a public who appreciated the 'killing for thrills' angle more than the satire of the relationship between the media and the myth of the killer.

Part of the problem with spree killing is that it is very easily adapted to the movie format. It creates an immediate dramatic tension, provides a regular stream of incidents, and sets up an inevitable denouement in which the spree is finally brought to an end. It is in this sense a perfect narrative arc.

But the truth is that most killing sprees are desperate, stupid affairs. They involve criminals who back themselves into a corner and then do increasingly stupid things as they attempt to find their way out of a net that is closing in on them. When two lovers find themselves in this situation, they may close ranks, as Alvin and Judith Neelley did (before betraying each other in the course of their trials), and this also feeds into the *Bonnie and Clyde*-style narrative form.

The truth of the Bonnie and Clyde case is that Bonnie Parker almost certainly never killed. She merely followed the man she loved with a loyalty that ended up costing her her life. Meanwhile, the other case featured in this section, that of Walter Kelbach and Myron Lance, is probably more representative of the grubby reality of spree killing. It also provides another example of the strange way in which the modern media's fascination with murder can feed back into criminal behaviour, as is shown by Kelbach's statement about watching his victims die.

248

As he talked to the camera, he sounded like someone who had merely been watching a television depiction of murder, rather than being a killer himself. The fact that he apparently found it hard to tell the difference suggests that the fictionalisation of murder is a more complex moral dilemma than we are sometimes prepared to admit.

Charles Starkweather and Caril Fugate

Rebels without a Cause

Dead people are all on the same level.
                                            Charlie Starkweather

In 1958, nineteen-year-old Charles Starkweather and his fourteen-year-old, underage girlfriend Caril Fugate went on a spree of killing that cost the lives of eleven men and women in the state of Nebraska, USA. Initially fuelled by robbery, the killings became more and more random as Starkweather doled out what he saw as his vengeance against injustice in the world. The country watched horrified as he and Caril Fugate carried out a string of frenzied, senseless murders.

It would seem that Charles Starkweather was always a troubled individual. Known as 'Charlie' he was the third of seven children, born to Guy and Helen Starkweather on 24 November 1938, in Lincoln, Nebraska. Although he was born towards the end of the Great Depression, he would later claim that he had no bad memories of his childhood home life insisting that the family never went without food or shelter.

Indeed the local community in Lincoln considered the family to be decent and respectable with well-behaved children. Charles's father Guy worked as a carpenter occasionally suffering unemployment due to bouts of arthritis in his hands and a weak spine. Because of this Charles's mother worked as a waitress to supplement the family income.

Things began to go downhill for Starkweather when he started school. His memories of school life were never pleasant. School became a problem initially because he had an undetected, severe myopia.

He was unable to read even the biggest letter on the eye chart and the undiagnosed short-sightedness prevented him from keeping up with his classmates. As a result, he was deemed to be slow learner and was frequently accused of not applying himself.

Unfortunately for Starkweather in addition to this he was born with a mild birth defect, Genu Varum, that caused his legs to become bowed and misshapen and he also suffered from a mild speech impediment. At Saratoga Elementary School in Lincoln, his short stature, speech impediment and bowed legs caused him to be the subject of bullying. Starkweather was picked on and beaten up from a very early age.

However, things were not all bleak at school for Charlie Starkweather. He soon discovered that he excelled at gymnastics, an activity that began to tone his body and give him unexpected strength. Starkweather began to use his newfound strength to defend himself against his bullies and from then on earned a reputation for toughness.

By this point though, he had gone from being a well-behaved schoolboy to a very troubled child. Initially he was fuelled by anger at those who had attacked him, but eventually his anger went beyond his bullies to those he simply didn't like. Turning from bullied to bully he began to attack his classmates sometimes beating them senseless.

He eventually began to carry a knife around with him to force any would-be attackers to back off. Slowly he developed a growing sense of anger towards what he saw as the injustice of the world around him. He was convinced that everyone looked down on him and that he would never achieve anything in his life.

Starkweather dropped out of school at sixteen. Given his poor academic performance it was always unlikely that he would ever graduate. Gaining a reputation as a rebellious spirit, he and his school friend Bob von Busch began to imitate James Dean in hairstyles and clothing. It would seem that Charlie empathised with Dean's rebellious on-screen character in *Rebel without a Cause,* thinking of him as a kindred spirit, someone who had suffered ostracism similar to his own and whom he could look up to. Starkweather's copper-coloured hair and striking green eyes, gave him an uncanny resemblance to James Dean, a likeness he revelled in.

After leaving school Charlie Starkweather initially worked as a lorry loader for a local newspaper business. During this time he became infatuated with a thirteen-year-old girl named Caril Ann Fugate, who was born on 31 July 1943.

Caril's high school was close by the newspaper warehouse where he worked and Starkweather began to see her every day. At this point his only interests were his guitar, guns, hot rods (his favourite possession was his 1949 Ford) and Caril Fugate. Caril was a bit of a rebel herself and her youthful innocence coupled with the fact that she was five years younger than him meant that she treated him like a hero figure in her life, a situation that Charlie delighted in.

He treated her as an adult and she became as entranced by him as he was by her. It has to be said that neither his nor her parents were happy with the situation. However, the couple were determined to stay together enjoying their reputation as teen rebels.

Charlie began to teach Caril how to drive, but it is unclear how successful this was because one day she crashed his Ford into another car. The legal owner of the vehicle, Charlie's father Guy Starkweather, was forced to pay damages to the owner of the other car. A huge row broke out between father and son and Guy Starkweather, having reached the end of his tether with Charlie's behaviour, kicked his son out of the house.

*   *   *

Charlie Starkweather was most definitely not considered to be a good worker. He was known for being lazy with a bad attitude. His boss at the newspaper warehouse later recalled, 'Sometimes you'd have to tell him something two or three times. Of all the employees in the warehouse, he was the dumbest man we had.'

After he was thrown out of his family home Starkweather moved into a shabby rented room and Caril Fugate became even more central to his life. He left the newspaper haulage job and found work as a garbage collector, but the poor pay made it impossible for him to pay his rent and living costs. He dreamed up ways to rob banks as he worked and retreated further into his nihilistic views of society and life. What he saw as the injustice of his poverty began to consume him.

At a mere nineteen years old Charlie Starkweather felt trapped. He saw his life as an endless road of hard, boring and badly paid work leading toward death. Feeling isolated, Starkweather developed a severe inferiority complex and became self-loathing and nihilistic. He began to believe that he was unable to do anything correctly, and that his own inherent failures would doom him to a life of poverty and misery.

Eventually, fired from his refuse-collecting job due to laziness, Starkweather was banned from his rented room for non-payment of rent. He wanted to marry his underage girlfriend and get some money for himself so he wouldn't spend the rest of his life in poverty.

Naturally, Fugate's parents would not allow the marriage and eventually banned him from seeing her. This enraged Starkweather even further. He became desperate to get out of Lincoln where he decided that everyone had him figured as a loser. It would seem that he genuinely believed that the world was always against him.

Throughout 1957, Starkweather was becoming increasingly convinced that crime was his only route to financial gain. He would claim his first victim within a week of his nineteenth birthday. On 30 November 1957, Starkweather went to a gas station in Lincoln and asked for credit so that he could buy a stuffed toy dog for Caril. The attendant working that day, Robert Colvert, refused him credit and Charlie left enraged with yet another sense of injustice.

Charlie returned to the gas station with a twelve-gauge shotgun at three o'clock in the morning the next day (1 December 1957). Leaving the gun in the car, he went into the gas station to buy a pack of cigarettes. Colvert was behind the counter working alone. Pocketing the cigarettes, Starkweather drove off down the road before turning around and heading back to the gas station. Once again he left the gun in the car and purchased a pack of gum, once again he left and drove away. He parked his car some distance away from the gas station, put a bandanna around his face and hat on his head as a disguise. He then walked back to the station with the shotgun in a canvas bag. Starkweather held Colvert at gunpoint and demanded money. Colvert told him that he did not know the combination to the safe and instead surrendered about $100 from the till, most of which was in change. Starkweather then forced Colvert into his car, drove him to a deserted area, and tried to make him get out of the vehicle. Fearing for his life at this point, Colvert attacked Charles and attempted to get hold of the shotgun. Undeterred, Starkweather overpowered him and shot Colvert twice in the head.

During the days that followed the robbery and murder Starkweather went shopping, spending large sums of money in small change on some new clothes for himself and Caril and purchasing a number of other things. The police so were convinced that the robbery had been carried out by somebody from out of town that local investigations were almost non-existent.

Charlie confessed to Caril that he had carried out the robbery – obviously he needed to account for the extra cash he suddenly seemed to have. He did however, deny the murder insisting that it must have happened after he left.

Whatever suspicions Fugate may have had, she nevertheless enjoyed helping Starkweather spend the proceeds of the robbery. The couple became closer than ever as Charlie Starkweather believed he had escaped undetected and crime really did seem to pay. After killing Robert Colvert, Starkweather believed he had become a new and different individual who was above and outside the law.

Charlie's euphoric mood and ready cash soon disappeared however, and by mid-January he was once again broke. Fugate's parents, who were convinced that she was pregnant tried to keep them apart.

On 21 January 1958, even though he had been banned from seeing her, Starkweather went to visit Caril at her dilapidated one-storey frame house in the poor Belmont section of Lincoln. By that point he had begun to take his shotgun everywhere with him. Finding her not home, he insisted on waiting for her in the sitting room where he fiddled constantly with the gun.

Caril's mother eventually started arguing about it with him and Starkweather responded by shooting Velda Bartlett (thirty-six) and Caril Ann's stepfather Marion Bartlett (fifty-seven) to death. Caril Ann came home from school into the midst of her family's massacre. Starkweather would later tell the court that Caril made them some sandwiches and then watched television whilst he fatally clubbed, strangled, and stabbed her tiny two-year-old sister, Betty Jean.

(Fugate would claim to have come home to find that Starkweather had shot and killed her stepfather, and her mother after whom Starkweather choked and stabbed her baby half-sister Betty Jean to death.)

The couple hid the stepfather's body wrapped in paper in the chicken shed behind the house. Betty was put in a box and thrown beside Caril's mother's body in another outhouse. Caril and Charlie spent the next six days in the house.

To keep away unwanted visitors, Caril pinned a note to the front door that read 'Stay a Way Every Body is sick with the Flu.' (sic) Caril Ann's grandmother attempted to visit but Caril turned her away without letting her inside the house. Her mother's boss also turned up to find out why she wasn't at work and he got turned away also.

The grandmother became suspicious and called the police, asking them to go round. The police initially performed a brief inspection of the property that didn't include the yard and concluded that there was no cause for concern. Further requests were made for the police to investigate, including one from Starkweather's father.

This time the police performed a more thorough search and discovered the three bodies behind the house. They issued a warrant for the couple's arrest but by this time, Charles and Caril had already gone and the police were confronted by a death scene that shocked the entire community of Lincoln. The two lovers were by this time driving across Nebraska in Charlie's battered old Ford on a spree of killing and stealing.

*　*　*

The couple drove to a Highway 77 service station to buy gas, a box of .410 shotgun shells and two boxes of .225 ammunition before heading to the rural farmlands of Bennet, Nebraska, sixteen miles south-east of Lincoln. Charlie had decided that a good hiding place for the two of them would be a farmhouse owned by seventy-year-old August Meyer.

Meyer knew the Starkweather family and frequently allowed them to hunt on his land. Starkweather and Fugate drove to Meyer's house planning to get more guns and ammunition. Seemingly unstoppable now, Starkweather killed the old family friend with a .410-gauge shotgun, then pushed his body into a washhouse. Later as they tried to make their getaway, the car the lovers were driving got stuck in mud and they decided to abandon it and continue on foot.

Unfortunately for them, two local teenagers Robert Jensen (seventeen) and Carol King (sixteen) drove by in their Ford and in misjudged kindness offered the killers a ride. Charles responded to this offer of help by insisting that Jensen and King drive back towards the farm where he forced them into an abandoned storm cellar. Starkweather shot them both in the head with a .22 rifle, and made an unsuccessful attempt to rape the girl, before leaving their bodies in the storm cellar. The girl was found partially naked. She had been brutally stabbed multiple times in the abdomen after being shot in an apparent moment of rage.

Charlie Starkweather's financial gain was a mere $4, the only money the teenagers had with them. The lovers then made off in Jensen's car, leaving Starkweather's old Ford behind. By now Starkweather's car had become the subject of a police search and was subsequently spotted at Meyer's farm. A search of the farm property revealed the three bodies, and a major manhunt was initiated.

Stupidly, given that most of the county was out looking for them, Starkweather and Fugate made the decision to drive home to Lincoln in Robert Jensen's car. They even drove past Fugate's home, where due to the number of police cars outside it was obvious that the bodies in the yard had been discovered.

From his days working as a garbage collector, Starkweather knew his way around Lincoln's expensive and opulent south-east district and decided it would be ripe for rich pickings whilst he was on his crime spree. The two drove on to this wealthier section of town, where Starkweather pulled the car into the garage of a large French provincial-style house. The house belonged to C. Lauer Ward, the president of the Capital Steel Company. Ward shared his home with his wife Clara and a housekeeper Lillian Fend.

When the housekeeper, fifty-one-year-old Lillian Fend, answered the door, Starkweather threatened her with his gun, forcing his way past her inside the home. He took Ward's wife, Clara, hostage and after gagging her, locked Fend in the basement.

Charlie insisted that Clara Ward get some food for him and Caril as they were hungry. According to Starkweather, after this Ward requested to be allowed to go upstairs to her room. He later claimed that she returned with a gun, tried to shoot him and missed. He said that he then threw a knife at her but denied stabbing her repeatedly.

Whatever did happen Clara Ward was found tied to a bed gagged and with multiple stab wounds. Lillian Fend had also been fatally stabbed. Later at their trial, with regards to the killing of the housekeeper, Starkweather and Fugate's accounts clashed, with each claiming that the other was responsible for her death.

Later that evening at around 5.30 p.m., C. Lauer Ward, forty-seven, a wealthy local industrialist returned from a conference with Nebraska's Governor, Victor Anderson. Unknown to him, by now his wife was already dead upstairs. Ward would never see her again.

Starkweather was waiting for him in the hall. As soon as he entered the house Ward was shot in the head and neck, and then stabbed in the back. He died quickly. After ransacking the house Charlie and Caril stole Ward's 1956 black Packard, along with a number of valuables from the house, and sped west out of Lincoln taking Highway 2 to Wyoming.

At some point during that afternoon, as they searched the Ward's house, a newspaper was delivered to the doorstep and Starkweather and Fugate were on the front page. They were delighted at their newfound infamy and took the newspaper with them as a kind of trophy.

*　　*　　*

The killing of the wealthy industrialist and his wife was greeted with panic and anger. The Wards were close friends with the State Governor who immediately called into action all law enforcement agencies including the FBI and the National Guard.

The small town of Lincoln was frozen with fear. Sheriff Merle Karnopp called on the townsfolk for help and 100 men turned out armed with deer rifles, shotguns and pistols. Parents held on tightly to their children, some were kept away from school. Around 1,200 law enforcement officers were by now out searching for the young lovers. There was even an aerial search for the stolen Packard car.

Even in the midst of all this chaos, Starkweather and Fugate tried once again to return to Fugate's home but on seeing the number of police still in the neighbourhood decided that they had to go elsewhere. They decided to drive to Washington State, where they intended to seek refuge in the home of Charlie Starkweather's brother.

They continued driving all that night and eventually crossed into Wyoming on 29 January 1958. Once daylight broke, they were worried that the expensive Packard would draw attention to them, so they decided to steal another car. Shortly after making this decision, they spotted a Buick parked by the road just as they approached Douglas, Wyoming.

The inhabitant was shoe salesman Merle Collison who had pulled over to take a nap. A scuffle broke out when Collison refused to swap cars with Starkweather. This resulted in Charlie shooting him several times at point-blank range. (Starkweather later claimed Fugate finished Collison off after his own gun jammed, as they blamed each other in the courtroom.)

The couple tried to drive off with Collison still dead in the passenger seat. No doubt they intended to find a suitable place to hide his body. However, trouble started when Starkweather couldn't fathom how to release the handbrake – the Buick had a push-pedal emergency brake – and kept stalling the car. Eventually a passing car driven by Joe Sprinkle, forty, a geologist, stopped to help whereupon Starkweather aimed at Sprinkle's head with his gun and threatened to kill him if he didn't show him how to release the brake.

Luckily for him, Sprinkle wrestled away the rifle just as Deputy Sheriff William Romer approached in his patrol car and stopped to find out what the trouble was about. At this point Caril Fugate started yelling, 'It's Starkweather, he's going to kill me,' and ran over to the Deputy telling him that Charlie Starkweather was in the vehicle, and that he had just killed somebody.

Starkweather immediately leapt back into the Packard and drove off at break-neck speed followed by the deputy sheriff who had by now radioed for help to set up roadblocks. A spectacular high-speed car chase ensued with Starkweather crashing through roadblocks at up to 115 miles an hour.

Police continued to chase him, firing at the car he was driving. One bullet shattered the back windscreen and the

flying glass cut Starkweather on the ear. He immed
pulled over yelling at the police that they'd 'shot
seemingly believing that he had indeed been mor
wounded. Sheriff Earl Heflin said at the time, 'He thought he
was bleeding to death. That's why he stopped. That's the
kind of yellow sonofabitch he is.'

Both Starkweather and Fugate were immediately jailed in
Douglas.

*   *   *

After their arrest Starkweather first claimed Caril had
nothing to do with the murders, but changed his story several
times, finally testifying at her trial that she was a willing
participant. She always maintained that she was a victim of
kidnapping.

Her betrayal of Charlie Starkweather when Deputy Romer
arrived on the scene was not forgotten and he eventually
claimed that most of the murders were her doing, claiming
that Fugate was 'the most trigger-happy person I'd ever met'.
At his trial Starkweather admitted shooting Jensen but
claimed that Fugate had stabbed Carol King in a jealous rage,
when he had implied that he found King attractive. Fugate
denied this, claiming that she had been in the car while the
attack took place.

Starkweather's options were limited. He could choose to
be tried in either Nebraska or Wyoming. Convinced that he
would be given the death penalty, he had two options of how
to die. He faced the gas chamber in Wyoming, while for their
executions, Nebraska used the electric chair. Charlie chose
extradition to Nebraska.

Ironically for him, had he chosen to stand trial for the one
murder in Wyoming he may well have got a life sentence
because the State governor at that time was opposed to the
death sentence.

During his trial his old high school friend Bob Von Busch recalled:

> He could be the kindest person you've ever seen. He'd do anything for you if he liked you. He was a hell of a lot of fun to be around, too. Everything was just one big joke to him. But he had this other side. He could be mean as hell, cruel. If he saw some poor guy on the street who was bigger than he was, better looking, or better dressed, he'd try to take the poor bastard down to his size.

Although his lawyer argued his case on a 'mental illness' basis, it was clear from the start of the trial that the Nebraska jury was convinced that Starkweather had been sane at the time of the murders. Starkweather himself tried to refuse the mentally disturbed label, perhaps because he thought that it carried a stigma that he didn't want. After all, he had been continuously picked on as a child for what were seen as his deficiencies.

It took the jury only a short time to find him guilty, specifically asking the judge for the death penalty. Starkweather was executed in the electric chair on 25 June 1959. He insisted that although he had personally dispatched most of the victims, Fugate had murdered several as well. The extent of her actual involvement is uncertain; Starkweather was executed still accusing her, and Fugate refuses to talk about it to this day.

Fugate was also tried for her role in the murder spree. Caril's defence was built around her hostage status, but the jury remained unconvinced because she had had plenty of opportunities to escape. They returned a guilty verdict on 28 November 1958. Because she was fourteen years old at the time, she received a life sentence and was sent to the Nebraska Detention Centre for Women.

Apparently, whilst there she was a model prisoner, and

was paroled in 1976 after serving only eighteen years. She now lives in Lansing, Michigan, and is a retired medical janitor. She never married. Caril still maintains that Starkweather was holding her hostage by threatening to kill her family (to this day she maintains she did not know they were already dead.)

One thing is certain. In the course of Starkweather and Fugate's notorious spree, they had taken eleven lives. The case has directly or indirectly inspired a variety of films and books, ranging from *Badlands* to *Natural Born Killers*. At times such films seem to glorify the spree killer and to underestimate the suffering and sorrow that their actions caused. Perhaps in this case, it would be better to end by remembering the victims.

The Victims

Robert Colvert, gas station attendant
Marion Bartlett, Caril Ann's stepfather
Velda Bartlett, Caril Ann's mother
Betty Jean Bartlett, Marion and Velda's daughter
August Meyer, Starkweather's family friend
Robert Jensen
Carol King, Robert's girlfriend
C. Lauer Ward, wealthy industrialist
Clara Ward, C. Lauer Ward's wife
Lillian Fend, Clara Ward's maid
Merle Collison, travelling salesman

Bonnie and Clyde

The Notorious Barrow Gang

When most people imagine Bonnie and Clyde they picture two young beautiful outlaws as portrayed by Warren Beatty and Faye Dunaway in the 1967 film *Bonnie and Clyde*. Directed by Arthur Penn, the film won two Oscars (Best Supporting Actress and Best Cinematography) and depicted Bonnie and Clyde as a romanticised twentieth-century Robin Hood and his companion, regularly robbing banks and sharing the proceeds with their family and friends.

The truth is that although Bonnie Parker and Clyde Barrow were alone in their stolen car when they were finally ambushed and shot by federal state officers in 1934, the history of how they ended up there is more complicated. The story involves a larger group of people known as the 'Barrow Gang' who were notorious outlaws, robbers, and criminals travelling the Central United States during the Great Depression, stealing cars and robbing small businesses and citizens.

They became famous, their exploits were known nation-wide and they captured the attention of the American press and its readership between 1931 and 1935. There is however,

264

some controversy regarding Bonnie's part in the crimes. Some argue that she never fired a gun, others that she was simply so obsessed with Clyde that she would have done anything for him, including helping during theft, murder and robbery and generally caring for the group when they were on the run.

*　　*　　*

Clyde Champion Barrow (people gave him the middle name 'Chestnut'), who also went by the aliases Roy Bailey, Jack Hale, Eldin Williams and Elvin Williams, was born in Telico, Texas, just south of Dallas on 24 March 1909. He was the sixth child of eight children, born into a poor, farming family. His father was a sharecropper.

On the whole, the family couldn't be described as law-abiding and most of the boys were arrested many times for various crimes. Clyde was first arrested in late 1926, after running away when police confronted him over a rental car that he had failed to return on time.

Clyde's school days were few and far between and he was never educated past the fifth grade. When he was twelve, the family gave up their farm work and moved to West Dallas where his father ran a service station and Clyde attended the Cedar Valley School. He quit not long after the move and became involved in selling stolen goods with his brother Marvin.

Clyde's new 'job' with his big brother Marvin 'Buck' Barrow led to his second arrest, this time for possession of stolen turkeys. Buck Barrow ended up in jail. Despite holding down regular jobs for the most part during the period 1927 through 1929, Clyde also cracked safes, robbed stores, and stole cars.

He was arrested three more times during investigations into auto theft and safecracking but released because of lack of evidence. Although now he is primarily known for robbing banks, at the time he focused on smaller jobs, robbing grocery stores and gas stations at a rate far outpacing the ten to fifteen bank robberies attributed to him and the 'Barrow Gang' by law officers.

Suspicions of him being a murderer date from the early activities of the Barrow Gang, too. During Buck Barrow's time in jail, Clyde had been the driver in a Hillsboro store robbery in which merchant J.W. Butcher was shot and killed. The murder victim's widow, when shown photos, picked out Clyde Barrow as one of the shooters.

It is unlikely that she was wrong – he was quite easy to pick out at a mere 5 foot 6 inches tall with a schoolboyish face. On 16 October 1929 he was arrested with William Turner and Frank Hardy at the Roosevelt Hotel in Waco, Texas. He allegedly told Chief of Police Hollis Barron through a stream of tears that the two men had picked him up hitchhiking and he was unaware of their reputations. It was a lucky break for Clyde, this time Barron let him go.

*   *   *

Clyde's future partner in crime, Bonnie Parker was born on 1 October 1910 in Rowena, Texas. She was the second of three children. Her father was a bricklayer by trade but was often unemployed. In 1914, when she was four years old, her father died and her mother, Emma Krause Parker, packed up the family and they moved in with her parents in Cement City near Dallas. Bonnie subsequently attended Cement City School where she was known to be an excellent honour roll student.

In 1924 she entered Cement City High School winning the Cement City spelling championship the same year. In high school she excelled in creative writing, won a County League contest in literary arts and even gave introductory speeches for local politicians. Described as intelligent and personable yet strong willed, Bonnie was a mere 4 foot 11 inches tall and weighed only 90 pounds.

She was said to be addicted to romance and confession magazines and dreamed of a future in the spotlight. Bonnie would get her dream but probably not as she had earlier imagined it. She would later write a poem, *Street Girl*, about the consequences of moving from the country to the city and the decline of her prospects.

On 25 September 1926, less than a week before her sixteenth birthday, Bonnie Parker married Roy Thornton. Always a romantic, she loved him to the point of getting a tattoo on the inside of her thigh of two intertwined hearts with their names in the middle.

The marriage was short-lived however, and in January 1929 they separated although they were never divorced. Parker was still wearing Thornton's wedding ring when she died.

In January 1930, out of work, she visited a friend in West Dallas, who had a broken arm. Clyde is said to have dropped by the girl's house while Bonnie was visiting, Bonnie was supposedly in the kitchen making hot chocolate when he arrived. From the day they met both were said to be immediately smitten and many analysts to this day believe Bonnie joined Clyde in crime simply because she was in love.

She remained a loyal companion to him as they carried out their crime sprees, even as they awaited the violent deaths they viewed as inevitable. She spent her days between crimes indulging her fondness for creative writing, producing poems such as *Suicide Sal* and *The Story of Bonnie and Clyde*, poems that would later appear to eerily predict her premature and violent death. (A selection of her poems is included at the end of this chapter.)

Though the public and the press at the time believed Bonnie Parker to be a full partner in the Barrow Gang, and thus its crimes, her role in the Barrow Gang crimes has long been a source of scrutiny. 'Barrow Gang' members William Daniel Jones (W.D. Jones) and Ralph Fults have both testified that they never saw Bonnie fire a gun, and described her role as 'logistical'. Marie Barrow, Clyde's youngest sister, writing with Phillip Steele in *The Family Story of Bonnie and Clyde*, made a similar claim: 'Bonnie never fired a shot. She just followed my brother no matter where he went.'

*   *   *

Whatever the true story was, and there are many versions, Bonnie and Clyde became a mythic couple in the early 1930s. Between 1932 and 1934, there were many incidents in which the Barrow Gang reportedly kidnapped lawmen or robbery victims, usually releasing them far from home, sometimes with money to help them get back, but not always.

They were a couple with whom the general public were simultaneously enthralled and repulsed. Notoriously, the Barrow Gang would not hesitate to shoot anybody, civilian or lawman, if they got in the way of their escape. In the myth, Bonnie and Clyde lead the gang; in reality Bonnie followed Clyde and therefore the gang.

Bonnie became aware of Clyde's past when the police turned up looking for him and took him back to Denton, Texas for questioning about some stolen merchandise. When they could not make the charge stick, they transferred him to Waco where he confessed to a couple of burglaries and several car thefts.

This time unfortunately, Clyde couldn't cry his way out. He was sentenced to two years on each count but the courts allowed the sentences to run concurrently. Bonnie, who visited Clyde every day, eventually smuggled a Colt to Clyde and that night Clyde, his cellmate William Turner and

268

another prisoner by the name of Emory Abernathy escaped. Freedom however, was short-lived. Clyde and Turner (Bonnie was not with them) were recaptured in Middletown, Ohio and Clyde got fourteen years in the Texas State Penitentiary.

Eventually, with the help and intervention of his mother, Clyde was pardoned and paroled from prison on 2 February 1932. Unfortunately, just prior to his release, he had asked another inmate to chop off two of his toes on his left foot so that he could avoid working in the cotton fields, a notoriously hard job in the Texan heat and dust. He left prison on crutches.

Clyde Barrow hated his time in prison and the treatment he received there. According to author John Neal Phillips in *My Life with Bonnie and Clyde*, Clyde's goal in life was not to gain fame and fortune from robbing banks, but to seek revenge against the Texas prison system for the abuses he suffered whilst serving time.

Trying to go straight, Clyde made a halfhearted attempt at 'real' work in Massachusetts. He lasted all of two weeks before he returned to Bonnie. Back in business, the couple set off together in a stolen car.

*   *   *

In March 1932 Bonnie was captured in a failed robbery attempt with the Barrow Gang in Kaufman, Texas, after which she was jailed. Bonnie remained in jail until 17 June 1932 when the grand jury for Kaufman County met in Kaufman and no-billed Bonnie (a procedure whereby charges are dropped by a Grand Jury and the person's record is cleared), which paved the way for her release. Within a few weeks she had re-connected with Clyde. They were once again on the road together.

On 5 August 1932, while Parker was visiting her mother,

Barrow and two associates were drinking illegal alcohol (this was during Prohibition), at a dance in Stringtown, Oklahoma. Without knowing what awaited them, local lawmen including Sheriff C.G. Maxwell and his deputy Eugene C. Moore assembled a two-car force to confront the suspected bootleggers living in the rented apartment over a garage.

Though caught by surprise, Clyde, noted for remaining cool under fire, was gaining far more experience in gun battles than most lawmen. He and W.D. Jones shot and killed Deputy Eugene C. Moore and fatally wounded another police officer. The survivors later testified that their side had fired only fourteen rounds in the conflict. That was the first killing of a lawman by the Barrow Gang, the start of a grim list that would eventually amount to nine dead officers.

On 22 March 1933, Buck Barrow was granted a full pardon and released from prison. By April, he and his wife, Blanche, were living with W.D. Jones, Clyde, and Bonnie Parker in a temporary hideout in Joplin, Missouri. The 'gang' now numbered five members. This new gang embarked upon a series of bold robberies that made headlines across the country. They escaped capture in various encounters with the law but because of their activities, law enforcement efforts to apprehend them became even more intense.

The gang knew they had to avoid any contact with the authorities but this did not always go in their favour. In June 1933, while driving with W.D. Jones and Bonnie, Clyde missed some construction signs and the car went off the road, dropping into a ravine. It rolled over and caught fire, Bonnie was trapped beneath the burning car, suffering third degree burns to her left leg.

After making their escape, Clyde insisted that Bonnie be allowed to convalesce. Once they had met up with Blanche and Buck Barrow again, they stayed put until

Buck bungled a local robbery with W.D. Jones, and killed a city marshall.

The gang had to go on the run again and needed a new hideout. On 18 July 1933, they checked into the Red Crown Tourist Court south of Platte City, Missouri. The courts consisted of two brick cabins joined by two single-car garages. Several yards to the south stood the Red Crown Tavern, managed by Neal Houser, who became intrigued by the group when Blanche Barrow paid for dinners and beer with silver coins instead of dollars. It was Blanche Barrow who would lead the local Sheriff to the gang's hideout.

As became common with the gang, their next brush with the law arose more from their generally suspicious behaviour than from being actually caught committing any crime.

The next day, Blanche Barrow went into town to purchase bandages, crackers, cheese, and atropine sulfate to treat Bonnie's leg. The owner of the drugstore contacted Sheriff Holt Coffey, who put the cabins under watch. Coffey had been alerted by Oklahoma, Texas and Arkansas law authorities, to be on the lookout for strangers seeking such supplies and had warned local merchants.

The sheriff contacted Captain Baxter of the highway patrol, who called for reinforcements from Kansas City including an armoured car. At 11 p.m. on 29 July, Sheriff Coffey led a group of officers armed with Thompson sub-machine guns toward the cabins.

A gun battle commenced but the law officer's submachine guns proved no match for the Browning Automatic Rifles (BARs) of the Barrows, who had recently robbed an armoury. (The BAR was reportedly Clyde's favourite weapon.)

The gang escaped once again, but Buck Barrow had been shot in the side of the head and Blanche Barrow had been nearly blinded by glass fragments in her eye. Their prospects for holding out against the ensuing manhunt dwindled.

271

In July 1933, the Barrow Gang was at Dexfield Park, an abandoned amusement park near Dexter, Iowa. Unfortunately, they were noticed by local citizens and it was determined that the campers were the Barrows.

Surrounded by local lawmen and approximately one hundred spectators, the Barrows once again found themselves involved in a shoot-out. Clyde Barrow, Parker, and W.D. Jones escaped on foot. Buck Barrow, however, was shot in the back and his wife hit again in the face and eyes with flying glass.

Buck died five days later at Kings' Daughters Hospital in Iowa of pneumonia after surgery. Blanche Barrow, with her left eye badly injured, was captured and jailed in the Missouri State Penitentiary for her part in the robberies. W.D. Jones was captured later in November 1933, in Houston, Texas, and Bonnie and Clyde went on the run together. Bonnie's leg, however, eventually became deformed for lack of good medical attention.

*　　*　　*

On 22 November 1933, a trap was set by the Sheriff of Dallas, Texas, and his deputies in an attempt to capture Bonnie and Clyde near Grand Prairie, Texas, but the couple escaped the officers' gunfire. Not long afterwards they held up an attorney on the highway and took his car, which they abandoned in Miami, Oklahoma.

A month later on 21 December 1933, Bonnie and Clyde held up and robbed a citizen at Shreveport, Louisiana. Throughout many other crimes they continued to evade capture, but they knew they had to be more careful. The Barrow Gang had left most of their possessions in the rented apartment in Oklahoma, including a camera with an exposed roll of pictures.

The pictures allowed police to clearly identify the

individual gang members and their cars. After this episode, Parker and Barrow used coats and hats to cover the licence plates of their stolen vehicles when taking pictures.

In January 1934, Clyde finally made the move he had been waiting for against the Texas Department of Corrections in what was to become known as the infamous 'Eastham Breakout'. Clyde Barrow was the mastermind behind the escape of Henry Methvin, Raymond Hamilton and several other prisoners. On 16 January 1934, five prisoners, including the notorious Raymond Hamilton (who was serving sentences totalling more than 200 years), were liberated from the Eastham State Prison Farm at Waldo, Texas, by Clyde Barrow, accompanied by Bonnie Parker.

The Texas Department of Corrections received a large amount of national negative publicity over the jailbreak and one has to assume that Clyde was at least partially satisfied that he had helped to bring that upon them. However, the revenge came at a price.

A prison officer (Major Joe Crowson) was killed in the breakout (by another escapee, Joe Palmer) and the Texas and federal governments subsequently pulled out all the stops in their manhunt for Bonnie and Clyde. As Major Crowson lay dying, Lee Simmons of the Texas Department of Corrections reportedly promised him that the persons involved in the breakout would be hunted down and killed.

He kept his word, except for Henry Methvin, whose life was saved, in return for his betrayal of Bonnie and Clyde. The Texas Department of Corrections contacted former Texas Ranger Captain Frank A. Hamer, and convinced him to accept a commission to hunt down the Barrow Gang.

Though retired, Hamer had retained his commission, which had not yet expired. He accepted the assignment immediately, as a Texas Highway Patrol Officer seconded to the prison system as a special investigator with the specific task of hunting down Bonnie and Clyde and the Barrow

273

gang. Frank Hamer put together a posse of Texas law enforcement agents, B.M. 'Manny' Gault, Bob Alcorn and Ted Hinton along with Louisiana officers Henderson Jordan and Prentiss Oakley.

* * *

Of course, federal officials from many states had by now been looking for Bonnie and Clyde for some time. They had first become interested in Barrow and his girlfriend as early as December 1932, through one piece of evidence. A Ford car, which had been stolen in Pawhuska, Oklahoma, was found abandoned near Jackson, Michigan, in September of that year.

At Pawhuska, it was learned that another Ford car had been abandoned after being stolen in Illinois. A search of this car, based on its abandoned contents, revealed that its occupants had been a man and a woman. A prescription bottle was found in the car, which led officers to a drug store in Nacogdoches, Texas, where an investigation revealed that the woman for whom the prescription had been filled was Clyde Barrow's aunt.

When officers investigated further, they discovered that the woman who obtained the prescription had been visited recently by Clyde Barrow, Bonnie Parker, and Clyde's brother, L.C. Barrow. They also learned that the three of them were driving a Ford car, identified as the one stolen in Illinois.

Apparently, L.C. Barrow had secured the empty prescription bottle from a son of the woman who had originally obtained it. On 20 May 1933, the United States Commissioner at Dallas, Texas, issued a warrant against Clyde Barrow and Bonnie Parker, charging them with the interstate transportation, from Dallas to Oklahoma, of the automobile stolen in Illinois. The federal law office started its hunt in earnest for this elusive pair.

As the gang eluded capture, the police death toll increased. In April 1934, they encountered two young highway patrolmen near Grapevine, Texas. Before the officers could draw their guns, they were shot. Henry Methvin is believed to have been the primary killer of both, although initially Clyde was also blamed.

Clyde Barrow did, however, fire some shots at the police. Once Methvin had begun a gun battle with law officers, Barrow was left with little choice in the matter, and fired at the second officer. It is now generally agreed that it was Henry Methvin who fired both fatal shots. Indeed, Methvin confessed in open court to being the sole gunman in both killings.

These particularly senseless killings shocked and outraged the public, who up to this point had tended to romanticise Bonnie and Clyde. Five days later on 6 April 1934, the gang killed again. This time the victim was Constable William Campbell of Miami, Oklahoma. They also abducted a police chief, whom they wounded. It was only a matter of time now before they were caught.

*   *   *

Frank Hamer had begun tracking Bonnie and Clyde on 10 February 1934. Having never before seen Bonnie or Clyde, he immediately arranged a meeting with a representative of Henry Methvin's parents in the hope of gaining a lead. Meanwhile, federal officials, who viewed the Eastham prison break in particular as a national embarrassment to the government, were providing all support that was asked for, such as weapons and information. Hamer obtained a quantity of civilian Browning Automatic Rifles and twenty-round magazines with armour-piercing rounds.

On 13 April 1934, federal officials uncovered some information that definitely placed Bonnie and Clyde as occasional visitors to a remote section south-west of Ruston, Louisiana. The home of the Methvins was not far away and Bonnie and Clyde had apparently been making visits there. Law enforcement had learned that Clyde and his companion had been travelling from Texas to Louisiana, sometimes accompanied by Henry Methvin.

Hamer studied the gang's movements and found they circled the edges of five mid-west states, exploiting the 'state line' rule that prevented officers from one jurisdiction from pursuing a fugitive into another.

Bonnie and Clyde were masters of that pre-FBI rule, but, unfortunately for them, they were also consistent in their movements, allowing them to see their families and those of their gang members. It also allowed an experienced man-hunter like Frank Hamer to chart their path and predict where they would go. He predicted that they were next due to see Henry Methvin's family. The net was closing in.

On 21 May 1934, Hamer, 'Manny' Gault, Alcorn, Hinton and Louisiana officers Jordan and Oakley were in Shreveport, Louisiana when they learned that Clyde had designated Methvin's parents' Bienville Parish house as a rendezvous in case they were later separated.

The officers put in place measures to ensure that the couple would probably be there that night. Hamer, Alcorn, Manny and Hinton (who had met Clyde in the past) separated Methvin from Bonnie and Clyde in Shreveport. Bienville Parish Sheriff Henderson Jordan, and his deputy Prentiss Oakley, set up an ambush at the rendezvous point along Highway 154, between Gibsland and Sailes. They were in place by 9.00 p.m. and waited through the next day (22 May) but saw no sign of Bonnie and Clyde. The police were becoming desperate. They turned to Henry Methvin's family for help.

Ivan Methvin, Henry's father, had in the past let Bonnie and Clyde use his place to hide. Now fearing for his son's life, he made a deal with Frank Hamer. The swap was a full pardon for his son in Texas for information on the Barrow gang.

Hamer was informed of a 'message board' that was used by the Barrows. It was a large board that lay on the ground near a stump of a pine tree on a farm to Market Road several miles from Plain Dealing, Louisiana. The 'message board' was used for communication among the Barrow gang and their friends and relatives.

Clearly this was a road used frequently by Bonnie and Clyde. Hamer had persuaded Ivan Methvin to betray Bonnie and Clyde and so lead the couple into an ambush. The scene was set.

At 1.30 a.m. Hamer's men set up a lookout on the desolate road near the Methvin's Louisiana home, using tree branches for camouflage. They hid approximately twenty-five feet from the road and about ten feet apart so that they had a good view of anything approaching. Much later, at about 9.10 a.m., they heard a car approaching at high speed.

Ted Hinton confirmed that the occupants of the car were Bonnie and Clyde. What followed has been the subject of much controversy. In the official report, when they saw Clyde's stolen Ford V8 approaching, the officers stepped into the road to challenge them and when the car stopped Bonnie and Clyde were told to give themselves up. Both reached for their weapons but never got the chance to use them. Ted Hamer's posse opened fire immediately.

The car leaped ahead and came to a halt in a ditch beside the road. By 9.15, the couple were dead but the firing continued even after the car came to a halt. After the trail of previous deaths amongst the police, they were taking no chances this time. The fingers on Bonnie's right hand were shot away. Her left hand held a bloody pack of cigarettes. She died with her head slumped between her legs and a gun across her lap.

Bonnie and Clyde were killed on 23 May 1934; Bonnie

was twenty-three years old, Clyde twenty-four. Inside the car, Hamer found a saxophone, three Browning automatic rifles, one 10-gauge Winchester lever-action, sawn-off shotgun, one 20-gauge sawn-off shotgun, one Colt 32-caliber automatic, one Colt 45-caliber revolver, seven Colt automatic pistols, and approximately 3,000 rounds of ammunition. They also found licence plates from Illinois, Iowa, Missouri, Texas, Indiana, Kansas, Ohio and Louisiana.

*　　*　　*

Although Bonnie and Clyde were now dead, questions about the way the ambush was conducted and the failure to warn the duo of their impending death have never been resolved. Much has been made of the fact that the lawmen, under Frank Hamer's direct orders, did not call out a warning, The officers emptied every weapon they had into the car to make sure its occupants couldn't return fire. According to statements made by Ted Hinton and Bob Alcorn:

> Each of us six officers had a shotgun and an automatic rifle and pistols. We opened fire with the automatic rifles. They were emptied before the car got even with us. Then we used shotguns . . . There was smoke coming from the car, and it looked like it was on fire. After shooting the shotguns, we emptied the pistols at the car, which had passed us and ran into a ditch about 50 yards on down the road. It almost turned over. We kept shooting at the car even after it stopped. We weren't taking any chances.

When later asked why he had killed a woman who was not wanted for any capital offence, Frank Hamer stated, 'I hate to bust the cap on a woman, especially when she was sitting down, however if it wouldn't have been her [sic], it would have been us.'

In the years following their deaths, Prentiss Oakley was reportedly troubled by his actions. He remains the only member of the ambush squad publicly to express regret for his actions. The officials, including Frank Hamer, took and kept for themselves stolen guns that were found in the death car.

Personal items such as Bonnie's clothing and the saxophone were also taken, and when the Parker family asked for them back, they were refused. Apparently, these items were later sold as macabre souvenirs.

In the grisly aftermath, the men who were left to guard the bodies (Gault, Oakley, and Alcorn) allowed people to cut off bloody locks of Bonnie's hair and tear pieces from her dress, which were also sold as souvenirs. Ted Hinton returned to find a man trying to cut off Clyde's finger and was sickened by what was occurring.

The coroner, arriving on the scene, reported the following: 'Nearly everyone had begun collecting souvenirs such as shell casings, slivers of glass from the shattered car windows, and bloody pieces of clothing from the garments of Bonnie and Clyde. One eager man had opened his pocket knife, and was reaching into the car to cut off Clyde's left ear.' The coroner enlisted Frank Hamer for help in controlling the 'circus-like atmosphere', and only then did people move away from the car.

*　　*　　*

In 1979, Ted Hinton's account of the ambush was published. According to Hinton, the law officers had tied Henry Methvin's father, Ivan, to a tree the night before the ambush, to keep him from possibly warning the duo off. In this version of the story Hamer made Ivan Methvin a deal whereby he would also keep quiet about being tied up, and his son would be pardoned for the murder of the two young highway patrolmen, a pardon that Henry Methvin did later receive. Hamer allegedly made every member of the group swear they would never divulge this secret. Hinton said:

> Ivy Methvin was traveling on that road in his old farm truck, when he was stopped by the lawmen, standing in the middle of the road. They took him into the woods and handcuffed him to a tree. They removed one of the old truck's wheels, so that it would appear to have broken down at that spot.

After their deaths, the bullet-riddled Ford containing the two bodies of Bonnie and Clyde, was towed to the Conger Furniture Store & Funeral Parlor in downtown Arcadia, Louisiana. C.F. 'Boots' Bailey did the preliminary embalming in a small preparation room in the back of the furniture store.

It was estimated that the north-west Louisiana town swelled in population from 2,000 to 12,000 within hours of the news of Bonnie and Clyde's deaths. The curious arrived in their dozens by train, horseback and buggy.

H.D. Darby, a young undertaker who worked for the McClure Funeral Parlor in nearby Ruston, Louisiana, and Sophie Stone, a home demonstration agent also from Ruston, came to Arcadia to identify the bodies. Both Darby and Stone had been kidnapped by the Barrow gang several weeks previously in Ruston and released near Waldo, Arkansas.

Bonnie Parker reportedly laughed when she asked Darby his profession and discovered it was an undertaker. She remarked that maybe someday he would be working on her. As it turned out, she was correctly predicting the future, Darby did indeed assist Bailey in embalming the outlaws.

Bonnie and Clyde wished to be buried side by side, but the

280

Parker family would not allow it. Bonnie's mother had wanted to grant her daughter's final wish, which was to be brought home, but the mobs surrounding the Parker house made that impossible.

Over 20,000 people turned out for Bonnie's funeral, making it difficult for the Parkers to reach the gravesite. The following words (from one of her own poems) are inscribed on Bonnie's gravestone:

> As the flowers are all made sweeter: by the
>   sunshine and the dew,
> So this old world is made brighter: by the lives of
>   folks like you.

The funeral service was held on Saturday 26 May, at 2 p.m. in the McKamy-Campbell Funeral Home, directed by Allen D. Campbell. His son, Dr Allen Campbell, later remembered that flowers came from everywhere including some sent by 'Pretty Boy' Floyd and the infamous bank robber John Dillinger. Initially, Bonnie was buried in the Fishtrap Cemetery, but in 1945 was moved to the new Crown Hill Cemetery in Dallas. The next year the service for Raymond Hamilton, also a one-time member of the Barrow Gang, executed on 10 May 1935 by the State of Texas, was also held at the McKamy-Campbell Funeral Home.

Clyde Barrow's family used the Sparkman-Holtz-Brand Morticians in downtown Dallas. After identifying his son's body, an emotional Henry Barrow sat in a rocking chair in the furniture part of the Conger Furniture Store & Funeral Parlor establishment and wept.

Thousands of people gathered outside both Dallas funeral homes hoping for a chance to view the bodies. Barrow's private funeral was held at sunset on Friday 25 in the funeral home chapel. He was buried in Western Heights Cemetery in Dallas, next to his brother, 'Buck' Marvin. They share a single granite marker with their names on it and a four-word epitaph previously selected by Clyde: 'Gone but not forgotten.'

At the time they were killed in 1934, Bonnie and Clyde were believed to have committed thirteen murders and several robberies and burglaries. Numerous sightings were followed up linking the couple with murders, bank robberies and automobile thefts across several states. The allegations include:

Murder of a man in Hillsboro, Texas
Robbery in Lufkin and Dallas, Texas
Murdered one sheriff and wounded another in
    Stringtown, Oklahoma
Kidnapped a deputy in Carlsbad, New Mexico
Theft of an automobile in Victoria, Texas
Attempted murder of a deputy in Wharton, Texas
Murder and robbery in Abilene and Sherman, Texas
Murder in Dallas, Texas
Kidnap of a sheriff and the chief of police at
    Wellington, Texas
Murder in Joplin and Columbia, Missouri.

Henry Methvin received his pardon from Texas as promised but not from the state of Oklahoma. He was arrested in Oklahoma for murder and sentenced to death, a sentence that was later commuted to life and served twelve years before being released on parole.

He was killed in 1948 after being hit by a train. Frank Hamer received thousands of letters of congratulations and was also honoured on the floor of congress, for his role in capturing Bonnie and Clyde. He died in 1955.

Roy Thornton's reaction to his wife's death was, 'I'm glad they went out like they did. It's much better than being caught.' On 5 March 1933, Thornton was sentenced to five years in prison for burglary. He was killed when guards shot him on 3 October 1937, during an escape attempt from Eastham Farm prison.

Blanche Barrow's injuries left her permanently blind in her left eye. After the 1933 shoot-out that left her husband mortally wounded, she was taken into custody on the charge of 'Assault with Intent to Kill' and was subsequently sentenced to ten years in prison. She was paroled in 1939 for good behaviour.

She returned to Dallas, leaving her life of crime in the past, and lived with her invalid father as his caregiver. She married Eddie Frasure in 1940, worked as a taxi cab dispatcher, and completed the terms of her parole one year later. She lived in peace with her husband until he died of cancer in 1969. She died from cancer herself at the age of seventy-seven on 24 December 1988, and was buried in Dallas's Grove Hill Memorial Park under the name Blanche B. Frasure.

In the end a total of twenty-three people were brought to trial on charges of harbouring Bonnie and Clyde. None of Bonnie and Clyde's possessions were ever returned to their families and most were sold as souvenirs. The grey V8 Ford riddled with bullet holes was shown for years afterwards at State Fairs for 25 cents a look. It is currently on permanent display at the Gold Ranch Casino in Verdi, Nevada.

Controversy still lingers over certain aspects of the ambush, and the way Hamer conducted it. Many historians have looked and found no warrants against Bonnie for any violent crimes. Archived FBI files contain only one warrant against her, for aiding Clyde in the interstate transportation of a stolen vehicle. For some, Bonnie's involvement in Clyde Barrow's crimes remains difficult to explain.

Jimmy Fowler, writing for the *Dallas Observer* on 9 September 1999 noted:

> Although the authorities who gunned down the twenty-three-year-old in 1934 conceded that she

was no bloodthirsty killer and that when taken into custody she tended to inspire the paternal aspects of the police who held her . . . there was a mystifying devolution from the high school poet, speech class star, and mini-celebrity who performed Shirley Temple-like as a warm-up act at the stump speeches of local politicians to the accomplice of rage-filled Clyde Barrow.

Bob Alcorn, one of Frank Hamer's men, continued to insist that Bonnie had been indicted twice for murder in Cases Numbers 5046 & 7 in the Criminal District Court, Dallas, Texas, on 28 November 1933. However, she had never been formally charged with these murders and hadn't been proven guilty.

It is more likely than not that Bonnie never killed anyone. What everybody seems to agree on, however, is that she did not want to leave her man's side. She would remain loyal to him no matter what, even as he murdered people and in doing so brought them both closer to their own deaths.

After their deaths, the life insurance policies for both Bonnie and Clyde were actually paid in full by American National of Galveston. Their legend has proved enduring, with four films, numerous songs and countless books and articles about the couple produced in the eighty-four years since they died.

Many cases of couples who kill raise the question of whether each would have been a murderer without the support of the other. This is one of those cases where this seems an easy question to answer.

Clyde was an inveterate criminal, who might have ended up as a prolific killer even if he hadn't been tipped further into rage by his prison experiences. However it is extremely likely that Bonnie would have been no criminal if it weren't for the fact that she fell in love with one. She was a roman-

284

tic, and she was prepared to forgive the man she loved anything, and do anything to protect him. But she was clearly not one of the world's 'natural born killers'. And to this day, Bonnie Parker's poems perhaps tell her story like no one else can.

The Story of Bonnie and Clyde

Bonnie Parker, 1934

You've read the story of Jesse James
Of how he lived and died:
If you're still in need
Of something to read
Here's the story of Bonnie and Clyde.

Now Bonnie and Clyde are the Barrow gang.
I'm sure you all have read
How they rob and steal
And those who squeal
Are usually found dying or dead.

There's lots of untruths to these write-ups:
They're not so ruthless as that;
Their nature is raw:
They hate the law –
The stool pigeons, spotters, and rats.

They call them cold-blooded killers:
They say they are heartless and mean:
But I say this with pride,
That I once knew Clyde
When he was honest and upright and clean.

But the laws fooled around,
Kept taking him down
And locking him up in a cell,
Till he said to me, 'I'll never be free,
So I'll meet a few of them in hell.'

The road was so dimly lighted:
There were no highway signs to guide:
But they made up their minds
If all roads were blind,
They wouldn't give up till they died.

The road gets dimmer and dimmer;
Sometimes you can hardly see:
But it's fight, man to man,
And do all you can,
For they know they can never be free.

From heart-break some people have suffered:
From weariness some people have died:
But take it all in all,
Our troubles are small
Till we get like Bonnie and Clyde.

If a policeman is killed in Dallas,
And they have no clue or guide;
If they can't find a fiend,
They just wipe their slate clean
And hang it on Bonnie and Clyde.

There's two crimes committed in America
Not accredited to the Barrow mob:
They had no hand
In the kidnap demand,
Nor the Kansas City Depot job.

A newsboy once said to his buddy:
'I wish old Clyde would get jumped:
In these awful hard times
We'd make a few dimes
If five or six cops would get bumped.'

The police haven't got the report yet,
But Clyde called me up today;
He said, 'Don't start any fights –
We aren't working nights –
We're joining the NRA.'

From Irving to West Dallas viaduct
Is known as the Great Divide,
Where the women are kin,
And the men are men,
And they won't 'stool' on Bonnie and Clyde.

If they try to act like citizens
And rent them a nice little flat,
About the third night
They're invited to fight
By a sub-gun's rat-tat-tat.

They don't think they're too smart or desperate,
They know that the law always wins;
They've been shot at before,
But they do not ignore
That death is the wages of sin.

Some day they'll go down together;
They'll bury them side by side;
To few it'll be grief –
To the law a relief –
But it's death for Bonnie and Clyde.

The Street Girl

Bonnie Parker, 1934

You don't want to marry me, Honey,
Though just to hear you say it is sweet:
If you did you'd regret it tomorrow
For I'm only a girl of the street.
Time was when I'd gladly have listened,
Before I was tainted with shame,
But it wouldn't be fair to you, Honey:
Men laugh when they mention my name.

Back there on the farm in Nebraska,
I might have said, 'Yes,' to you then:
But I thought that the world was a playground,
Just teeming with Santa Claus men:
So I left the old house for the city,
To play in its mad, dizzy whorl,
Never knowing how little of pity,
It holds for a slip of a girl.

You think I'm still good-looking, Honey?
But no I am faded and spent,
Even Helen of Troy would look seedy,
If she followed the pace that I went.
But that day I came in from the country,
With my hair down my back in a curl,
Through the length and breadth of the city,
There was never a prettier girl.

I soon got a job in the chorus,
With nothing but looks and a form,
I had a new man every evening,
And my kisses were thrilling and warm.

I might have sold them for a fortune,
To some old sugar-daddy with dough,
But youth calls to youth for its lover –
There was plenty I didn't know.

Then I fell for the 'line' of a 'junker',
A slim devotee of hop,
And those dreams in the juice of a poppy,
Had got me before I could stop:
But I didn't just care while he loved me,
Just to lie in his arms was delight;
But his ardour grew cold and he left me,
In a Chinatown 'hop joint' one night.

Well, I didn't care then what happened,
A chink took me under his wing,
And down in a hovel of hell –
I laboured for Hop and Ah-Sing,
Oh no, I'm no longer a 'junker':
The Police came and got me one day,
And I took the one cure that is certain,
That island out there in the bay.

Don't spring that old gag of reforming,
A girl hardly ever comes back,
Too many are eager and waiting,
To guide her feet off the track.
A man can break every commandment,
And the world still will lend him a hand,
Yet, a girl that has loved but unwisely,
Is an outcast all over the land.

You see how it is don't you, Honey?
I'd marry you now if I could,
I'd wish to go back to the country,

But I know it won't do any good.
For I'm only a poor branded woman,
And I can't get away from the past,
Good-bye and God bless you for asking,
But I'll stick it out now till the last.

Walter Kelbach and Myron Lance

Thou Shalt Not Kill

When one considers the history of serial killers in the twentieth century, one question raised is the degree to which the depictions of death and murder in popular culture have fed back into the mentality of those individuals who are capable of murder. Looking at the number of killers who have kept film or photographs of their own actions, or who have seemed to be acting out the part of a serial killer, following characteristic Hollywood clichés, one has to question whether the modern mind has become inured to the horror of murder, by repetitive exposure to the imagery of film, the news, and television drama.

The early 1970s was a period in which this problem was at the forefront of public attention. Television news had become a stream of daily horrors presented as entertainment, while the imagery allowed in Hollywood films became steadily more disturbing. An iconic and tragic milestone came in 1974, when the Florida newsreader Christine Chubbuck killed herself live on air. After announcing that 'in keeping with Channel 40's policy of bringing you the latest in blood and guts, and in living colour, you are going to see another first: an attempted suicide', she shot herself in the head. (This was one of the inspirations for the film *Network*, which satirized our increasing alienation and the degree to which television trivialises tragedy and turns it into a spectacle.)

In 1972 there was a very different example of the way that television makes death and tragedy seem anodyne, or anaesthetised. The murderer Walter Kelbach, who had killed six people in a remorseless spree was interviewed by NBC News for a program entitled *Thou Shalt Not Kill*. Millions of people watched from the comfort of their homes as this vicious killer smiled into the camera and said: 'I don't mind people getting hurt because I just like to watch it.'

At the same time as this confession was being treated as just another piece of 'infotainment', the audience was given an insight in Kelbach's mind. For him, the pain, suffering and death of his victims was no more than a spectacle, something that amused him as watching a horror movie or a television re-enactment of a serial killing spree might do. Kelbach was letting the audience know that death was nothing more than an entertainment. He had been the audience to his own killing spree.

*   *   *

Kelbach's reign of murder had occurred in Salt Lake City, Utah, six years earlier in December 1966. He was accompanied in his murderous activities by his homosexual lover Myron Lance. At the time, Kelbach was twenty-eight years old, and Lance was twenty-five. Both had been in jail, for petty crimes, both had addictive personalities and abused alcohol and drugs on a regular basis. Kelbach in particular regularly swilled down a variety of narcotic pills with his drinks, and spent most of his waking life under the influence of one stimulant or another. And as their relationship developed they discovered that they also shared sadistic, violent tendencies.

Their fantasies spilled over into murder on 17 December 1966. They had been drinking wine and taking pills, and drove to a late-night gas station, where the attendant, eighteen-year-old Stephen Shea, was working the night shift alone. Kelbach and Lance kidnapped him at gunpoint. They stole $147 from the till, but they were there for more than the money.

Shea was forced into the back of their station wagon, and they drove out into the isolation of the desert that surrounds Salt Lake City. Once they were there, both Kelbach and Lance assaulted Shea sexually, raping him and forcing him to perform sex acts on them. When they were finished, they tossed a coin in front of the victim, to decide which of them would be the murderer.

An insight into Kelbach's mind comes from the way that he described the fact that he was chosen for this act as 'winning the toss'. He stabbed Shea five times in the chest with a stiletto knife, and then they threw his corpse into a ditch that ran beside the road.

It often seems that once an individual or group crosses the line into murder, it is all too easily crossed again. And there is something about the dynamics of a couple who kill together that can make the act of murder into an addictive and symbolic act. The two individuals can relive the moment together, talk it through and normalise it. And also they may want to impress one another or bind the other partner more closely into the shared guilt. For whatever reason, couples who kill are often repeat offenders. The two men were in this together and they killed again as soon as the next night.

They used the exact same modus operandi. This time the unfortunate victim was Michael Holtz, who was working alone at a different gas station in Salt Lake City. He was also kidnapped at gunpoint and forced into the station wagon.

Like Shea he was abused and raped in the desert before being stabbed. This time Lance won the toss and he stabbed Holtz a single time through the heart, using the same stiletto, before the couple disposed of his body.

Police recognized the pattern of a spree killing and an order went out across the city requiring all gas stations to be closed overnight until further notice. The police were aware that this would not guarantee that a motivated, deranged killer could not strike again, but in the short term it was all they could do in the absence of evidence.

* * *

Kelbach and Lance spent three days debating their next move, before killing again, this time in a rather different scenario. On 21 December they hailed a taxi and told the driver to take them to the airport. They were clearly under the influence of alcohol or drugs and were exchanging looks with each other in a way that made the driver, Grant Strong, feel suspicious.

He actually stopped off at the control office to discreetly tell his supervisor that the couple were acting strangely. It was arranged that if anything happened he would send a signal by clicking the microphone switch. Unfortunately, he then got back in the car and proceeded in the direction of the airport.

Strong sent the signal via the microphone switch just a few minutes after leaving the supervisor, who immediately called the police and other taxi drivers. What had happened was that Kelbach had pulled a gun and was demanding money, with his gun pressed against Strong's head.

Strong handed over all the money he had, expecting that the pair would simply take it and go. But he only had nine dollars and Kelbach and Strong weren't satisfied. Probably they had never had any intention of merely robbing him; the money for them was just a prelude to the murder.

Kelbach shot Strong in the head. In the NBC interview six years later he would give a graphic and repulsively enthusiastic account of the thrill this gave him, saying, 'Oh boy! I never seen so much blood!' There were police and fellow taxi drivers within a few blocks, on their way to answer the distress call. Some of them even heard the shot, but they would arrive too late to help Strong or catch the killers. They were only in time to discover Strong's dead body in the cab.

The two killers were now in a frenzy, and decided to move on and get some more money, as the nine dollars from the taxi was insufficient for the drink and drugs they planned to buy. They had also tipped over the edge into recklessness, apparently in the belief that they were invulnerable now that they had got away with three previous murders.

They went to a bar called Lolly's Tavern, not far from the airport that they had been driving towards. They intended to make up for the low profit gained from robbing Grant Strong. On entering the bar Kelbach played pinball for a few moments, while Lance walked around behind him. Then they started shouting that they were holding up the bar, and to prove that they were serious, Lance shot a random customer in the head. The unfortunate victim was James Sizemore, who was forty-seven years old. He was killed instantly.

The pair forced the bartender to open the till and stole $300 from it. Then, still shouting incomprehensibly, they backed out of the bar, firing at random at the remaining customers and the bartender. Two more victims died in the hail of bullets, Beverly Mace (who was thirty-four) and Fred William Lillie (who was twenty).

The other customers feigned death, and waited in sheer terror for the two maniacs to stop shooting and leave. As Kelbach and Lance finally decided that they were finished and turned to leave, the manager of the bar grabbed a gun that was kept behind the bar for emergencies and shot at them. They escaped without injury, but fled in panic.

The two were now the subject of a city-wide manhunt, but they were panicking and behaving irrationally. Rather than flee, they returned to their car, which they had parked before hailing the taxi. Within a short distance they had driven into a police roadblock, and were immediately identified and apprehended.

At the trial, both Kelbach and Lance were found guilty on five counts of murder and sentenced to death. However, after a long wait on death row, the US Supreme Court ruled in 1972 that the death penalty was unconstitutional, and their sentences were commuted to life imprisonment.

Neither of the pair expressed any remorse or understanding of the suffering they had caused to the families and friends of their victims, and the fear they had engendered in the citizens of Utah. Lance's attitude was as repulsive as Kelbach's – he was quoted as saying, 'I have no feeling towards the victims.'

In 1992, Michael Sibbett, the chairman of the Utah Board of Pardons and Parole, was a member of the board that had to decide whether or not Kelbach and Lance were eligible for parole. He recalled that Kelbach, at an earlier interview, had said, 'I don't know how you could ever let us out.'

For Sibbett, this was evidence that Kelbach understood the horror of the crimes the couple had committed, but that he still had no remorse. Sibbett and the rest of the board decided that the pair would never be released. The nature of their crimes were such that they could not safely be allowed to return to society.

It's safe to say that no one who had witnessed Kelbach's 1972 television appearance would have disagreed with the verdict of the parole board.

Alvin and Judith Ann Neelley

The Bride of Frankenstein

When couples or teams of killers are finally caught, it is not unusual for them to blame one another for the crimes. In many cases, one can feel that there is a dominant partner who was the prime mover, but in the case of Alvin and Judith Ann Neelley, one has to suspect that either of the two would have been capable of murder in their own right. Judith was an unusually vicious woman, and it may even be that she was the more dangerous of the two.

The final death toll from their killing spree is uncertain – Alvin suggested that the total might be as high as fifteen at his trial, at which he would inevitably blame Judith for most of the deaths.

The pair were criminals long before they started to kill. Judith Ann was born as Judith Adams in Tennessee in 1964. Her father died when she was nine years old, and she was raised by her rather unstable mother. At the age of fifteen she met Alvin Neelley, who was in his late twenties, and the two became involved in a relationship.

At that time, Alvin Neelley was on his second marriage. His first had ended as a result of his violent abuse of his wife, which had included firing a gun at her. His second marriage was no happier, and his wife was not sorry when he left her for the young Judith.

Alvin was a petty thief, who specialized in car crime. Together, the two embarked on a three-year crime spree in Alabama, Georgia (Alvin's home state) and Tennessee. They occasionally took on temporary jobs but for the most part they lived off the proceeds of robbery, petty cons and cashing stolen cheques.

In 1980, after they had threatened a woman with a gun and stolen from her, they were apprehended trying to cash the stolen cheques. Alvin was sentenced to five years in jail, while Judith was sent to the Youth Development Center in Rome, where she would give birth to her twins.

Her time in the YDC seems to have flipped her over the edge. She hated every minute of her time there, and wrote to Alvin complaining that she was being sexually abused. It is impossible to know if this was true or not, but either way she became obsessed with gaining revenge on the YDC and would later launch several attacks on members of staff.

Judith came out of imprisonment before Alvin, and spent time living with his parents. In 1982, he was released and they set back off on their rolling lifestyle of crime. But now there was a new agenda. Judith wanted her revenge.

During this period they installed CB radios in their cars and they would co-ordinate their criminal activities over the airwaves. Alvin called himself the Nightrider, while Judith was Lady Sundance (or Lady Sundown, according to some reports). They would be operating under these names when their petty crime spilled over into murder.

*   *   *

One of the members of staff at the Rome Youth Development Center was Kenneth Dooley. In September 1982 there was a

298

phone call to his house in which a female voice claimed to know his wife, and asked for directions to the house. This was Judith, who was trying to track down members of staff so that she could attack them.

Dooley thought no more of the call, until 10 December, when there was another call. This time a male voice told him that he was 'going to pay'. That night four shots were fired into the house, but no one was hurt. Dooley was lucky, as his wife and two children were asleep in the house at the time.

Shortly afterwards there was a second attack on Linda Adair, another member of the YDC staff. Once again their house had been phoned in advance by a woman obtaining information about its whereabouts. This time there was more information. A brown car with white stripes was seen speeding away after a Molotov cocktail was flung at the house.

After the attack, when the fire had been put out, there was a call to the house, while the police were there. The same voice, that of Judith, threatened the lives of Adair and Kenneth Dooley. Judith also made an anonymous call to police in which she stated that the attacks were because of sexual abuse that had taken place in the YDC.

The police recording of this call would later play a crucial role in the capture of the Neelleys. But at this stage no one was able to identify Judith as a suspect. The slightly cowardly nature of the attacks also misled police into thinking that the attacker was not particularly serious in their intent.

*   *   *

It is not clear when the Neelleys first killed. Alvin would later claim that Judith had been involved in people-trafficking without him and had killed eight to fifteen times. The first documented murder occurred in September 1982.

The Neelleys had apparently been roaming the streets trying to pick up young girls, sometimes with their own children in the back seat. There were at least two reports of their car having stopped while Judith tried to entice girls to join them in the car. She would pretend to know the girls, then act as though she had been mistaken, but strike up a conversation anyway.

The couple didn't look especially threatening. Judith was a slight, wiry redhead, while Alvin seemed an affable wimp, with the ability to be charming and friendly to strangers. The first few girls they approached turned them down anyway, but Lisa Anne Millican was less lucky.

She was on a day trip to Riverbend Mall, near Rome, from the home for girls that she lived at. This was the mall where Judith had held up a woman at gunpoint two years earlier, the incident which had led to her stay at the Rome YDC. Perhaps in her head this was still all part of a psychotic revenge mission against the entire world, or at least anyone associated in any way, no matter how tangential, with her incarceration.

She seems to have been tempted into the car without a struggle. Lisa completely disappeared and there was no sign of her for a few days. Then the police in Georgia and Alabama received a series of anonymous calls from a female caller. She directed them to Little River Canyon, near Payne in Alabama, which was where Lisa's corpse would be discovered. She also claimed that the murder was being covered up by police officers associated with the detention centre. Once again, this was Judith trying to get back at the YDC, but she had gone to extraordinary and horrific lengths this time. She had also helped once again to build a trail that would eventually lead back to her, by allowing her voice to be recorded.

The police found Lisa's corpse on the floor of the canyon, partially lying on a tree. Nearby there was a pair of bloody

300

jeans. Both had been thrown from the edge of the canyon. The autopsy revealed a range of terrible injuries. The girl had been raped and assaulted, then injected with a substance that had caused terrible damage to her subcutaneous flesh. Finally she had been shot three times.

The substance would turn out to be Liquid Drano. After they had abducted Lisa, the Neelleys took the poor girl to a hotel room. For three days they kept her captive here and in another hotel room in Alabama. Alvin would later deny he had been present, but both of the couple were spotted by witnesses at the hotels. There they assaulted and raped her for two to three days.

A horrific detail of this crime was the fact that the Neelleys' two-year-old twins were present during this assault. When they decided to get rid of Lisa, Alvin told Judith to inject her with drain cleaner as he believed this would kill her without leaving any forensic evidence. The drain cleaner almost certainly caused the unfortunate girl terrible pain and suffering, but it didn't succeed in killing her.

So Judith took her to the canyon, shot her, and pushed her from a cliff into the canyon. It is unclear whether she acted alone or with Alvin in disposing of the body. Alvin's later attempt to blame Judith for everything means that very little of the evidence he gave at his trial holds up to scrutiny. He even tried telling the police that he had not only not been present at the hotel rooms for these assaults, but that Judith had gone so far as to masturbate him to obtain sperm which she could leave on the corpse to implicate him. He didn't stick to this obvious fabrication under closer questioning, and finally admitted he had assaulted the girl, but it is an example of the nonsensical lies he tried to tell to save himself at Judith's expense.

*   *   *

301

Detective Kenneth Kines was assigned to the case. The only solid piece of evidence at this stage was the recordings of the calls Judith had made. No one had yet connected the calls to the attacks on YDC workers, so the only theory they had was that Lisa had been snatched by strangers. The police followed up every lead they could think of but they wouldn't make progress until after the next murder.

This happened shortly afterwards, on 3 October. A cemetery worker called John Hancock and Janice Kay Chatman, his fiancée, were picked up by Janice, who was not with Alvin – it seems that they took pity on her and decided to keep her company. Whilst they drove, she started chatting to someone with the handle 'Nightrider' on her CB radio. They were exchanging information in code as their intended victims sat unknowingly in the back of the car.

Judith stopped the car at an agreed rendezvous outside town, where Alvin, the Nightrider, joined up with them. They drove off in the two cars, claiming they were going to buy some drinks to share. Once again the children were present throughout the events that followed.

John asked for the car to stop so he could go to the toilet. In a deserted area of the countryside, he got out, and Judith followed him out of the car. She pulled a gun on him and told him to keep walking down a lane. Alvin started shouting at her to get on with it, and at this stage she shot John in the back. The bullet hit him in the shoulder and threw him to the ground.

At this stage Judith made a fatal error, in that she didn't check to see if John was dead as she assumed. He was left wounded but was able to wait for the cars to drive off, then he ran back to the road and flagged down a passing truck driver. He wanted to try to chase after his girlfriend, but they were not in sight and he was losing a lot of blood, so the trucker took him to the hospital, where the police were called.

To start with the police didn't connect John's shooting with the recent attacks. However there had been other reports of a woman in a brown car with a white stripe who had been driving around town trying to offer lifts to strangers. The story of John's attack reached Detective Kines, and he played the tape of Judith calling the police to John. He gave a positive identification of her as the woman who had shot him.

Now Kines had a description to work with, as well as an identification of the types of cars he was looking for. The other connection which fell into place was the realisation that the female caller was the identical voice that had called making allegations about the YDC after the earlier attacks.

Linda Adair and Kenneth Dooley were questioned to see if they could think of anyone from the YDC who might be holding a grudge. Kines went methodically through the records of girls who had been held there and came up with a shortlist of five girls who had previous convictions. One of these was Judith Ann Neelley.

Linda Adair was also able to confirm that Judith had two children of about the age that John had thought the children in the car to have been. Kines found a photograph of both on file. John was able to give a definite identification for Judith and a tentative one for Alvin.

Everything was now in place for the apprehension of the Neelleys, but for the time being they were still at large.

*　　*　　*

The unfortunate Janice Kay Chatman was subject to an assault that was similar to the earlier attack on Lisa Millican. She was raped and beaten in a motel room, before being taken to a woodland area near Chattanooga and shot dead.

Even now the Neelleys might have escaped justice for longer if it weren't for their persistent addiction to petty crime. They tried to pass some bad cheques in Murfreesboro,

Tennessee, and were picked up on this minor charge by police. Their details had been circulated by Detective Kines, and as soon as it was realised that they were wanted for murder, he was contacted.

Alvin immediately confessed to the crimes, except that he blamed Judith for all the worst details. He told them where to find Janice's body, and insisted that it had been Judith who pulled the trigger of the gun that killed her. He stated that his wife was a dangerous woman and that he was scared of her, and intimidated into helping her in her killing spree. Most couples who are caught killing take a little while to start blaming each other, but Alvin couldn't blame Judith fast enough. He also claimed that as well as the abuse she had allegedly suffered at the YDC, she had been involved in a prostitution ring, trafficking women for immoral purposes, and that in that role she had killed on numerous occasions. He described her as carrying round a deep-seated rage that she was taking out on the world.

This latter statement certainly seems to have had some truth. Judith's behaviour speaks for itself. But it seems likely that Alvin was a more willing participant than he wanted to pretend. Judith was more forthcoming about the details of the crimes and to some extent accepted the responsibility. But she made it clear that Alvin had joined in with the rapes and claimed she had only procured the girls for him. She would develop this story further in her eventual trial.

The legal situation was complex as the crimes had been committed in different states. Alvin was most clearly implicated in the murder of Janice Chatman, and as a result he was kept in Georgia to face charges of murder.

Meanwhile Judith was taken to Alabama to face charges of the murder of Lisa Millican, knowing that she might also face further charges back in Georgia. She gave birth to her third child early in 1983, before the trials began. She now had three children, all of whom were born while she was incarcerated.

Both attempted to strike plea bargains, but eventually both came to trial on the charges. Judith tried to have her case considered as a juvenile, which would rule out the death penalty, but as an eighteen-year-old it was ruled that she would be tried as an adult.

So her defence attempted to portray her as a battered wife who had acted against her own will. She claimed to be terrified of Alvin, and to have been scared that he would harm her children if she didn't do as he said. Her lawyer brought in Alvin's first wife, who testified to Alvin's violent temper.

Judith claimed that Alvin had ordered her to find him girls to rape, that she had only injected Lisa Millican with Drano in an attempt to put her out of her misery, and to have been subjected to serious abuse by Alvin herself.

Her attorney depicted her as being like the 'bride of Frankenstein', acting only through the will of Alvin. He invoked the idea of 'coercive persuasion' to explain the actions she had taken as being entirely the responsibility of her husband.

District Attorney Richard Igou believed she was play-acting and that she was simply a cold-blooded killer. He did everything he could to reject the argument that she was a battered wife.

One of the most fascinating parts of the trial came in the later stages when psychiatrist Alexander Salillas gave his opinion on the whole issue of coercive persuasion and battered wife syndrome. The whole philosophical question of moral responsibility became the key issue as the defence attorney, Robert French, tried to depict Judith as being effectively brainwashed. Salillas was a highly effective witness for the prosecution. He was able to accept some of French's examples of how a battered wife might behave partly under someone else's control, but he was careful always to point out that the moral choice still lay with the battered wife, even where one might perceive an element of coercion. By asserting the basic notion that we are all responsible for our actions, he did some damage to the battered wife defence in this case, even though it is clear that in some cases it is fair to invoke the idea of coercive persuasion to explain someone's actions.

Judith was found guilty and the jury recommended a life sentence, but the judge sentenced her to death. To avoid receiving a second death sentence she then entered a guilty plea to the murder of Janice Chatman in Georgia. This provoked Alvin to finally settle his plea bargain and plead guilty – if Janice had given evidence against him he might have ended up with a death penalty, but instead he was given a life sentence.

*   *   *

As is common with female killers, Judith Ann Neelley's time in prison has been a complicated one that has received a lot of media attention. The appeals process initially delayed the prospects of execution, and she remained on death row. She became a prolific correspondent, writing many letters to people on the outside, had an affair with a fellow prisoner which ended in a suicide pact that only Judith survived. But the biggest controversy of her time in prison came in 1999 when Governor Fob James of Alabama commuted her sentence from death to life, without parole.

There was a public outcry at this decision which many Alabamians disagreed with profoundly.

Responding to the criticism in 2003, James said that he had thought long and hard about the decision. He continued, 'It would be impossible for me to give you all of the reasons without showing you a lot of information and documents on the matter . . . That DeKalb County jury – which heard all the facts of that heinous crime in the months right after the events took place – convicted her to life in prison. Then, the judge changed the sentence to death.'

It is impossible to know what information James was going on, but it seems that he felt that the decision of the jury, who had taken the possibility of battered-wife syndrome into account, that a life in prison was punishment enough should be respected. It seems that the efforts of the defence attorney to depict Judith as a mere female victim were not wasted after all.

Following further legal judgments, it is now possible that Judith Ann Neelley will be released from prison on parole. However, if she is ever freed, she may simply be retried for another of her alleged murders, as her life sentence is based on the murder of Lisa Millican alone.

Alvin will never be released as he died in October 2005 whilst serving his life sentence.

Afterword

Love and Death

So many victims. So many lives cut short and so many grieving families and friends left behind to mourn their loss. The overwhelming feeling one has while writing a book about killers is melancholy about the pointlessness of so many murders.

Many writers have pondered the reasons why murder, and serial murder in particular, seems to have become more common in the modern world. Of course there are many possible contributory causes. One that has been mentioned in the accounts here is the prevalence of violent imagery in modern media, including film and television. To a large degree, murder has been robbed of its true meaning and turned into a mere narrative element in a story.

Secondly, we live in a world where pornography and especially sexually violent imagery has been increasingly normalized. It is hard to point to a single murderer and say with certainty that his or her mind was warped by exposure to sexual imagery. But when one considers the number of murders here that ape the imagery of rape and domination that is so common in pornographic materials, and even in

309

mainstream entertainment, it is hard to miss the fact that ideas that might be acceptable as private fantasies, never to be acted out, become extremely dangerous where an individual fails to observe the limits of acceptable behaviour.

It is also worth considering the fact that we can overestimate how much the world has changed. Violence and sexual aggression have always been a part of the human race. In days gone by, wars and local conflicts were the occasion for horrific violence, and in many cases sexual violence. The Vikings travelled to rape and pillage, and that was the model for the behaviour of many armies for whom casual violence was the norm.

It is true that in the past many people lived in small communities, in which stranger murders were not common. But outside of the tight-knit community, murder and violence were always possibilities.

What has changed in the modern world is that few of us live in such small communities, and many people live in large cities, where everyone is a stranger. We also live in a world where we are promised glamour, easy sex and wealth by the blandishments of the modern media. So when people feel themselves not to be getting their share of love, sex, money, or whatever, a few twisted individuals find it relatively easy to turn to crime against those around them.

When it comes to couples who kill, it is often the case that there is mutual support in this attitude to the world. For whatever reason, a couple comes to see their own needs and desires as more important that morality, and decide to do whatever it takes to get what they want. The results can be tragic. They are also travesties of the idea of love.

Sometimes in this book we have referred to the guilty couples as being in love. But anyone who can kill in the name of love is profoundly failing to understand what love is. For the final words of the book I'd like to return to the words of St Paul in 1 Corinthians 13.

After reading this beautiful passage, perhaps it will be easier to remember that love is not the twisted version that is represented in some of the accounts in this book, but something that can be pure and that can elevate mankind to a higher level of existence.

When we read of the most evil deeds of mankind, it is easy to lose hope and to lose faith in people. But in the end the one thing we must remember is that our salvation will come only from real love.

If I speak in the tongues of men and of angels, but have not love, I am only a resounding gong or a clanging cymbal. If I have the gift of prophecy and can fathom all mysteries and all knowledge, and if I have a faith that can move mountains, but have not love, I am nothing. If I give all I possess to the poor and surrender my body to the flames, but have not love, I gain nothing.

Love is patient, love is kind. It does not envy, it does not boast, it is not proud. It is not rude, it is not self-seeking, it is not easily angered, it keeps no record of wrongs. Love does not delight in evil but rejoices with the truth. It always protects, always trusts, always hopes, always perseveres.

Love never fails. But where there are prophecies, they will cease; where there are tongues, they will be stilled; where there is knowledge, it will pass away. For we know in part and we prophesy in part, but when perfection comes, the imperfect disappears.

When I was a child, I talked like a child, I

311

thought like a child, I reasoned like a child. When I became a man, I put childish ways behind me. Now we see but a poor reflection as in a mirror; then we shall see face to face. Now I know in part; then I shall know fully, even as I am fully known.

And now these three remain: faith, hope and love. But the greatest of these is love.